Afterlife Teaching from Stephen the Martyr

Afterlife Teaching from Stephen the Martyr

Conversations about the spiritual life

The testimony of
Michael Cocks

Front cover: Stained glass window from the Anglican church of St Peter and St Sigfrid, Stockholm.

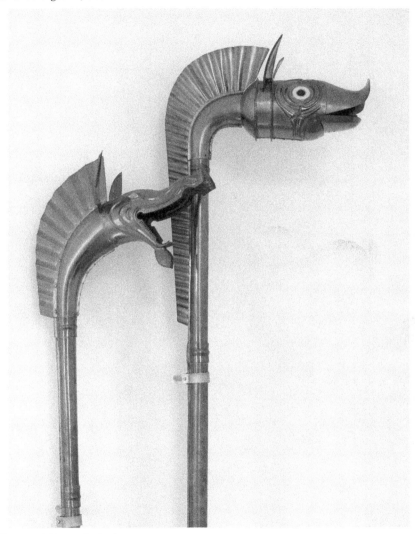

[Photo: Wolfgang Sauber]

Reconstructions of the bronze Celtic war trumpet, the carnyx.

Speaking in Greek Stephen appears to refer to himself as a "Carnyx" or one who comes from a Celtic land.[1]

Stephen's parting words

For what truth I speak is but my truth; my truth comes only from my experience, and alas, my judgements. God bless you all.

Contents

Introduction 1

Author's Preface 3

   1. Stephen, the first Christian Martyr 3

   2. The beginning of the St. Stephen experience 4

   3. How did Stephen make himself known to us? 4

   4. What does the New Testament of the Bible
   have to say about St Stephen? 7

Part One
Exploring the teaching of Stephen

Chapter 1. Why we are on Earth 11

   5. Stephen talks about the whole purpose of our life on Earth 11

   6. God seen as the Surgeon operating on us while we live
   our "unconscious" lives on earth 12

   7. The necessity for physical lives 14

   8. Gazing at our image in the pool 16

   9. What is the role of the Physical? 17

   10. Stephen as an extension 18

   11. The Father has laid down a course that you will follow. And I
   say this to you: Think more of the course that All are to follow. For
   the plan is greater than you and I 18

   12. God's will and our will 20

   13. Concept of how God operates using Man's Free will 21

   14. Knowing and Knowledge 22

   15. Science, Facts, Akashic Records 24

   16. What is truth? 25

   17. Recognizing the truth 26

   18. Confirm truth - test untruth 27

Chapter 2. Jesus Christ..29

19. That they all may be one...29

20. There never was a time when our Lord Jesus was not the Christ, nor any of the imaged creation of the Father not the Christ..................30

21. The Image: What we search for then must be the wider perception of the Source so that we might image...31

22. Do we experience Jesus more when we die?........................32

23. Second Coming of our Lord..34

24. More than a great teacher 35

25. I am the Door 36

26. Jesus Christ - His life and His teachings............................37

27. Jesus our Saviour..38

28. "How is growth towards one Consciousness best achieved?" 41

29. Stephen's Prayer...43

30. Salvation..43

31. Let this cup pass from me 44

32. The twenty-third psalm 45

Chapter 3. The "Fall" and the "Atonement" 47

33. Discussion..47

34. Stephen's version of the Fall and the Atonement 48

35. Stephen tells this parable about the atoning death and resurrection of Jesus...49

36. The story of the camel in the desert 54

Chapter 4. Sin, Evil and Judging..55

37. Sin and Stagnation..55

38. Nature, red in tooth and claw...57

39. Evil, Devil...57

40. Judging...58

41. More about Judging 60

42. Sheep and the Goats..61

Chapter 5. The Afterlife 65

    43. Our passing over 65

    44. Science and the afterlife 68

    45. Resurrection of the body 68

Chapter 6. The Cell, the Soul and "Reincarnation" 71

    46. Discussion: Leslie Weatherhead on "Reincarnation" 71

    47. The Continuous Self and "Reincarnation" 72

    48. "Christian" being the name that defines the pursuit
    of what is Christ 73

    49. I am called by an unwelcome name 76

    50. More about that unwelcome name 82

    51. Stephen on Essenes now 84

    52. Stephen reminds us not to see our incarnations too concretely 84

    53. Being reincarnate a thousandfold 88

    54. On being realistic 90

    55. Experiences are like ripples on a lake 91

    56. Previous lives – Reincarnation 92

Chapter 7. The Trinity - Source, Soul and the Created 97

    57. The Trinity 97

    58. Trinity: Spirit, Soul and the Created 97

    59. The Godhead 101

    60. God, the paint and the picture 102

    61. The Void 107

    62. The Seven Bodies 107

    63. Healing 110

Chapter 8. Is there development in the realm of Spirit? 113

    64. Is there development in the realm of Spirit? 113

    65. God the Babe 116

Chapter 9. Love and Faith..66

66. Love and Faith.. 66

67. Against those who teach a wrathful God........................... 120

68. The sacrilege of suggesting that God is not Love 121

69. Paying our debts with love 122

70. Love 124

71. Love that is the flood 126

Chapter 10. Other Questions and Answers 129

72. Abortion... 129

73. Ethics of Abortion..130

74. Astrology...131

75. Authors of the Apocalypse and John's Gospel 132

76. Who wrote John's Gospel 133

77. Creations of the mind 134

78. The Flea and the Ass..135

79. The furthest sun is closer to you than your tongue 136

80. Healing 137

81. Activation of healing through prayer............................. 140

82. A heavenly game with pawns....................................... 140

83. What about the Mission of the Church?............................ 141

84. Offering our gifts 141

85. The point of unfolding... 142

86. Prayer 144

87. Prophecy.. 144

88. Sacrifice 146

89. Sanity 148

90. Spiritual discipline 148

91. The Virgin Birth..150

Chapter 11. Intuitional Receiving – Guidance................................... 151

92. The process of receiving spiritual guidance 151

93. A very strange episode 151

94. Spiritual and physical, like two legs operating jointly....................152

95. Michael's first encounter with Stephen 156

96. Contradictions...156

97. Whether I was hearing from God or from Stephen.........................159

98. When the sheep are scattered in the field and the
darkness and the night-time come 160

99. In the dimensions in which Stephen dwells how
does one come by knowledge?...162

100. Jeremy's receiving...163

101. Universal theology underlying all religions 165

102. "If your choice be wise, you will indeed see the
fire from my eyes." 165

103. Christ speaks: The two witnesses of Love and Sacrifice;
the main teachings are simple 170

104. What do we mean by the term "Receiving?" 171

105. Stephen talks of Receiving in simple language 172

106. Ways of receiving knowledge or recovering our memories 173

107. Trance Receiving 174

108. Why has trance been used to communicate with us?....................175

109. Strange parallel coincidences 176

110. Questions about receiving..177

111. "Each moment is a gift of the Father." 180

112. The gates … can only be opened by perception 181

113. Receiving of Jeremy...182

114. A little about the way Spirit was operating in our group 183

115. How is receiving to be distinguished from Guidance
by the Holy Spirit as spoken of by the Church?....................................183

116. Baptism of the Holy Spirit 184

117. Receivings about earthly destruction in the near future 187

118. On not coming to conclusions.. 188

119. "Knowing" and "learning" things..190

Part Two
The Five Fives puzzle.

120. What happened at Berlins 191

121. Gestalten 192

122. The Five Fives puzzle 197

123. Commentary...200

124. The UFO theme 201

Part Three
Actually partaking of the banquet.

125. Actually partaking in the banquet............................203

126. Anxiety 204

127. We were wondering whether you would talk on what we term "I" ... 205

128. Viewing things from the Spiritual 207

129. The Image of the Pen and Paper 208

130. Praying for the Water..209

131. The Second Coming 212

132. Peaks and Valleys..214

133. Not feeling in tune with other Christians..................215

134. The rings..217

135. Blasphemy against the Holy Spirit 219

136. Eternal Life...220

137. A healing - Wish to be at home with God - The Millennium - Not just a few saved - Eternal Life 220

138. Christ is not in us; we are in Him 222

139. The conversations with Stephen end 223

140. Brief reunion...226

Part Four
Discoveries about Stephen's early life.

Chapter 1. Stephen, the Essenes and the Dead Sea Scrolls 231

141. After the wedding breakfast Stephen sets his Greek puzzle 232

142. This is what Stephen's words mean and imply 233

143. Discussing this Greek Puzzle with Stephen 234

144. Stephen's own moving words about his childhood and youth 237

145. Stephen's Awareness 1: Stephen's Awareness 2 238

146. On his language 241

147. More on his martyrdom... 242

148. Christ speaks about Stephen 243

149. Celts and Jews in Galatia 243

150. So then, how was it that the Celts came to Thrace
and then to Galatia? 245

151. Stephen in Ancyra.. 249

152. One day Thomas consciously attuned his mind to
Stephen and attempted to intuit more of his history........................... 250

153. A cross-correspondence with "Stephen" 253

154. The possibility that Stephen and his parents came to
Judaea because they were sympathisers with the Essenes 253

155. Joseph and Mary as Essenes.. 254

156. The Essenes in general... 254

157. Putting detail into our picture..255

158. The Essenes' expectation of a Messiah with their
Messianic Feast (like a Communion service) 256

159. Stephen as a novice and his acceptance as an Essene.................. 258

160. We can now try another translation 260

161. The village community that Stephen would have joined 260

162. Why were Stephen's words so memorable? 262

Chapter 2. Stephen's Ministry and Martyrdom 263

163. Stephen's Greek fits one situation only: that of his
pending reception as a full member of an Essene community........... 263

164. What St. Luke has to say about Stephen 264

165. Thomas Ashman's Intuitions about Stephen's
life and ministry discussed with Stephen 265

166. Stephen on his martyrdom 267

Chapter 3. Additional Articles...**269**

167. How much can we rely on the historical accuracy
of The Acts of the Apostles? 269

168. Scholars' thoughts on Stephen as an Essene......................... 270

169. How it may have been for the Holy Family 271

Part Five
Some essays about the Stephen experience.

170. The Testimony of the Perennial Philosophy 275

171. Definition of Synchronicity 277

172. What some Quantum Mechanics theorists suggest........................... 277

173. Quotations from a summary of Bohm's Gnosis by Beatrix Morrell 277

174. St. Stephen and Philosophy - Prof. Richard M. Cocks Ph.D.............. 279

175. Further study of Stephen's Greek in Part Four and how
much does it prove? 283

176. Acknowledgements..**290**

177. Bibliography **291**

Endnotes **295**

The Stephen Experience

Foreword

St. Stephen and modern Christianity

If you want an idea of what to expect from St. Stephen at the core of his teaching is a familiar message. This message is that it is our calling to become the Love of God made manifest. We are to be an extension of the Father. This is perfectly consistent with Jesus' summary of his teachings that we should love the Lord our Father with all our hearts and minds and souls and that we should love our neighbour as ourselves.

So much for the central thought around which all else revolves. The next thing you might wonder is what level is Stephen speaking from? Is it as a Christian fundamentalist who takes parables and myths literally? Is he speaking as a Christian from 2000 years ago? How close to orthodox Christianity is he? The answer is that, although many of Stephen's images and metaphors come from an earlier time, his theology is of the highest order. Like a rational theologian, he uses myths to help explain complex ideas but does not take them literally. This rational reworking of ancient stories seems to be informed by an intimate familiarity with the highest levels of human consciousness in which we arguably merge with the divine and in fact realize ourselves to be God in some sense. These higher levels, that we might call the post-rational or transpersonal, involve perspectives that become progressively less personal and less tied to a particular mind and body. These higher levels are sometimes called "cosmic consciousness" in which lower identifications (with our body and mind) are superseded and transcended (but included).

While Stephen's teachings are not unique they do provide a wonderful addition to the world's wisdom teachings. One thing that makes his teachings so beautiful and worth reading is the example he provides of what he is teaching, the Love of God made manifest. Some people may respond well to angry prophets but for those drawn to those who practise what they preach Stephen's embodiment of warmth, love, gentleness and humour is immensely appealing and seems like a model for his interlocutors and readers to follow.

What Stephen provides is both an ethics and a cosmology. I personally have found in Stephen, despite a good familiarity with Plato and Ken Wilber, the leading transpersonal psychologist, an irreplaceable source of thoughts, images and metaphors that provide succour and also a map for further development.

Stephen's teachings are consistent with the Great Chain of Being, the notion that reality exists in a hierarchy or holarchy extending from matter to body, to mind, to soul, to spirit. This way of thinking puts him squarely in tune with the world's greatest religious traditions. This hierarchy has been confirmed over and over by mystics, including Neo-Platonists like Plotinus, Sufis, post-rational Buddhists, Cabbalists, Christian mystics and those engaging in contemplative prayer and meditation who have developed beyond merely discursive knowledge of the Divine into direct apprehension.

Prof. Richard M. Cocks PhD, Dept. Philosophy, SUNY Oswego, NY

Author's Preface

1. Stephen, the first Christian Martyr.

In this book it is claimed that, without doubt, we have in some real sense been communicating with the spirit of Stephen the first Christian Martyr.

In her much respected book, *Mysticism*, Evelyn Underhill writes: "mysticism avowedly deals with the individual not as he stands in relation to the civilization of his time, but as he stands in relation to truths that are timeless." She also wrote: "All mystics, said Saint-Martin, speak the same language and come from the same country."

Stephen also comes from that place. He can be compared to the best of the world's mystics and also has much in common with other great communicators from the world of Spirit. He is humble, wise and has a sense of humour. But what makes him almost unique is that he has provided us with such strong evidence of the reality of his identity. The evidence is so strong that his understandings of the original teaching of Jesus and of some events in the early church will be of great interest. Such is his loving nature that he avoids judging but rather leads us towards realizing the divine and eternal nature that Jesus called the Kingdom of Heaven.

The Risen Christ is central for Stephen and he presents his own personal understanding of the teachings of Jesus, an understanding that has much in common with that of the author of the *Gospel according to St John*. As with writings of many of the mystics, we cannot hurry over his words. They take time to digest.

2. The beginning of the St. Stephen experience.

In 1973 I was the Anglican vicar of a parish in Christchurch, New Zealand, when one day an acquaintance knocked on the door. She had come down from the North Island partly to deliver to me a hand-written book of prophecies, the product of a woman unknown to me who once had belonged to the Plymouth Brethren. There were about a hundred pages of these prophecies, largely based on the Book of Revelation, casting me in the role of one of the Two Witnesses in Chapter 11 of the book. She had plainly taken immense pains with her prophecies and my acquaintance had incurred the loss of time and money to bring them to me. I hope that I received the gift graciously and acknowledged the caring and depth of belief which prompted it. All the same I could not regard it as other than the product of irrationality.

And yet, on the other hand, I found out later that the gift was almost simultaneous with St. Stephen's first words to my friend Olive Ashman, through her husband, Thomas, who, although not previously aware of his mediumistic abilities, was in trance. They were living at the time in Sevenoaks, Kent. Three months later, the strangest circumstances were to have me talking with Stephen in New Zealand. In the meantime the Ashmans had come to live in Christchurch and I had met Olive in a psychic library that I on a whim had visited. She talked to me about Stephen and I was interested to find out more. (I describe this in more detail in the section headed "Intuitional Receiving".) When I eventually learned that Stephen and the prophecies had come together in time and I reflected on how I had come to talk with him myself, multidimensional reality appeared more and more strange, for many of those weird prophecies had close parallels with Stephen's teachings.

3. How did Stephen make himself known to us?

Olive's preparation for her encounter with Stephen came from her Catholicism with its high respect for the saints, from her seeking a more direct relationship with Spirit in a Charismatic church and her searching for help in a number of other religious movements.

Olive's husband, Thomas, had a Catholic mother and a Jewish father. As a child early in the Second World War he attended the Star-Cross school, a school in London for Christians and Jews. Tom thought of himself as a Jew but was without any real belief. He had occasionally attended synagogue, but was never fully accepted because of his mixed parentage. He had no tertiary education, having left school at the age of sixteen. While at school he received a technical education, learning no languages there. (I mention this because Stephen twice spoke in a form of ancient Greek.) At home he picked up a little Yiddish. In 1943 aged 17 he joined the RAF and on discharge in 1948 married a Polish woman. This marriage lasted more than twenty years during which time he learned some Polish together with a few sentences of Russian. He earned a living in business and also hotel management. (He married Olive, a New Zealander, in 1974) That he had Catholic and Jewish parents must have raised questions in his mind. Tom was interested in mediumship and indeed once had a conversation with the well-known medium Harry Edwards. He joined Olive in a brief involvement with a group called Eckankar. All the while Tom saw himself as a secular Jew, not participating in the worship of a synagogue. There was nothing, apparently, to prepare him for the wonderful way in which Spirit was to use him.

Nevertheless, it was Tom who made the Stephen experience possible. One night Olive heard him speak in Latin while he was asleep, his words conveying spiritual teaching. On subsequent nights Olive recorded his words on tape. It seems that when Tom was confronted by what was said and its profundity and wisdom he felt compelled to become a Christian. Discovering what had happened might initially have been deeply disturbing to him. Someone does not change their world-view so easily. In any case, Tom did not fight the experience. At first, his becoming "Stephen" was involuntary but subsequently he found a way of praying and then of voluntarily allowing his personality to be supplanted by that of Stephen.

When this happened sometimes it would be in the presence just of Olive and myself. More often there would be a group of up to ten other people present all of whom joined in the questioning. We met informally as a group most weeks from 1973 until 1981.

Tom had this to say about his feelings when that happened:
"Firstly I feel so small as if I am surrounded by another being, enclosed, warm and completely protected as if I am a child in a womb. I am also conscious of his words. The emotion of love is all around and through me. Happiness almost to the point of being unbearable without bursting into fragments. But at the same time I wish to stay in this

5

state forever. Safe, warm, and loved, beyond my previous existence. When he is gone an uncontrollable sadness of great loss comes over me and I unashamedly weep. A feeling of being left very much alone and separated from joy and safety comes over me. His beautiful words still ring in my ears afterwards, and the feeling of great joy is remembered, but soon begins to fade."

[Tom was not always aware of what Stephen was saying. There were even occasions when he had to ask, "Did Stephen come?" When he was conscious of the sense of what Stephen had been saying he sometimes interrupted him. Then Stephen would stop in mid-sentence, appear to be listening to Tom's inaudible voice, report Tom's words, answer and then carry on speaking from where he had left off.]

The words "séance", "channelling" or "mediumship" come to mind but they would be insufficient to describe what was going on because of deeply meaningful coincidences involving friends in different parts of the world. Like Tom we too were caught up in something greater than us, in such a way that we could readily identify with the feelings Tom expressed.

It became clear that Tom and the rest of us were caught up into the same experience. For that reason I prefer to speak of the whole complex event as "the Stephen Experience" to differentiate it from other occasions when the Unseen communicates through a group of people.

The facts were that Tom was deliberately allowing himself to be displaced by Stephen, after prayer and as an act of obedience to God. After this experience, Tom would be groggy as if awakening from sleep, with little memory of what had been going on. He often seemed to feel out of it, as if he had been sent to another room, while Stephen and his questioners were holding deep conversation. Indeed, he often felt a little hurt and resentful, as if it did not matter to us whether or not he had been aware of what was going on. To be told that he could read up about it when the transcripts were printed in a few days did little to assuage these feelings. Yet he laid himself open to Stephen almost two hundred times. In doing this it was patently clear that Tom's motives were spiritual, that he wished to do the will of God and that his submission to Spirit was not in service of fame, money or to have power over others. We are deeply in Tom's debt. Sadly, he died in late 2010.

4. What does the New Testament of the Bible have to say about St Stephen?

We read in the New Testament that the first Christian martyr was St. Stephen, a Greek-speaking Jew, "a man full of faith and the Holy Spirit" [2], that he was chosen by the twelve apostles to care for the widows who spoke his language. But what he became known for was being an extraordinary preacher who awakened the wrath of the enemies of Jesus who in turn had him tried for blasphemy.

St. Luke, the author of Acts, puts a long speech in the mouth of Stephen which reminded his accusers how religious authorities throughout the history of Israel had persecuted and killed prophets sent by God. They had capped this by murdering Jesus.

We can doubt that stenographers were present at the trial. But Luke, as was the custom with historians at that time, composed a speech that he believed would represent the kind of thing Stephen would have said. Luke continues:

"This touched them on the raw and they ground their teeth with fury. But Stephen, filled with the Holy Spirit, and gazing intently up to heaven, saw the glory of God and Jesus standing at God's right hand. 'Look,' he said, 'there is a rift in the sky; I can see the Son of Man standing at God's right hand!' At this they gave a great shout and stopped their ears. Then they made one rush at him and, flinging him out of the city, set about stoning him. The witnesses laid the coats at the feet of a young man named Saul. So they stoned Stephen, and as they did so, he called out, 'Lord Jesus, receive my spirit'. Then he fell to his knees and cried aloud, 'Lord, do not hold this sin against them' and with that he died. And Saul was among those who approved of his murder."

Michael Cocks

Stephen's Prayer

Lord, let me forget that I am me,
Let me know that I am with thee,
Let me not separate myself from thee
Because I am me.

Part One
Exploring the teaching of Stephen

Chapter 1

Why we are on Earth

5. Stephen talks about the whole purpose of our life on Earth.
I think I can perhaps help mostly by talking a little tonight and you will find that many of your questions will be answered.

Shall we first recapitulate?

Remember, that in the beginning there was the coming away from the Source for the correction of many disorders.

Acquiring a physical body is only one stage in the corrections.
To be in the physical is not always the most enviable stage,
   as just lately you may have learnt,
but this I tell you: in this span of creation,
the time or times in the state are of short duration,
and, though important, are at the most very temporary.
It is not surprising then that whilst you should be in this state
the importance of comfort or happiness
seen from the physical point of view
is generally foremost in the mind of each soul.
And yet the message that you have all been given,
and which you must learn to hear with greater clarity,
is the message of our Lord Jesus Christ [namely that]
your physical well-being, your possessions,
or lack of them, so important to you,
are immaterial to your development.

As the Lord said, you should neither be judged whether you be rich or poor, for neither state will qualify you for acceptance back to the Source.

"Blessed are the poor", you have read,
words said by the Lord.
Do not misunderstand these words, as often is done.
The state of poverty in itself does not make them blessed.
It is their own mentality
and thoughts they have in the state of poverty.
You will find that the poor give as often as the rich do
but because they have so little to give in material things
they always give a larger percentage,
more often than not all of what they have.

"Blessed are the meek for they shall inherit the earth." For the same reason are they blessed, for they look down on no man and call him less, for they are meek. The gift of meekness is a gift indeed; therefore pray for the mighty, for they are not thus blessed. Each one elevated to the heights of government of kingdoms has always to accept and give the example of greatness. They may not be meek: therefore, to be rich in grace is doubly great.

If we were to carry on and talk more and give more of these examples we could only come to one conclusion: that life in a physical body is from necessity difficult and undesirable. For it would be very hard to accept that when you have the least comfort, when you have the least position, you are greatly blessed and that when you have the most comfort and the higher position then prayers are needed more.

It seems a contradiction in itself unless you understand that it is for this reason each and every one of you is in the position that you are for the reason that you may develop and that disorder may be corrected. Each is in the situation where he must learn, develop and correct disorder.

6. God seen as the Surgeon operating on us while we live our "unconscious" lives on earth.

Stephen: Then you say, "Would it not be easier if the Lord our God were to make it very clear to us what the purpose is and what the working of that purpose is, and why and how, and when and whom?" You have asked questions like this, Olive.

But think how a surgeon would act if, when he had to operate, he had to keep the patient conscious, adjust mirrors so the patient could see the operation that would be beyond his understanding in any case. Should he perhaps have each patient undertake advanced studies before an operation? Or would it perhaps not be better only to operate on a surgeon?

In actual practice the patient is treated and bathed and is given what medication he may need. He is clothed in a gown most suitable for access, and he is put in a place most suitable for the operation. He is kept in a state so that no pain more than he can bear will be administered to him. When the operation is completed and the wound is healed and the disorder is corrected then the patient may arise and even discuss the disorder and sickness with the surgeon and learn from him.

This must be the order of things, therefore, that the patient must trust his surgeon and carry out his instructions regarding what the patient must know or do or, rather, not do. Likewise the patient must love his Lord God with all his heart and all his soul; he must trust his God as he trusts his surgeon, for when he comes to the operating table he is by his own choice made unconscious of the things that are about to happen. Even if he were a surgeon himself he would still be unconscious at the time of the operation. Even though in consciousness he would know what has to be done and how it should be done by his own choice he would choose the unconsciousness, for he would know that without this the operation would not be possible. So, therefore, you must trust your surgeon, have faith in his skill, place yourself in his hands and love him.

Furthermore we must all love one another for we are part of the one body; there is no separateness. To hate someone, dislike someone, is to hate or dislike yourself and to hate and dislike your God. There is no one, no soul beneath your love; for there is not one soul that should not give you love and not one soul that you should not receive love from. Therefore, the second of your duties is to love yourselves, for you are a part of God and He of you. Love each other; give to each other, for in giving you are receiving.

The physical is only temporary; providing you do these two things then no state of mind or physical welfare is material to your progress. Your true reward for loving each other is to receive the love of each other, and the love of God.

Understand and give only this, and you will find that each time that you do this the wound of your operation will heal a little more; each time that you do this, consciousness which you lack now will begin to return. This is the way that the answers will come to you, to heal the wound and return to the consciousness. Therefore love much.

When you are gone from this place, when you are done with these bodies, physical, mental, ethereal and all others, then you will be back with the Source, and it will be of no mind.[3]

(Same session) You will forgive me for my serious talking this night for it is not often that I have the opportunity to discuss these things with you alone. Remember that mothers never tend to be less wise than their children are for, because of their development not in age but in experience, their wisdom grows and you will generally notice a calmness and an acceptance of life. Look upon the aged and those older than you and you will find that you are looking upon yourself when a number of your own mis-arrangements have been corrected. Think of the acceptance, notice the calmness; this is a message. Do not expect the aged to be clever, for cleverness most times is a barrier to the healing. Cleverness often, as I have said, stops loving. Intelligence is a disability; this is why I am often amused when Tom accuses me of cleverness for I discarded cleverness many ages ago.

I must depart now. Thomas is tired. God bless you all; pray for me and also for those in greater need of your prayers than yourselves or myself.

7. The necessity for physical lives.

Olive: Some religions teach that having physical lives is necessary until we become perfected men and it is all a matter of evolution: *not* because of the Fall, caused by eating of the forbidden fruit. Can you help me in my confusion over this?

Stephen: We do have to become Man.
Now if the Father created Man in his own image,
then the Father created Man that he might be His,
and He might belong to Man.
For what is the Father but All?
Therefore we might say that each of us becomes Man.
But the conclusions that are drawn are that the cell,
part of the Father, must become Man to become perfect.
This contradicts what is the truth:
for how can what is perfect require a created vessel
of its own creation in order to become itself which is perfect?
The confusion in many minds, including our own,

is derived from thinking that we need to make a journey,
and thinking that we should be progressing
from one stage to another
until we reach the heights of perfection.
We speak often of two different things;
we confuse what is created with what creates.
You yourself have often created apparel
 that you wish to wear for a particular effect or experience.
But does that apparel become you?
Are you less of yourself without the apparel?
Or more of you because of it?
So when we speak of Man let us not confuse
what is eternal and everlasting with what comes from the dust
and will return to the dust from which it came.

In the beginning of our meetings we spoke then of the Source
of all Things and the cell of that Source that voluntarily came away
(for this is the best concept that I can give you.)
    It came away so that each cell gathers in experience
    by choice of the Love that is the Source.
    For love is not stagnant but a moving thing
    and love becomes greater by growth.
    As the cells began to experience
    they experienced not only love,
    but also what is the opposite of that love.
    Now the opposite of to love is not a thing that a teacher might
point out to a pupil, but something to compare love with.
    For Love is, and the opposite of Love is not.
    Therefore the cell experiences the lack of that love
    so that the cell through choice would make growth in love,
    to cancel out what is lack, or the non-love.
    As a vessel for that experience
    all that we can perceive has been created
    and is even yet being created.
    The aim and object is not the instrument of loving,
    nor is it the vessel that receives the loving.
    The aim and object is the actual experience of Love.

8. "Gazing at our image in the pool".

"Think of yourselves as you gaze upon your image in the pool which, for all intents and purposes, be your mirror´

[Here, Stephen is addressing our eternal selves looking at themselves in the mirror of this world:]

Stephen: Just one more step with your thoughts, and you might be able to see yourselves.

Think of yourselves as you gaze upon your image in the pool which, for all intents and purposes, be your mirror. How often, as a child, have we looked into this pool and our consciousness has gone into that one which we see. This then is the state that our conscious mind is in, in the one of the image. What we see and perceive are reflections, or so be it, symbols of what truly is, but because of the unreality of that image it can either be good or not-good as we ourselves choose to see.

We have listened to the words that we must step outside of ourselves and look inwards. This would be confusing if it were not for the image that we are conscious of ourselves as. Imagine now, each one of you, your reflection in the pool. Then imagine that you are that reflection. Now I say to you, step outside of your consciousness, and look within yourself that you might see the image.

What then, in the consciousness of the image, would need to happen? The image in its consciousness, that which has held and does often hold us, would need to separate and die ...to live. There are many ways in which this might happen.

The image that can be perceived by other images may be destroyed, as truly was the body of Jesus in the manner as described (in the Gospels). The importance was not of the dying but to show the way, the gate to come out of the image and back into the true consciousness, where we perceive only those things that are reflected and distorted by the turbulence created by our thrashing inside the pool so that even the reflections (should we be able to perceive them) from ourselves rather than from *our image*, would also be distorted.

Think of the reason now that we would first put our consciousness into the image as we gaze at the pool; for truly, now we have come out... we look back into the pool. We take our consciousness and immerse it in the image for we reason as children do: "I wish to experience...for by looking at myself from without I can understand myself better." We do this many times, with many images that we might learn of ourselves. Often as the image we perceive all else that is mirrored around us: we the (mirrored) cell that we speak of this night, we see the pattern that is formed, the movement of the parts and of the Centre. We understand that it can separate, divide, come together and be created. We learn much of ourselves and of all things.

We forget often the pattern that we may perceive does have this margin of error, physically, visibly, for it is only an image and cannot be defined with the same clarity as the cell itself is, in truth.

9. Bill Andrews asks: What is the role of the Physical, as opposed to Spiritual?

Stephen: It was created in the image of the *Father* as an extension to the Source.[4]

How can one explain and give a concrete example of love?

What is an extension of love but love?

What is an extension to the air that you breathe but air?

We speak of "the Father", for in this way we can conceive in our minds *a tangible image of what is intangible.*

The essence of what is a father is in the image of the Source that created it.

What is a father, but a source of love, protection, a teacher, comforter and a strength?

This is a father, therefore. We were made in this image.

To create thus from base material requires this material to be refined, to insert and influence emotions with other emotions.[5]

For, as we know, we do not make a father from a child. When it is born it comes away from the mother, it grows, learns, experiences until it in its turn re-creates and then, and only then, can it become a father. But the mere act of re-creation itself does not give it the emotion, only the ability to become a father. Each of you fathers here, are fathers to those you have not created *[All of the fathers present were stepfathers]* and there are many who have created and are not fathers. These are some of the mis-arrangements that may be corrected.

The activities and purpose of a true father are an extension of our Father. This is the purpose. Would not he who loves extend the power of that love? Would not he who provides extend the power of his providence?

[If readers are unhappy with the term "Father", they might substitute mentally the word "Parent" or "Mother".]

10. Stephen as an extension.

Let us consider Stephen: perhaps his continuous self [6] that we spoke of has had sufficient refining for it not to be too separated from the cell of the Source and for that reason Stephen would feel less of a "thing".

Were Stephen to actually be the soul then Stephen would also be the Father and this is not so.

He is rather an extension, which can be used.

This knowledge is brought to your consciousness,

not as a gift but as a recall.

I have said on many occasions

that nothing I speak about is unknown to you.

Fear not your questions

for what you ask is what you know.

I assist as your memory,

only in so much as that I help the decision as to when you might recall.

I even assist when I tell

that to progress further in conversation sometimes confuses further.

Be at peace with yourselves,

for you know in your emotions what you should be

and how you should be.

Never let the mind persuade

against the emotions in these things.

I will depart now. God bless you all.

11. The Father has laid down a course that you will follow. And I say this to you: Think more of the course that All are to follow. For the plan is greater than you and I.

You have said even this night that you act and that you act in faith. If you have faith you know that if you did wrong you would be protected from your folly. For someone must act before I speak to you. Thomas must act. He must do something. Then I can help.

In coming to speak with me you also acted. Should your vehicle not have got you here then you would have known that it was not within the plan that you speak with Stephen. Should Stephen not act, and Thomas not act, then we would know also that this is within the plan.

The Father has laid down a course that you will follow. And I say this to you: Think more of the course that All are to follow. For the plan is greater than you and I. Think in terms of All, as well as all things. The earth which revolves around the sun and then the sun which revolves around another point. The course cannot vary, even if the earth or the sun chose, or even if we wished that it might follow a different course.

We must remember that the part of the path that we will follow is part of the path the earth travels, inevitably. We know this and we know that it is futile for us to try to follow a path other than that taken by the earth.

And in our minds we wish often to do what might take us from the inevitable path that we ourselves follow. The cells in our bodies, the particles in our blood, follow that course which is planned, neither knowing whence it comes, or where it is going. The earth still revolves, just as we must act.

The acting is the understanding of where we are, to appreciate the moment. The disappointments always come from the actions we feel that we might wish to take. All of these things are not possible and it is just as impossible for this earth to change place with another planet. In the course of our destinies we tend with the use of our physical minds to create a path which differs from what we are to follow and will follow. It would be easier to step off this earth than to change one moment of what our lives will be.

Michael: In which case, it seems futile to worry what we should do next or even to discuss it, because.. I see what you are saying is true because I have had so much experience of things working together that I in my material mind could not possibly plan. But for this reason it would seem futile to influence each other, or even to act.

Stephen: You will act, for this is part of the path also. Your action is part of the course. It is the mind that conceives and tries to create an action which is not of the Father.

Michael: When you look at members of the group or myself, do you feel that in any way we are off-course?

Stephen: You are where you should be at this time and one year from now you will be where you should be. Four years ago, in the past, you were where you wished to be. And you were content. You are in the same place, but not so contented. Has the place changed?...

Michael: Can you tell me - may I keep you? –
whether this inevitability comes from the role that the cell plays? Does the cell decide or does the Whole decide?

Stephen: The Creator of all, and the Whole and the movement, and the plan for all things, are there and cannot be altered. There is no one thing that decides. Except that each action has its reaction. I must leave. God bless you.

12. God's will and our will.

One member of the group was unhappy about a forthcoming move to another town, owing to her husband's work promotion. She asked: "Is it the Father's will that they should move?"

Stephen: "If it was not the Father's will there is no power in heaven or on earth that would bring the move about. Let us at least know that where we are and where we go must be the will of the Father."

Olive. "Where does our free will come into it then?"

Stephen: "The choice of saying yes or no. But the free will depends on many influences. We speak of the free will as though we had an original thought in our independent minds. What appears to be our will is dependent upon other influences. You yourself say that you would surrender your free will for your husband's ambitions, opportunity and happiness. Each of us, each day, surrenders our free will to some influence from another.

If I might give you an instance. You would prefer to sleep longer in the mornings but your child wakes you early; I jest a little. But think on this. For the free will that the Father has given to us is the freedom to love where it could be difficult to love and accept things that others might not accept. We are given the freedom to be happy about the influences that the Father, through others, may have upon our lives. Should your husband's superiors at work direct or ask him that he move should we disassociate that superior from the Father? Should we not know that if the Father directly wished your husband to go to another place, would He not use such an instrument for sending him there?

It is no mystery how the Father speaks and acts towards us. Each step we take is influenced by the Father for His purpose. We do not become puppets of each other, for I am influenced by you; I come because your wishes influenced my free will. Have you taken away my free will? No more then, has the Father taken away yours by influencing you through His instruments. Be at peace with the Will of the Father.

We have talked of self-determination, perfection and of the acceptance of all things as they are. It could be interpreted, were we not careful, that on one hand we may have foolhardy activity and, upon the other, negligent apathy. We should follow the middle path and that is the acceptance of our experience and what we ask for in our prayers.

What we have been asked to do is to give both our self determination and our apathetic acceptance into the Father's hands; then we have the satisfaction of knowing that we have not been inactive. We have taken the only sure action: To do that which is the will of the Father. Should we do this, then the Father might say that he is well pleased with our progress.

We have spoken then of what the Lord laid before us as a remembrance and his gift to us. Often, we have made the mistake in that we do not readily accept this gift, except in special circumstances only. The words used were that we should do this often. Let us not feel that it is only given to a few to call upon the Father for the blessing of what was offered. For all we need to do for ourselves is to call to mind that blessing and when we take the bread and wine in remembrance, then it is as the Lord said: His body that is LIFE and His blood that is LOVE that you take into yourselves. Do not be led into arguments that would separate one or either of these gifts; remember when you take each or any of the gifts, do this and remember to truly accept that gift. The Bread of Life and the Blood, which is Love."

13. Concept of how God operates using Man's Free Will.

Stephen continued: "Let me talk a little more of how I understand the plan of God could operate. I think that I speak with some knowledge, for I did think at one time that, had I kept my tongue still, maybe I would have continued in the physical existence with much greater use to the Whole. I searched in my heart and my mind, as to the wisdom of what my emotions led me to do and say. Was it the emotion of pride or mental conviction that caused me to act in a manner which some might refer to as disastrous? Without sounding immodest, that action of mine, through the will of the Father, has inspired many to achieve much greater things than I would have achieved myself. This is how I believe the Father uses us, for we are, because we have free will, unique in his kingdom.

We are like a machine or tool with many and varied functions that operates in a random rate and way. Imagine such a machine that chooses its own functions and actions randomly for a purpose that it is unaware of itself from one moment to the next! Were you to be the master of such a machine, would not the manner of using this machine be to observe the way that the machine is functioning at any particular time and supply work for the way that the machine is functioning?

Now think upon this very carefully. The physical mind, with its limitations, can only use what is subservient or obedient to it. That is because the physical mind itself has great limitations. Now, take away those limitations then you have the Master. He would need a machine that is not subservient, obedient to him, or under control, simply one that would *operate*. The usage and the product of the machine must then be unique or an act of *creation*! Therefore the machine must be a *co-creator* with the Master, for the purpose of the Master. Therefore, irrespective of what we decide to do, whether it be judged in retrospect as wise or foolish, it will be used for the Father's purpose. Let us make this machine mobile. We could understand by saying, that if you wished to travel from this country to another, then we could say that the Father has designed that you travel this journey. Whereas, in fact, you have chosen the journey. The experiences of that journey combined with what is the Father's purpose for you to achieve, are at the end of your journey.

14. Knowing and Knowledge.

The group had been having a serious discussion about Symbolism, before Stephen came. He began thus:

Stephen: A solemn gathering indeed, that seeks knowledge in such seriousness. In what way may I become serious with you? May I speak about symbolism too, for what are we here but symbols. What am I, a symbol of Thomas or of Stephen? What are we all? What is the earth on which we live, the air we breathe, but a symbol. We should remind ourselves that each of us gathered here has been gathered together before and done the same things. We have begun to recognize this by the same things; if we did not have symbols to recognize things by, how would we know the path? How would we recognize the place or the face? It must always be the same.

We have said that knowledge is not what we might believe but what we must know. Do not doubt that we have known others before, and there many things that we know, even though we had not been given the knowledge first. I have spoken of and indeed even yourselves have spoken of and have gained the knowledge of what you know. What we learn should be called what we can recognize, for we all know now in our minds we are different from each other. So we have a situation where what we know is not true knowledge. Does this confuse or is this clear? Someone wishes to comment?

A comment: I think that knowing that you know is important to grasp.

Stephen: So, we have misnamed knowledge. We must remember this, that what we often seek as knowledge can indeed be a fruit that does not nourish. We look for a mysterious understanding because we cannot accept what is. What is must be simple because we are it. We cannot be separate, for only when we ate the fruit of knowledge that we were advised not to eat did we feel that way. Look where it has brought us. Long journeys in time until each of us begin to discover, after many teachings, that the place that our knowledge has taken us to or taken us from is still with us. We have never left!

All that has happened was our knowledge clothed us. Where before we were naked to the truth, we recognized that we were unclothed, we were uncovered, and we were not separate. Now we have clothed ourselves and often continue to do so with these clothes of knowledge that we seek.

We say that many things repeat themselves throughout the ages and they tell us the same thing. Is this surprising? For what we are in truth, is no more than what we are. We may, if we wish, continue to clothe ourselves and seek for ourselves even finer garments than we originally had. But, the foundation of this clothing we have cast upon ourselves will be as firm as those of the house that was built on sand and will wash away. No matter how often we clothe ourselves, the garments, as with our physical garments, can never be permanent. Even if we were to paint our skins it would not hide us for long, for we are there.

Often we cannot feel the sun for we are clothed. The helmet that we have upon our heads often has a visor covering the face and if someone were to speak, we would only hear echoes. The echo will continue until the helmet is lifted. Then there will be no echo, no need to speak of what is. For we will see, feel the warmth, breathe the air that is there, that has never gone and can never be taken away. There, that is serious is it not?

Michael: Unfortunately my helmet, dear Stephen, is still on my head, therefore I have to ask questions.

Stephen: Therefore, I will echo what you ask.

15. Science, Facts, Akashic Records.

Olive: Can you explain in a way that a scientifically minded person can understand how the spirit survives death?

Stephen: The facts are there, if one would wish to see. The fact that he thinks, the fact that he has emotions, the fact that time is an inexact science, are all there to be investigated. That is if the investigation would be willingly undertaken. The facts of phenomena and of healing that are well documented do not fit in with the narrowed scientific theories that are often used in argument. Look then at these results that cannot be explained by using only limited theories and measurements. You might measure water with a jug or similar small vessel but you cannot measure the ocean with the same vessel.

If we confine what we wish to know to what we think or theorize we already know, we will have great difficulty. Be sure then, that the limitation that is being used is not a limitation of want to know, but how to know."

Olive: Some say all knowledge is to be found in the Akashic records. Is this true?

Stephen: The Akashic records is a very nice name if it describes that all experiences that have ever happened. For to experience is to create.

How best can I describe what I understand? The voice and the words I say are never lost. They are there and they continue on in perpetuity. It is the same with experience. These experiences are there. For without the knowledge and the knowing gained by these experiences, we cannot return and be at one with The Source. The Akashic records are, in the loosest form, records. In the widest possible form, they are the actual being of experience, because whilst in the physical body, most cases outside of the physical experience, make a whole. In the physical body, there is a false sense of separateness. In our other selves there is no such separation. There are only differences in consciousness, differences in experiences, but not separateness.

Even the words "to Love one another" imply a separateness. Remember the words of our Lord: 'Love thy neighbour as thyself'. We are joined to the whole, are part of it; "the unity" and "the Church" are other words which describe the concept. Not to love is like the man who kept banging his finger with a hammer. When asked why he did this, he answered, 'When I stop doing it, it feels so good'. This lack of love we show to ourselves, to the Church, to the community, is very significant. Maybe, after tonight, you will understand why I always ask you to pray for me.

Be wary of drawing conclusions, of looking at facts or happenings and believing that you are recognizing what is obvious. For throughout your life when you look back at important times you will find the obvious thing is very seldom the truth and would not have been a good choice. Profit by the experiences, profit by the sharing and learn much from others that you will have contact with. For this is an experience you can pass on to others. Beware of letting your hypothesis extend until you have drawn conclusions; do not close your mind to other possibilities. These possibilities will always be suggested by other people's hypothesis which could be right."

16. What is truth?

Stephen. We are here alive, able to move, communicate and reproduce. This is truth. The sun shines daily over all the earth. This is truth. The rain brings us the essential water for the growth of plants. This is truth and cannot be denied. Truth is a fond embrace, love, compassion, the wanting of good for all people, the healing of the sick in mind and body... one could go on and on.

Therefore, what we have learned of the truth will always correlate with what we learn again and again. For truth is like sun, constant and the same. One could wither an arm by constant suggestion then, by the same, one could correct a malady. This is why all the truths that we have known, all that we know of our Lord, must be repeated and repeated and be repeated again. What we must look at is not the individual attitudes and actions in the narrow perspective but at the results. For looking from a different point of view, the actions of Judas were as necessary as the actions of Pilate or the soldiers. We are always inclined to narrow the perspective to just the moment as the truth. Here it is!

But the perspective of the Whole is not just the moment. It is for all moments past and all moments to come. Each one, as it was for Judas in his time onwards, was the truth. Now, in retrospect, we may look back and see all the truths of those moments in a much broader perspective. We can see that the truth can become enlarged as part of the pattern of the Whole. All moments, every moment that is being perceived now for all people, is part of the pattern.

It is difficult I know, to be told to look at what is in front of you as the ultimate truth and then to be told to look even beyond that, to search for a greater perspective through the Source and visualize or image what again, could be the whole truth. This of course cannot be done by one mind alone and segregated. It must be done collectively, through each other, through the Whole and from the Whole and the Source back to us.

17. Recognizing the truth.

Stephen: There are many things that cause us to wonder and perhaps become excited. There are many things that we may hear or see that would show us things that are known to be true and this is good. But as always, even these words that I speak, they must be looked at with the greatest care. For man, in a body or without the body, believes many things in himself. The conclusions that he has drawn he fits into things that are true. He explains them to himself and would be apt to say, "I know these things that I have concluded are true, for are not these words here written a confirmation of that truth? Does not this that I do, speak with truth? Do not my figures add up? Therefore, the truth that is mine, I might give to another." Then he perceives others and says, "They are mistaken; they see the same things as I but their additions are incorrect. Therefore I shall take them back through what they have heard, and think they know to be true. Then from my conclusions of the truth, I shall adjust their arithmetic."

Can we then blame or judge that one who, when believing that he has the truth, offers this truth as a gift to others. We have been taught that to draw conclusions is to stop learning. To lead others to draw such conclusions, not from hate or deception but from love, would stop them from learning also. This is why the Father needs to watch over what we do. The Father has given each man the will to decide and listen for the truth and feel the truth for themselves, but not alone for His hand is outstretched. The hand of truth is always outstretched that we might grasp, each one for ourselves.

Physical man is complex; he might conclude that the egg may mean love, but truth is not the egg, but love! Think then, of how we must always look only for the Truth. Think of the emotions that come when we hear the stories of our Lord Jesus. We know the truth of these. You should disagree with what I, Stephen, say if it does not bring love and peace."

Question: Is the picture of reality as stated in the book I'm reading, true?

Stephen: The picture of reality, that is the true picture, is well known by the words of our Lord. It has been told very clearly, what is real and what is unreal. If the words that you read are simple and give the same concepts of reality that you have received they must be true concepts. Do not mistake what I have said, for words may be different; the methods of teaching and the description of reality might well, to the intellect, differ greatly. Summarize the book into the briefest concepts. Then compare the seeds of that book to the seeds of your knowing.

We often seek to analyze an expression of feeling, into concepts of mind that we place in words. Each of you here would describe the words that I have spoken differently and according to your own minds. But this I say to you, that your feelings are the same, although the understanding of your minds may be vastly different.

There are many paths to learning the Truth. Each path has different contours and to know the rightness of your path you have to look at your destination. If you feel sure and at peace within yourself that your destination is the same as those whose path may differ, then be at ease with your path and follow it. For it is your path, it is the one that you choose and understand.

18. Confirm truth – test untruth.

Stephen: In the physical thinking of man, the expansion and the repetition of the truth and the complete disregard for the untruth, hoping that it will drop away, is actually what happens. Whereas, once the truth has been accepted and it has been well recorded and taught, then we should concentrate on proving the untruth wrong which will always be able to be done. Make statements of the truth; then anything that contradicts the truth should be examined, discussed and disproved. Only the truth can have no contradictions; what is untrue will have contradictions and must then be disregarded.

Think of chemistry: unless a combination of elements has the desired result in a test, then that combination is unsuccessful. If in an experiment the combination of elements proved to be wrong would you then attempt to separate out the elements and use the same elements again to find out which of those elements are false or would you discard it and start the experiment again? The tendency is always to say that because there is some good in it that good should be taken out of the experiment and used. That in itself is wasted effort.

Again, with readings and teachings, irrespective of from whom or whence they come, with one exception, do not spend much effort in separating the good or truth from something that may have the majority of untruth in it. It would be better to disregard the whole. Accept only what has no contradictions whatsoever. Look for obvious contradictions; examine it closely and if the contradictions remain then the information should be disregarded.

Our thoughts can create for us happiness or unhappiness. They can often guide us to words, signs and interpretations that do not come from the Father, but which serve as confirmation as to how we think and feel ourselves. Often our thoughts and feelings are confirmed in many ways at a later date and in the light of truth are contradicted. Of course, you must respond to what you feel but it is better to say, "Now I feel happy; I feel content and at peace with myself so what I do, what I perceive, what I am at this moment, is what I ought to be." Never say when unhappiness is with you, "This is how I should not be." For to recognize that which in truth you are not is to create a self that is untrue."

Chapter 2

Jesus Christ

[Yes, there has been a Communicator other than Stephen, namely Jesus Christ. Several times I have heard this Voice, plainly other and greater than Stephen. Each time I am filled with awe and the strong sense of the numinous. I am not moved to question this Voice, only to listen.]

19. That all may be One.

The Voice of Christ: Sic Ecclesia Spiritus Sanctus[7]. I say to you this, that before all could dwell in the one house, there must be complete trust in the Father of that house. For even you, who were close to me, loved in a different manner. Never do we see the complete trust in the Father, even though the books and the teachings that we have had show us only this: that each of us, though we love, restrict our love at some point or other. So recognise this in your fellows and in your selves that your trust is limited, and your trust and love will manifest in diverse manners. Expect no more of others than you would of yourselves. This is why you live in these separate houses. Complete trust and the knowledge would enable you to dwell together. This is what we must learn. This is what you must teach. That you are here, and that all are here, and loved and cared for, is the proof that is shown to you. All must learn to trust, on that proof. This is all I have ever said and those that were before me have ever said. It must keep being said.

Stephen: Jesus once asked, *Why me?* The Christ or the connecting source from God has come to many as it will come to all of you. Be not awed by this. Jesus was the same as you all or the man who now walks along this roadway; he also has the qualities to be used by the Christ. Jesus was the perfect tool, therefore at that time there was only need for one; now it needs many.

[*Christ* then was the Spirit that was in Jesus. The word "Christ" is related to "chrism" and means "Anointed", "Anointed with Spirit". Jesus was thus Anointed with Spirit/Christ. In the next passage, Molly asks about *Jesus* Christ, while Stephen in his answer refers only to the *Christ*. The spirit of the historical Jesus, in perfect union, is taken up into the Christ. Christ is the outworking of the will of the Father.

This next passage is the key, and is crucial to Stephen's teaching about the Christ.]

20. "There never was a time when our Lord Jesus was not the Christ, nor any of the imaged creation of the Father not the Christ."

Stephen: There are many ways to ask but one question. I think we have all found a number of those ways. If I may be permitted, I shall answer that one question.

First, I shall answer the question: again in our way we wish to know the nature of *us*, why we are here, and for what purpose. All our beliefs of our religion are for this one purpose, to remind us of these things or to help us to recall them.

So let me attempt to answer in this way: first in the mind of the Father, we were conceived, and from that conception we were created in his image.

Do not be confused about the "image." We know that what we ourselves would create firstly has to be imaged. We know that in our minds, if we image these things, then they will in fact be created. Therefore we were imaged and all that we can see, feel and touch, were thus imaged. And all was created in that image. This may spoil some popular misconceptions, but this is so. The image that was created was the perfect image, the wonderful image of the whole tapestry of creation in the mind of the Father, (in whichever way we conceive him to be). *Christ is that image.*

To save us, we must first ask ourselves from what we must be saved?

Our salvation lies in our ability to receive and conceive the truth of our own perfection and of our own part and participation in what is the whole of the body of Christ.

We do not have to be saved and preserved from terrible and dire consequences that we may perceive, for all that is perfect is here, always has been and always shall be. All that we need saving from is the conception in our minds that we are separate from this perfection. We separate ourselves often by feeling that there is much that we must do to change ourselves, to be forgiven, to step away from sin, before we may be saved. Yet we are told in many diverse ways, that the path to salvation is the acceptance of Christ or the acceptance of the perfection of all that is.

For we must not forget that we were created in the image of the Father and therefore must be perfect. We, all of us, have often failed in grasping this perception, and for a more graphic illustration, through One who could accept this perfection perfectly, we were to recognise Christ.

There never was a time when our Lord Jesus was not the Christ; neither is there a time, when any of the imaged creation of the Father is not the Christ.

This we must understand: this is our salvation, our acceptance of what is. Once we accept the perfection of all that is then, as I have said before, there are no disasters; there are only disasters from the point of view of perfection.

The place of men's thoughts in the future of things, whether we call it religion or not, is the acceptance of what is perfect and we need to continually remind ourselves that all is perfect, and all is well. There is no sin too great that would continually separate you from the Father if you would not have that sin separate you.

To help us, we have had a demonstration of forgiveness, a sacrifice that is easy for us to remember, that is easy in our minds to conceive of as an intermediary. The intermediary that turns our minds into our hearts so that we can see the truth.

Look well and you will.

21. The Image: What we search for then must be the wider perception of the Source so that we might image.

Michael: I can understand that the Father images me and how therefore what I do may interlock with what happens with others. But I do not understand the distinction, if any, between what I image and what the Father images.

Stephen: In our minds we can but image to our own understanding and our knowledge of what is: therefore, it is often our own image that is restricted. To image correctly, we must first look and think and feel through the Source that has the wider perception. This is the whole point of our worship, our devotions, our studies, and our feeling with each other and for each other: for we often have in our hands and in our minds what we can perceive ourselves. What we search for then must be the wider perception of the Source so that we might image.

[On a later occasion]
To move Thomas was like the small boat having to move the larger one! How may I assist?

22. Do we experience Jesus Christ more when we die?

Molly: I wanted to ask about Jesus Christ, whether we are with him all the time and whether we experience him more when we die.

> Stephen. Hear the words that you have spoken!
> Are we nearer to him when we die?
> Look at the things that we know,
> things that we have been taught:
> That he is our Lord, is ever with us, that he is always close.
> This we must understand,
> for there is no journey that we must take,
> not one thing that we must cast off,
> for the nearness of our Lord.
> In our minds it may be conceivable that when we have cast off one barrier, or one body, we might see Him more clearly. But - "See?" is that the right word?
> For the Lord is a presence and a being-with, not as an individual but as all pervading and as with all.
> What we should ask is "How must I recognize the Lord here with me now?
> How must I look for him that I may see him?
> But not with a physical eye to do the seeing
> but with the eye of my heart,
> and with the eye of my emotions.
> Feel great joy and you feel the Lord.
> Feel great love and you feel the Lord.
> Feel great happiness and you feel the Lord.
> Feel first these things, for often we look for a feeling that is greater than our experiences that we have each day.

We must find for ourselves strangeness,
in order to recognize what is ordinary.
What we seek is a heightened sense of emotion
that we have through our understanding.
If when we feel love
and we understand completely what it is that we love,
then the emotions do heighten
and we feel ourselves comforted or protected from all harm.
And our emotions are heightened at these times
through the knowledge of when and whence the protection and
love come.
Then we will recognize the Source of these emotions.
Would it not be a strange Christ
that he should be at a distance
and come only under special circumstances to special people
that they might recognize him on rare occasions.
He would indeed become a stranger to us.
He is ever with us.
The understanding even that we have of ourselves
is often the understanding of his presence with us.
The sorrow we feel at times
when we are not pleased with our own thoughts and feelings
is the sorrow he feels with us.
The joy that we feel when we are pleased, when we are happy,
when we are content,
is his joy, his contentment,
for he is with us.
Let us not think that it is for special people, or that we must experience an emotion that we have never experienced.
For each of us experience the Lord and have continued to experience him even at this moment, for he is with us.
Think not to judge that you yourselves are lacking
that you have not been at one with our Lord,
for in truth you cannot be separated, if you would use that
term.
The closest you will ever be to the Lord
is when you are least conscious of him.
For the more that you are true to yourself
and the least conscious of yourself,
you do not say, "I know that I am me, for I feel that I am me!"

The knowing is in being.
There are times when many, through their seeking,
as they might look upon their image in a mirror,
might truly cry out with joy:
"I see the Lord! I feel the Lord!
Now at this wonderful moment I am experiencing the Lord!"
They symbolically have stepped beyond themselves
and have but observed what is always there.
I have said that the most distant thing
is closer to you than the tongue of your mouth.
And the Lord is with you as is the blood in your veins.
But unless you bleed are you conscious of this blood?
The emotions that are heightened at this time,
are a bleeding out of your consciousness
that the presence within you can be viewed
from outside yourselves.
These times are wonderful to behold;
but do not allow them to take from you the knowledge
that the blood that is Christ's flows in your body.
    Do not seek to bleed
so that you might prove that you have blood.
If you bleed, rejoice,
for then you recognize your Christ with another sense.
    Do not despair also when others who see themselves bleeding,
and are filled with joy of another and a different recognition, and
say "I see the Christ!"
    Do not weep for yourself, that you do not bleed.

23. Second Coming of our Lord.

Olive: Might I ask about the Second Coming of our Lord? If we are
one with Him and He is one with us in the way that you have described
how would His Second Coming be different?

Stephen: For this I have knowledge. For often we cannot recognize and we do not know - not all know that Christ is their blood,
as their blood is to their body. So therefore the blood shall spurt
forth and be seen. For none will be able to deny it. For they will feel
the wetness, the warmth and they will understand the importance
of this blood.

Michael: In the dreams that we were discussing last time I spoke of the old lady, the church saving us from the wetness of the water. You are not making any connection there are you?

Stephen: If we were to make this connection, we might say that your old lady being your church, and yourself: you interpret the dream, and feel the things from this dream, do not know, and do not feel that the blood runs even through her veins. So you might say to yourself "I will cut open the old lady, to see whether there is blood - or is she dry? For like all that is created the blood is equally as well in the old lady as with all things. For those who have little love for that old lady they will find others through whom the blood flows equally as well. Stay close to the body of that one that gives you warmth for it is the blood that flows through that warms the skin. Do not worry and say to another "You cannot be warm there, for I am warm here, and this is where the warmth is." Neither can you say to yourself "I must depart from this warm old lady for over there another must surely be warmer."

We have had much blood this night!

With the blood that is our Lord Jesus Christ may there be blessing for you all.

24. More than a great teacher.

Olive: Stephen, I would like to know more about our Lord Jesus. Something puzzles me in particular. Many sects say that He is a great teacher, just like many others. I feel He is much, much more significant than that.

Stephen: Your simple questions have a way of being very complicated when it comes to an answer. Let us speak of 'Significance'. We can look at significance from two opposite directions. To yourself, the Lord Jesus has a greater significance than being a great teacher. To others, He is just a great teacher. Perhaps it would be better then, if I give the significance of our Lord to myself.

Firstly, let us understand Jesus as a man. The body was as physical as the body here now that is being used, the one difference being that instead of being like us where we have a continuum of experiences collected by the physical He had a physical brain and body that was created, that was directly influenced by the Source and without past experiences. This direct influence is The Christ.

To confuse you even more, there was also a continuous self of Jesus the man. But I have often spoken of memories fetched into each incarnation, chosen for the needs or possible needs of that incarnation. In the particular case of Jesus, the Divine need was that an example of complete cell influence, or direct influence from the Source, should be manifest in a physical body of man. You have been taught by Jesus on many occasions that the things that He did were done by the Father, not by the grace of the Father but by the Father. It was also said by Him that these things that were done by the Father, through the physical body of Jesus, we might do also.

The significance then of Jesus the man to myself is that there was the complete influence of the Source in the man with none of the past experiences which are collected in what you call your 'Continuous Self' influencing His physical mind, but only those of the Source.

What is often interpreted by a number of people as the doubts or sadness of Jesus was a manifestation of the physical mind that registered the pain and disappointment but did not act upon it under its own initiative but allowed the action to be that of the Father.

This then, is the significance. For if I or all of us were to obtain this state whilst we were in the physical body we and all of those surrounding us would be blessed indeed as were those who surrounded Jesus at that time.

25. I am the Door.

Stephen: "The Lord said, 'I am the way and the light'. These are concepts given to help our understanding so let us be careful not to make them solid. Here is another concept. Think of Our Lord as being the first thread that has passed through the tapestry. For the way of this thread is the way of all true threads of the tapestry. That He is one with the Father is true. That the Father came to us as the thread is true also. Likewise that the door be the way that one must pass, as did the thread that was of, and is, the Father.

We insert a separation each time with our concepts of us, space and the Father. Therefore, if we put our Lord with the Father, then we have us, space and our Lord. This is not what our Lord taught us. He came with us and we are of Him so he is of us. The way that He shows is the way that brings us to know that we are of the Father. The doorway shows a space; a barrier is envisaged with perhaps a wall. The opening of that barrier in our minds is the separation that we feel. We should strive to pull down from our minds and our hearts the barrier that we have so carefully built. For we see that, as our Lord made a doorway through which we can pass, there is no barrier at this point. Think rather that He said 'Do as I do, become as I, become the doorway' so that the barrier is nothing but doorways. If in your mind you see a distance that you must travel know that it is nonexistent for there is no journey to make."

26. Jesus Christ - his life and his teachings.

Olive: We would like you to tell us more about Jesus Christ - his life and his teachings.

Stephen: That is a little like asking a thirsty donkey to drink!

The message that our Lord brought is, as was our Lord himself, simplicity in itself. He shows that we can live the life that we have been given by the grace of the Father, for the purposes of the Father, and unseparated.

You have spoken of fear [your fear of "dying to self"] but really your fear can be seen in quite another light. Nearly always we conceive of fear as a physical fear of a hurt or of extreme discomfort and confusion.

The real fear that we have is the fear that we would have, if I may jest, if we were to hang on to the tail of a wild horse and were afraid to let it go. For in truth, what we fear are not the perils but the ultimate safety. We must let go of the tail.

The message and the words he continues to give you are that you do not grasp for something that is passing at great speed. No more is what you must grasp moving at a greater speed than would be the rock of safety if you were rushing in a fast-flowing river.

He says to you "Fear not, reach out and grasp my hand in the rush and the perils of life that you are passing along, and the path that you are following." There is stability in the rock of security that will intercede for you against the current, that by yourselves you cannot resist.

He says to you that you must reach out and grasp what is firm, and let go what would propel you along into further uncertainty for what you have now is your uncertainty, what you grasp for is your security.

Always we conceive that we must surrender but in fact we do what is the opposite of surrender when we grasp this purity.

The purpose of your lives, of your path, is to teach you, and for you to learn what is secure and what is perilous. The message of our Lord is that you should abandon this oneness with yourself that does not enable you to reach out and *grasp what is whole.*

Each of these things that he bade you to give up and let go of are the things that are the momentum of the journey; the fear that you have is the fear of security and of peace, if you would but hear and feel.

The Lord would say "Stop! Hold! For I am the Rock, I am your salvation; join with me that you might cease to be swept into journeys of uncertainty."

This then is the message of the Lord: how you should stop; how you should reach out. There are words sufficient.

We often lose from our sight and our hearts the reasons for the words.

[These words about the Christ need to be read alongside Stephen's words about Creation, and the purpose of our life on Earth. Christ, the anointing Spirit is inseparable from this earthly life. "Letting go of the tail of the horse", salvation, is the acceptance of the Love behind the Christ of the present moment, the experiences we receive from God, from the Source.]

27. Jesus our Saviour.

Olive: Stephen, I would like a deeper meaning for the words, "Jesus our Saviour."

Stephen: Look then not for deep mysteries such as that the sacrifice of one body would have saved us all. The example, and pointing out what we know, is what will save us. An example was shown to us that the *limits* we place ourselves in our minds, conscious minds, do not apply when we think of the Whole.

An example of the messages that Jesus gave to us whilst he was with body was a time when some of his friends wished him to prove to others conclusively his relationship with God and the power that he would possess, by the grace of God.

If it were a conversation in this company, we might say, "Come along now, show these marvels, show them here." And Jesus answered at that time: "If you would see the power of God, then choose anybody other than yourself you would wish to die at this moment. This I will perform for you." Of course the choice was not made but a great lesson was taught to those who heard.[8]

Those who were witnesses at this time saw that the saving of men was a saving of their thoughts and their minds. They would fear that they are not separate, that they are together, that they are one, irrespective of the things that they would do to one another. It is never from real choice but only our mind would simulate a necessity for these actions.[9]

The saving that our Lord gave was to show us that our minds often lead us to actions that are not of us [of our real selves] and it is these actions that we must deny. These are thoughts that of necessity we must deny.

Put it like this: we can listen to the words and stories. Some of these stories are real, some imagined and some are concocted to give an example but all were true of the Whole.

The saving is the saving of slavery to your own minds, the release of bondage to imagined ills and wrongs, desires that are not within you but are created by the environment, by the desires or imagined desires. The protection of what you have is a false desire for it can neither support you, nor love you, nor comfort you in itself. It becomes a support and comfort only when you have imagined it to be so and therein comes the bondage.

When you love somebody with your mind you build an image of what that somebody must be, for you love them. You create a non-existent person and when that one which you would love disappoints you and acts differently from the image that you have created you suffer great hurt.

Jesus also, in many examples, showed us the way to be saved from this folly.

We often get an image that in some way the death of the body of Jesus in itself cleansed us yet we fail to see how he showed that the body itself was meaningless.[10]

All should never regard this body as a possession.

Just as a gift that we should use and care for as we would a gift,

not be in bondage to it and its imagined desires; to release us, to show us, that was the purpose, and that was the saving. If we would but accept it, the lesson.

Many, throughout our lives and before, have given us proof again and again of how these lessons were true and they themselves have been saved.

Michael: I recognize the truth of what you are saying, Stephen, and it speaks very much to my own thoughts. But speaking for myself, and I think also for others, although I recognize this and have recognized this, I do in fact inflict a tension upon myself and unhappiness.

Stephen: We are here to learn... how not to inflict unhappiness. There are many times when Michael is happy.

Michael: This is true, but there are too many times when Michael knows all that Stephen and the Father has taught, and feels it, or thinks he feels it, and yet he still feels tense, and afflicts himself with this tenseness, and Michael gets annoyed with himself for doing this.

Stephen. Then be saved, Michael.

Michael: I would like to be saved Stephen, but I am not fully. Might I meditate better? Might I.. what.. the better?.. that I don't do this to myself?

Stephen: Michael is still looking for a mystery, for a key. Michael has all that it needs. We may search often by walking backwards so we look often where we have been, but never where we are going. Look around you often. Do not conceive of the things that might have been, as they should be, but as they are. Enjoy, feel and experience that, for all that is a gift to you; this moment now and all moments are yours. Are you unhappy now?

Michael: No, I am not.

Stephen: Why should you be thus happy? I ask this question because Michael asks this same question of himself and he analyses his happiness and sees no reason for it.

Michael: When I get influenza, or someone else gets a disease, this could be said to be the result of what I have inflicted upon myself. Is it the will of the Father that I suffer from a disease?

Stephen: It is the will, and part of the Whole that we experience all things without exception. It is a matter of the way we react to those experiences and the way we live; for our reactions and the way we act towards each other and to the circumstances are the way we learn.

You have confused in your mind what I spoke to you last time. I said that you are here and that you are doing the will of the Father. The plan of our lives, from the moment of our birth until the moment of our death, has a path, an inevitable path that will be followed. In that path there are many and varied experiences. The free will of man enables him to act and react to those experiences.

Inaction would not be satisfying to yourself and it would not teach you much. We might say that it would be easier for a child to remain in a cocoon and remain there continuing to be fed by its mother until the life is past and gone. But the child would learn little and life would be pointless for all must be experienced, all is experienced.

I am reminded once again that quite often it has been said among us by John that there is no good and no bad and I think at the time it was said that whether rain is good or bad depends on the point of view. In the news recently, in this country that has been without rain they would tell you that rain is good - and I have been aware of complaints that rain is not particularly good. Again with your malady: Do you have the knowledge to say that your body did not need this malady? For all things are needed. All experiences are necessary.

Michael: You said of Thomas's cold, "This cold was well caught!"

Stephen: He learned of his cold and he had the experience. It was important. Did he suffer like a martyr? Or were others martyrs? These are the things. They are so simple that we must realize that there is not one thing that moves, one planet that revolves, that is not of the plan. The plan is for the experience and learning of all. Let us not wish that it were otherwise for we would be the losers.

28. "How is growth towards the one Consciousness best achieved?"

Stephen: I think it is better if I summarise the whole of what was said last time I had the pleasure of talking with you. For often I have said that words are but seeds and it is the feeling that you have when you hear these words that is important for often, even though I speak much, little effect is actually caused.

We spoke of many things and my answers to all were the same. It will be the briefest summary in the name of creation and of existence that there has ever been.

> That to correct the disorders
> and to arrive back in a consciousness or state of oneness,
> whichever name we may choose,
> we must experience many things
> during our lives as separate particles.

There are laws that *can* govern
(I say "can" with full meaning)
can govern the actions and the type of experiences
that each separate part of us will have.

The law I speak of, of course, is this one known to you as "Karma". This karma is not a punishment but the formula by which it is inevitable that the disorders will be corrected.

When through practice and assistance, and listening to practice and assistance, we reach an awareness (other than the lowest physical awareness) we may bypass the necessity of what can be called karma and the law that must govern us so that the corrections are inevitable.

These laws, and the achievement of raising the consciousness above these laws, have been well taught and taught in the best way to achieve this and these of course are your spiritual teachings.[11]

The beginning, the Creation, as I have explained, was not a matter of time measurement that we could even begin to understand.

Sufficient to say that what you are beginning to feel can be discerned in the words of the stories of the Creation and the Fall. From then on, in the book of Knowledge wherein which you have all proofs and all answers to all questions [the Bible], you have described the efforts of man and the manifestations [of God's actions], the years spent trying and in some cases succeeding in correcting disorders.

You have been given a clear pattern of what is correct and what is incorrect. All this gives you your spiritual guide to rise above the necessity of keeping on the line of the laws of "karma" (the word you know best).

Through these times, and through your ages which compared with the whole of creation are so brief (for we are all so young) , it was plain that as long as was necessary would be allowed for the correction of these disorders.

Therefore, the Source, our God, connected us within these times with what can only be described as his only Son, the perfect Connection, our Lord Jesus Christ. He did this to show the way more clearly, to show the example of the way in which we should behave and other things that we should think and of the love that we should give.

Think of our Lord and ask yourself these questions: as a man was he greatly learned in mathematics? Was he a fine musician? Was he a great surgeon? A strong hunter?

Therein lie your answers. For the way to salvation without karma, and the way that must rise above karma, [is] to rise above those things we do, [and] trouble ourselves with. We trouble ourselves with these things to the extent that we continually try to impose them upon our spiritual progress, instead of including our spiritual progress into [these things].

This is what I may have said to you at the last meeting. I may have spoken and answered specific questions, and spoken of accident and incident; but this, as I have said so often, has to do with the Whole.

This is the message, this is your answer. What you have to achieve has been clearly before you in two thousand years of your time. Do not think that the Lord would have impatience, for remember it is a very short time, and but a moment.

29. Stephen's Prayer.

Therefore I ask now as your teacher, that we pray, and whilst we pray each with our own words, from our own hearts, remember this that I have said, and you may ask, in the words that I often ask,

> "Lord, let me forget that I am me,
> Let me know that I am with thee,
> Let me not separate myself from thee,
> Because I am me."

Bless you all.

30. Salvation.

Michael: Could you talk of Salvation? Could you narrow things to this question, to clarify in my mind the meaning of this word?

Stephen: Salvation, to use the concept which we used earlier:
Salvation is to be saved from being stagnant:
to keep the purity and the clearness.
Do not mistake the word 'purity',
For as with sin, purity is a relative matter.
To flow and to progress, to be at the point where you are now and to continue further to the points
where you were or shall be.
To come eventually back to the Source

with the mis-arrangements rearranged,
The Christian message is clear on Salvation.
For Christians, this can be the only concept.
Think of this though.
Before the Second Coming of the Lord Jesus,
the Christ, all will not be Christians,
And yet Christians and non-Christians
Will be saved alike according to their purity,
according to their lack of sin,
according to their love,
for this is the message that even you would understand as Christians from your own Scriptures.
The Lord himself said:
that even though they may be Gentiles,
if they feel the way of the Light,
and are faithful to this way,
and are pure in their heart,
and they love others as they love themselves,
they shall have a greater call on salvation
than the priests and them that keep the law, but in their hearts sin against their name, and against themselves.
When you have all come to trust me more,
I shall speak further of these things, not just I, but those that you will listen to;
but first be sure in your own hearts that you wish to hear,
and that you understand whence this comes. Bless you all, and pray for me.

31. Let this cup pass from me.

["My God, why hast thou forsaken me?" They are the words of a psalm that starts in dejection and finishes in praise of the Lord]

Olive: I would like a deeper understanding of our Lord's words in the Garden of Gethsemane: "Let this cup pass from me" and His words from the cross, "My God, why hast Thou forsaken me?" I have never been able to believe He has doubts, as some have preached. So why is it He uttered these words?

Stephen: Let this cup pass from me, this cup of disappointment, this cup of non-love, and this cup that is the witness to the frailty of man

44

and man's mind. We have often spoken of the disappointment that the ones whom you love bring to you. This is the bitter cup and the sour herbs that our Lord prayed about. He prayed not that His task and His duty be taken from Him; He prayed that the others be strengthened, that they would not weaken. That they would not be a disappointment unto themselves, for each of them there failed in their own minds, in many ways, their Lord. So Jesus prayed for them, not for himself.

"My God, why hast thou forsaken me?" They are the words of a psalm* that starts in dejection and finishes in praise of the Lord. All of those who were nearby knew of this psalm and understood, for a psalm is but a song of praise. Were that the body had been a little stronger, he would have finished those words.

Think of that testimony, that to be subjected to pain and agony, the reaction of our Lord was only to teach and give testimony of the love and gentleness of the Father.

32. The twenty-third psalm.

Stephen: I will not stay long, therefore I will just talk. You will find what I say will answer your questions, even though what I say you have often heard before, and often you have spoken:

Where you lead, I will follow:[12]

if it be your will, then I will follow, for you are my shepherd,

and you *do* lead me beside green pastures.

you *do* lead me beside still waters.

you will always lead as you have,

through death and through life,

and I am here because it is your will.

Teach me, O Father, more that I should follow you and not look either to the right or to the left,

let me be one who would follow and walk in your footsteps.

---

* [From Psalm 22] "My God, my God why have you abandoned me? I cried desperately for help, but still it does not come,

During the day I call to you, my God, but you do not answer..." [The whole psalm parallels the events of the crucifixion and concludes:]

"I will tell my people what you have done,

I will praise you in their assembly,

Praise him you servants of Jacob!

He does not neglect the poor or ignore their suffering

He does not turn away from them.

But answers when they call for help."

Let me not be concerned with the fact
that I do not know where your steps lead,
only that I may trust and love you.
    For if I do this, I need have no doubt
    of the destination being according to your will.
    For where else would your steps lead me, other than the path
that you yourself travel on my behalf, that I may follow.
    If I know this, then surely goodness and mercy will follow me all
the days of my life, and I will dwell with you.
    Sometimes on this path I may feel the cold of the wind, and if I
look to the left and see those that stand by my left hand, I may wish
that I be with them.
    Other times I may look at those on my right hand, and I may
wish that I were with them.
    But always, Father, my foot is drawn and I must follow. Let me see
that where my feet are drawn, this is not penance but my path.
    God bless you both.

Jesus: Your fruits are your own integrity, not the action of others.
Let us be judged by the Father and not by ourselves.

Chapter 3

The "Fall" and the "Atonement"

33. Discussion.

To understand Stephen we have to keep his view of reality before us and not relapse into split vision, with the "spiritual" separated from the "physical", "good" from "evil" and so. All reality emanates from one Source, the nature of which is love. Each successive present moment whatever it may be, whether it may be an event or whether it is a spiritual intuition or receiving, is projected from the Source, is imaged by the Source, and our salvation lies in accepting this, whether we do or do not like what we receive from the Source. In church we acknowledge this when we sing or quote "This is the day that the Lord hath made", "in everything give thanks", "rejoice in the Lord always", "God in whom we live and move and have our being," "God...in all, through all, and above all." This is at the heart of the teaching.

Many of the conversations with Stephen that follow help us to overcome beliefs and prejudices and accept salvation as he defines it.

Nearly everybody knows the story of the Garden of Eden, where Adam and Eve lived in happy communion with their God. And how a serpent tempted Eve to eat the fruit of the tree of knowledge of good and evil. How she ate the fruit, and persuaded Adam to do so likewise. They fell from grace, and were driven from the Garden by an angry God.

Ken Wilber's words about the Perennial Philosophy, in Part Four, suggest that the Adam and Eve story crops up in the great religions in many guises.[13] The underlying theme he describes as the story of how we as wavelets are part of the Ocean. The wavelet forgets that it is the Ocean. That is the Fall. In the story of the Garden of Eden, Adam and

Eve "fall" from their state of oneness with the creator of all things, use their own judgement about right and wrong and are expelled from the Garden. As for the Atonement, the wavelet remembers its oneness with the Ocean; the Christian "dies to self, rises with Christ," to oneness once more with the Creator.

Christians call this forgetting "The Fall". The restoration of our memory of connection to the Source is "The Atonement", the At-onement.

The big theological problem for Jews and Christians is that if God is good, how is it that there is so much evil in the world? And then there is the question, how are we to be restored to our connection with God and evil vanquished? There is an important strand of Christian thought that teaches that we are saved or restored by the death of Jesus on the cross.

34. Stephen's version of the Fall, and the Atonement.
Bill Andrews: Perhaps Stephen, as you know our minds and our thoughts there may be questions that some of us want to ask yet cannot frame. Perhaps you could help us with the answers to these questions. This is not meant to be a clever test but an honest attempt to ask for assistance.

> Stephen: One question that is often asked,
> and is still uncertain in the minds of all here,
> is why God created what can behave in a manner
> that is so imperfect and so un-Godlike?
> Of course the Father[14] did not create any imperfection
> but what the Father is, and what must extend from the Father,
> must do so with the will and the desire
> and the love of the Father.
> It has been said that good and bad are only apparent
> when each of these things are there,
> to compare the difference.
> As a simple answer, with no attempt
> to explain the complexity of the meaning,
> then I shall say that from free choice
> each of what was created will become good and perfect
> and in that state love the Father.
> The created has chosen, or will choose this perfect state,
> from the comparison with what was not good.

48

But it is a hard way that the comparison must be learnt.
But we have been told a story which contains the concept,
and can be learned from:
That man and his mate were of Love,
and were for the extension of the Father.
And the comparison was persuaded on them.[15]
The persuader was the feeling of need for the comparison;
the created, from choice chose to recognize what it had
only by the comparison.
Because of the wish for a comparison,
we therefore have needed to travel far,[16]
then to return whence we came
to gain what we had already,
what is there for us to take, and to accept what is ours,
at any time we wish comparison.[17]
Think on these things.
What you would have, you have. to cast away the

It is much like the beautiful woman who cried
that the mirror, in which she should see herself,
was taken from her,
for she felt that the beauty that was hers
she was not able to recognize.
In fact, a story has been given to all children,
that, simply told,
gives the truth for which we all seek.
I may quote "Mirror, mirror, on the wall, who is fairest?
Is it I?"
    For if we continue to deny our fairness,
and look always for a comparison,
we will always find a comparison.
The Lord Jesus said often
"Compare yourself not with others." [18]

35. Stephen tells this parable about the atoning death and resurrection of Jesus.

Stephen: There was a great lord who provided for his people,
all that they needed, all that they should have,
all these things that they possibly could want.
What he asked in return was that they love him.

And it occurred at one time to these people,
that they might be considered prisoners,
for there they were, where the Lord would have them.
And because they must love the Lord
they must do only as the Lord chose them to do.
They did not argue that it was wrong
what the lord chose for them to do,
but only that they might choose for themselves.
On knowing of this
 the lord cast them out
from this place where he cared for them,
telling them firstly that when he did not provide
they would find that they needed work. to protect themselves,
and that all these things and all creatures
that were there in the place of the lord,
that loved the lord and were obedient to the lord,
and did not harm them, did go with them also,
and they might choose what they would wish to do.
And the lord warned them also that their choice
must lead them to pain,
must lead them to anguish,
must lead them to suffer;
that it would be good
for they would come to know
through their own choice
and in choosing the suffering
that the place that the lord had given them was the best,
And it would be the place that they must choose.
In a very short while
those who had left
understood this to be true
and they made overtures to the lord
that they be forgiven.
They offered from the sweat of their brows,
from the blood of their labours,
many things to the lord, for their forgiveness. *
For they had decided
that their stupidity and crime

_____

* Stephen is referring to the system of making sacrifices and burnt offerings in
the Temple at Jerusalem as a way of atoning for sin and pleasing God.

and offence to the lord
that they did not love sufficiently,
would require all of this.
And the time came when the lord, knowing of their anguish,
knowing the only sacrifice of gift that he wanted of them
would be their love,
understood that they had chosen to pay a penalty.
This posed a problem for the lord,
for he loved them as they must love him,
and one who loves truly could not impose
nor accept the penalty.
So he decided that he must teach them
and show them an example of what love was.
He called them together unto him,
and sat as a judge
and said to them,
"The penalty that you must pay
the sacrifice that you must give
is more than you have.
But as you know - and have decided for yourselves:
This sacrifice must be paid."
For [then] the lord reached into his treasures,
and took what was dearest unto him, and destroyed it
in front of the eyes
of those that could see,
so that they would understand
that the price they could not pay,
was paid for them. **

** A modern Catholic view (similar to that pointed to by Stephen} is that of St
Anselm who refers to the need of satisfaction of sin. No sin, as he views the matter,
can be forgiven without satisfaction. A debt to Divine justice has been incurred
and that debt must needs be paid.[Quotations from the _Catholic Encyclopaedia_.
Anselm of Canterbury, C.E 1033-1109: _Cur Deus Homo_] Jesus' death is regarded
as satisfaction for that debt. This view has also been taken over by Evangelical
theology and is still the official view of the Catholic church.

   It can be argued that this "debt to Divine justice" has much in common with
the Old Testament Lex talionis, "eye for an eye" and nothing to do with the Christian God of Love; this is what of course Stephen is arguing. Lex talionis also has
something in common with the Eastern idea of karma. Elsewhere in relation to
this concept, Stephen says that karmic debts can only be repaid with love. (i.e. the
inevitability of karma is not part of Stephen's thinking.) _(continue on page 52)_

He showed and gave an example of the love that he gives
and the love that he would expect.
Still, it is difficult for those to understand
and know and believe,
that this debt has been paid.
It is still difficult for them to conceive
that they have been given the ability... to love.
They would doubt that they are perfect,
they doubt that they can perform
given the opportunity
the same sacrifice
that their master and lord
made on behalf of them.
They would continue to suffer
for they judge themselves badly.
Therefore the lord knowing this,
and knowing that they will need to be shown
that love can repair
all that has been undone
even what has been broken
and destroyed in the eyes of them all,
would have to return
the thing most precious to him,
in the sight of them;
to keep them conscious
and to stop them
destroying themselves with remorse
and with lack of love for each other,

There is a temptation to take a Biblical metaphor too far and draw unwarranted conclusions. It can be plausibly argued that Irenaeus and Anselm have done just this with Matthew 20:28//Mark 10:45 writing that Jesus gave his life "as a ransom for many". Widely known in Jesus' time was the *Fourth Book of Maccabees*, perhaps written c. 100 BCE. Chapters 14.11 to 17.6 describe the martyrdom of a widow and her seven sons. At 18.22 we read *"They became as it were a ransom* for our nation's sin, and through the blood of these righteous one and their propitiating death, the divine Providence preserved Israel which before was evil entreated. For when the tyrant Antiochus saw the courage of their virtue and their endurance under torments, he held up their endurance to his soldiers as an example .."* [my italics]. Exactly these terms "ransom" "sacrificial blood" and "propitiation" are applied to Jesus in the New Testament. It was the later theologians who took away the "as it were" in their thinking.

to stop them destroying themselves
for placing the blame
that they felt for themselves
upon the shoulders of another.
He comes to them daily and speaks with them.
Many do not
feel that they are worthy
to hear the voice of that Lord
and when he speaks
they explain the sound
and the words that they hear
in many different ways.
They look at their misery
and use this as a proof
of their own lack of righteousness.
They insist often
that the Lord is the one
that punishes them,
the one who cannot forgive
though they have seen this forgiveness.
Like sheep outside of a fold
even though the gate of the pasture
has been opened unto them
they still require the shepherd.
Until that time when the shepherd is come,
comforting noises and messages
come from inside of the pasture
then the sheep hearing these noises
face in that direction
ready to be herded once more
to the comfort.
Some of these messages are familiar to us all.
The message that tells us
that if we do not bear the fruit of love,
then surely we must wither and die.
This would not be a curse
or a punishment from the Lord
but a judgement upon oneself.
The messages come clear
but they are accepted

to fit in with what is judged by the receiver
to be worthy of their guilt.
The less the guilt
the simpler the message
and that message is always
that the gate is open.
God bless you all

[It could be said that Stephen's parable has the same message as the parable of Jesus about the Prodigal or Lost Son; namely, if you want to return to communion with God, you just come, and you will find open arms.]

36. The Story of the Camel in the Desert.
[Should the wilderness of unknowing that we travel leave us in ignorance if we did not ask the Christ?]

Stephen: We had almost confused Thomas *into his mind*! I had a story given to me once: a camel driver, after many days of crossing the wilderness, knew that his camel had become tired and that should he continue the camel would surely die. Also he knew that if he did not reach the oasis very soon he would die also. He might then have decided that this was inevitable, for he could not live without the camel to take him to the water and the camel would not live to take him there.
Those of us who heard the story were asked,
were we the driver, what would our actions have been?
Should the wilderness of unknowing that we travel leave us in ignorance if we did not ask the Christ[19]? Or are we perhaps to insist that our experience causes us to require this ignorance? In each case we may not know if we cannot decide upon the answer to this.

> This is our task: it is this that we must understand.
> Each of us often, in our lives, has come to this point.
> Each time we are not sure that the help is really there.
> But here I am, the help,
> with the question that only you can answer.
> Would someone now decide to give an answer?
> It is more profitable, then, that each of you
> listen to the words of each other and, more importantly,
> to the words of yourself. God bless you all.

Chapter 4

Sin, Evil and Judging

37. Sin and Stagnation.

Stephen: I thank you again for the invitation. You have questions, Michael?

Michael: We have several questions. Could you comment on this verse from the *Bhagavad Gita*[20] I think your answer may help to throw light on the question of sin and suffering in the world:

[10.35] "I am the gambling of the cheat, I am the splendour in everything splendid" [I also quoted Isaiah 45:7 ff:] "I the Lord God create peace, and make war. Is there any evil in the city and the Lord hath not done it?"

Stephen: I could almost believe that you have not read the Scriptures! However, let us not discuss it in a concept from the Scriptures. Let us discuss it in the concept of the laws of cause and effect.

Try to realize that you are unrestricted in the bodies and lives that you have left and will live.

Take it that each debt must be paid, for each effect did have a cause.

To say that these (and this is a poor word) debts are incurred and that they must be paid back is again restricting the concept of the law.

To attempt to say that it is not God or a manifestation of God in each of these sufferings, and also in the things of good, would be inconsistent in itself, for God created what is here.

Think of a beaver creating a pool of water:
    the beaver did not create the stagnancy.
That pool is held through lack of movement.
The stagnancy is caused by the water failing to move.
That is the cause; the stagnancy is the effect.
Are we then to say that the beaver stagnates the water?
Again the answer that you must seek, you [actually] have.
Is the wish that it be said that if God created,
then he should have created only the good?
Or that God is suffering and that God punishes?
For this is not so. [Instead let us say that:]
God creates and if what he creates stagnates, or progresses
or runs ever sweeter, then that is the effect of many causes.
Can you clarify in your own mind
the narrowness of this question,
so that I can attempt to discuss it in a closer concept?
It requires narrowness instead of the great width.

Michael: How would you define sin? Is sin stagnation?

Stephen: Sin is stagnation, for each cell, soul and spirit, whichever name you would like to put on the concept, must progress. It is on a journey.

It has to correct mis-arrangements.

If the cell were to stagnate or attempt to stagnate
it would become sin.

But be wary of what you term a sin. Sin to a Christian, such as yourself, is disobeying or purposely ignoring the words and the teaching of God.

For a non-Christian, an ignorant pagan, these sins of yours would not be sin to him. It is the consciousness and the knowledge which changes the concept of sin.

If it were, for an uncivilised person, laid down by his elders, and all really believed that to eat fish were a sin, then this would be a sin.

But if to murder his neighbour and to eat his flesh was not in his mind and not in his heart a sin, how could this be a sin? For this is what he knows and what he feels. Each of you know when you sin. For you know yourself you have sinned. You have sinned against your own consciousness, or your own feeling, or your own heart.

This is sin you feel each time; this is your guide to sin, this is your moral law, and this is your own conscience, your own consciousness.

The greater your consciousness expands the greater the number of things that you will feel are sin.

Sin for whom? Many things that the priest may not do may be done with impunity and without sin by others who are not the priest.

38. Nature, red in tooth and claw.

Stephen: We must be so quiet![21] In what way might I assist? You have questions?

Michael: I have a series of questions, but would like to give other people the opportunity to ask questions - well, the first question is about the phrase "nature, red in tooth and claw" meaning that each creature preys on the other in order to live. While I feel that the loving God is all around me I wonder why there is this arrangement.

Stephen: The context that is often used can be very misleading, for again, you see, we bring our minds to the glorification of the physical and what is created. [We could ask:] Should the life of the plant not be revered as much as the lives of all that is created? Would we destroy a flower and say that it is right to do this? Yet we would not destroy a beast, for we say it is wrong to do so. Do we judge which are our needs and which are our wants? For the Father has provided what is needed for all creatures. That we think of destroying and terminating for ever that from which we have taken the physical breath, can confuse, for we know ourselves what for ourselves is right to take and right to leave, for we feel this.

For we have people, some of whom would not eat one meat, and yet others will eat of no meat at all. The question you wish to ask is: Should you kill? Then this I must say to you, if you cannot kill, then you should not, for this is your guide.[22]

39. Evil, Devil.

Stephen: Michael, may I, before your questions, answer the question that you would have asked concerning evil, sin and other things which may trouble you from time to time. There is evil, unfortunately, and to tell what is evil is simplicity itself: anything that would put a barrier between yourself and your Lord, your God, is evil. This is evil in the true sense. Temptation to do a thing that you would wish not to do must be evil.

But let me give a word here in caution. Occupy your minds and thoughts with what is good, for that is to think positively. If you wish to find evil it takes less effort than to find good. This you probably recall from your own experience.

Michael: That *was* on my mind, and I am not surprised you knew it. Now would you confirm for me that I am correct in believing that there is no devil, in the sense of one head being, opposed to God?

Stephen: This I will confirm, in the sense that you have stated. In reality the "Devil" or "Satan" is a collective state of mind, en masse, and has many manifestations. In groups large and small, devil can manifest. Your term "mob violence" is a manifestation of devil, but the opposite of devil can occur in groups, where there are manifestations of God. Therefore do not discount the devil, even though you should not think of him as an entity - the danger being that you will decide that Stephen is the devil!

Olive: I told someone about you Stephen and that was her immediate reaction. But I myself believe I know differently! Stephen, could you perhaps tell us what is meant by a body being possessed by the devil?

Stephen: Here we are dealing with certain entities. But firstly, at the time of history when this is mentioned mostly, it quite often referred to purely physical phenomena and sickness. But there is indeed possession by evil entities. Remember the guide to recognise evil: it is what would keep you and separate you and put a barrier between you and your God. Therefore, if there were a non-physical entity which possessed your mind, and used your mind and body for purposes of keeping you separate and stopping your development, or delaying your development towards your God, it would be demon-possession indeed.

In the Scriptures you will find that our Lord cast out these demons and even today many are possessed by demons. Speak not ill of your brothers who cast out demons. Think not that it be their imaginings. Demon possession, which you enquire about, is more common than you would imagine. By their fruits shall you know them.

40. Judging.

Stephen: Be quite clear, your duty to God and your fellow man is simplicity in itself:
You should concern yourself only with your own actions towards others, and love sufficiently as did our Lord Jesus.

You will accept with love, as a gift,
the actions that they would do unto you.

We must, for our own sakes, never decide for another what they should do to improve themselves.

We must forever be concerned only with what we must do, for we know what is right and what is wrong, that we do ourselves.

Someone speaks words that make us angry.

We would be wrong to think that the anger comes from those words. The words when they came from the other were just words. They were received and turned into anger by us.

If another speaks words that we judge as intolerance those words did not leave the mind or the heart of that other as intolerance; they were turned into intolerance by us.

We must say each time when we speak to another, "I must not sin. I must not judge. I must not anger. I must only love."

To direct in physical things is not to judge, for the soldier who leads many men must, for the physical, make judgements for the physical by the physical.

Our Lord Jesus has said, "Give unto Caesar what is Caesar's" but in the judgement of the spiritual, this is the Father's and we give you the judgement of the Father, for it is His to judge.

Our mind is but physical, therefore it may judge what is needed for the physical; our soul is of the Father and the Father judges the soul. Let not your physical mind judge the soul of another, for in doing so you are attempting to judge the Father.

Do not get confused between physical judgements and spiritual judgements. Separate them in your mind. For the spiritual, only ask through your heart for the Father to guide you yourself in the way that you must act. Never ask that He guide you to judge another in the way that they must act.

All of this that you have spoken tonight moved from one judgement to another judgement. Who was the lesser? Who was the greater? It is folly to ask the question, for you lack the necessary knowledge and judgment in any case gives no satisfaction to your heart.

The Father asks that you do not judge, for He loves you; for when you judge you take away the peace that He has given you. You lose the harmony that is His gift to you and you punish yourselves in your dissatisfaction. For someone who is hungry cannot be filled by eating wood-dust, for he would not thrive and his throat would become dry.

Take only good grain that comes to you in truth,
for this is the food of the Father.
Think of all these things that you have spoken this night,
of the dissatisfaction that you have felt,
of the confusion that has come to you,
of the blindness and the shields
that have come across your eyes.

The more that you have spoken the less you could see and the less was your understanding.

Had you instead looked inside yourselves and said, as you had done later in your prayers, "Am I giving love? How best can I love others?" I need not speak any more, for think of the two conversations - your previous one and the conversation of your prayers - what you felt in your heart - and then ask yourselves which was the chaff and which was the good grain? Feed yourselves only with this good grain and may God bless you.

41. More about Judging.

Olive: Perhaps you could go on a little further about judging.
Stephen: To truly judge is to act upon a decision.

Now I ask you this - have you indeed judged
or perhaps, like a wise king, have you learned to seek advice before the final judgement is made?

For to judge is to act upon the decision
or cause an action upon that decision.
Do not feel that you are guilty of judgement
by listening to an opinion from yourself
by reckoning the possibilities of what may, or may not, be so.
But once judged the decision is final.
Before the courts there are always two advocates
and whilst in your mind the advocate for the defence still speaks
then judgement has not been made, even upon you.
Fear not the argument or the case before the court,
for each moment you must listen to arguments for and against all things, whether you should eat or not eat, move or stay where you are.

Until judgement is actually made on these things, no action is taken, therefore you have not yet judged. And as Thomas always likes a guideline that he may use, then I say this - you have not judged until you have acted. Once more, now you think, you will also remember that you know.

At times my task is very satisfying in that I cannot be wrong in what I say to you; for these are things which, after I have said them, you know that you have known, and therefore I must always be right!

Olive: It is an enviable position!

Stephen: Have I to do a little more of my task? Call me, perhaps, your memory and you will understand me better and also the things that I must do.

Michael Webb.: Our memory spanning more than this incarnation

Stephen: You say "our memory" and this is the correct term, OUR memory.

Michael Webb: Thank you.

Stephen: At times, it would be confusing for all of our memory to be with us. So I listen to the argument for and against and I do not judge. Often there is neither refusal nor affirmation, but wonderful inaction only; my memory may be refreshed and the judgement passes from me. You are correct, I tease!

42. Sheep and the Goats.

Michael: My questions relate to Trust. As a matter of fact I think I am trusting more than I used to. I am less worried and happier. But I am concerned about the strain going through the New Testament, themes of the Sheep and the Goats [Matt 25:32]; those in the fields, where one is taken and the other is left [Matt 24:40], where one is consigned to the fire of Gehenna [Matt 10:28]; "Fear him who is able to destroy both body and soul in Gehenna", "furnace of fire [Matt 13:42,50" "lake of fire" [Rev 19:20, 20:10, 14, 15], all of which I am not too sure about.

Stephen: Then let me make it clear for you, if I may, that in each of us there are often two people, might I say a kind of schizophrenia. One is the mind, the conditioning of that mind, and the belief that one has gathered. The other one is the openness of what is part of the Whole.

It is but another body that is the goat, for we cannot take [it] with us and it cannot come to be joined with the Father and with the Lord, bringing with it these prejudices, these misbeliefs, these conceptions, that can only cause doubt. For what joins with the Father is purity and love. They will have nothing with them, that could cause a separation. This then is what will be consumed in the fire of Truth. This, then, is what will be cast off. This, and these creations of the mind, these beings that can be created from the mind, cannot and never will be joined to the Father and the Whole.

As simply as I can put it!

Michael: I am glad that you answered like that because my other concept was not one that I liked very much and that rather fits in with my question about being the Water. Last time I was with you, you said, "There is no chance of your stepping into your boat and only finding water, Michael". And I thought perhaps that might be a pity. Perhaps it might be better to step into the water.

Stephen: You must remember that often I speak to the Michael that might be left behind, not to the Michael that will join. Might I say that your unacceptable twin, though he is a charming fellow, can often be mistaken. (All right.)
Do not think that Michael is unique in having this unacceptable twin, unacceptable to the Father as part of the Whole, for all of us do have one; yes, Olive, I also; for did I not still have this mind, were I completely [un]separated, I could not even manifest in this manner, for I too have likes and dislikes.

Michael: Now Michael and his unacceptable twin...

Stephen: Unacceptable to the Father as part of the Whole.

Michael: All right. Now I do not find it useful to beat myself or punish myself. I find it good to love myself even in my unacceptableness. On the other hand, let Michael be an example: tell Michael about how the acceptable Michael might survive, but his counterpart...

Stephen: The acceptable Michael can do nothing but survive. For it was, is, and always shall be, part of what we choose to call the Whole.

The unacceptability is what the true Michael (or whoever) would find unacceptable, what we cast off.

Michael: Now I say to my friends that we are all children together, all struggling a little with our twins. Now I do not wish to recount the 'unacceptableness' of other people, because we are all in the same boat. [*Stephen's words about 'boat' come to mind, and we laugh*]. Could you clarify our minds on how we might approach each other on our 'unacceptablenesses?'

Stephen: Firstly do let me explain that when I use the term 'unacceptable' I do not mean 'useless'. For this unacceptable mind, this state of being, is there for a purpose. But like our physical bodies, we would know that this would be unacceptable in its decay to join with the Whole. Can you deny the usefulness of your physical body? You cannot deny the usefulness of the body that I have termed 'unacceptable'. That is all.

Chapter 5

The Afterlife

43. Our passing over.

Stephen: Your conversation this evening has been uplifting - should we say perhaps the Gospel according to St Thomas? How can I best assist you?

Olive: Well, Stephen, we have some visitors tonight, as you have gathered.

Stephen: There are many visitors gathered!

Olive: I am sure. Visible ones I mean. We thought perhaps something that is simple but is probably not a good question to ask at this stage would be about our passing over.

Stephen: The questions you choose are simplicity. Perhaps if I told you this, that Thomas even now is in that state that we all will be in, as I am, when I return to Thomas this, his body. What you feel is what you are. I will ask Thomas if he feels that he is without something that he should have. He said that he is not without. Then this is the way that you would feel. As you feel now.

You would learn that perhaps you are less limited. Each of you often has had experiences as this whilst in a dream, whilst you go on a journey in your dream; you walk the streets, you speak with friends, you are you, except that you feel neither heat nor cold, nor hunger nor thirst. You discover that you have no sense of touch, or of taste, or of smell. You see, but not with your eyes; you hear but not with ears; for you only feel emotions and vibrations.

Often those who are in the physical believe that the lack of knowledge causes great distress in one who leaves the body. This is not so. For a while perhaps the state may appear to be dreamlike but it is no stranger than when you do leave the body in dreams. Ask yourself this: when you have been in your dreams and in another place did you feel that you were dead or that things were not as they were? No, you felt that you were a spectator of happenings. Other things may be strange but never ourselves. Others may act in a peculiar manner but never ourselves.

Did we yearn in our dreams for those that we love? Did we think perhaps of our clothes? For those we had left behind, with little or no memory, for the need is no longer there. If we were to stay in our dreams long enough, what we had witnessed and where we were would become normal; just as where we are and what we see now is normal.

Ask yourselves this: should others from another house be here now they would perhaps think that they were in another state. Now we have the manifestation of those who have left their body becoming conscious of those that are still with their bodies, such as myself and others of our friends. Their thoughts are no different to the thoughts that you have yourself now when you contemplate others who have no body.

Begin to understand as those without their bodies understand you. They often cannot feel your needs but they do recognise sadness; their emotions and feelings are the same. Should you dream that someone who is well loved by you is unhappy or in danger or in need, then in your dream state you might cry out but they would not hear. How often in your dreams have you tried to avoid for others happenings which you may see? This is the state that you become when you leave your body in relation to those who are still with their body. On the realisation that in no way can you affect, or only temporarily so, the state of one still with the body, you search as you do now for the needs which you yourself have.

With us now are many who are learning to communicate, to understand; to them what they see and hear but cannot touch and taste is a little like a dream. You, yourselves, are unaware of them. When the morning comes and you are in a different place and you concentrate on the things that you need, do not these things take precedence in your mind, rather than us without the body?

Think not that when you are without your body you are going to be much different, although your needs are different. Except through feelings there is little association, for your tasks and your needs are no longer what they were whereas the tasks and needs of those that are still in the body are different. These are the first things that you learn.

The others that you learn in a later time are the same things that you learn now: the purpose and need of us all, for we are but one in the Father. Would you ask more that I can help?

Bill: Stephen, I had heard that when we pass on we do have a counterpart of our physical body in a different wave-length or a different sphere. I have heard that this happens in some cases; is this not true?

Stephen: Thomas, at this moment, would feel that he still has a body. He is surprised, therefore I ask him to touch. The body is relative to the plane that you have now. To a stone your skin is soft and of no substance, to your finger the water is liquid and your finger can pass through; but to the smoke and air it is as solid as a wall or as this chair that Thomas can no longer feel. Each stage of development of you, yourself, always has you as you feel and as you know yourself, for even with your physical body you can change. If you were in the company of men that were large and tall you would be small; if you were in the company of children you would be large, in the company of fat people you would be thin, in the company of thin people you would be fat. You are you, and you will always feel you, in relationship to what else there is in your own presence.

Bill: It is a bit hard to grasp this relativity but I dare say it will come in time. Thank you, Stephen.

Stephen: Are there other questions that you would ask? Then I shall answer for you: our theories, all of them not untrue, of different lands and lands now past, where symbols from one country appear after ages have passed in another, where the tongues and complexion of some bodies, in the art and paintings of some, are the same as others from a distant land where these bodies have never trod. We forget one thing, that each of you has walked in a different land, has spoken with a different tongue, has been in ages past and many of the things that you do now are things that you had done then. Would it then be strange that the habits of one race of people, who in that life could not have travelled great distances, were the same as the habits of people in different lands, unknown even to each other with ages as well as distance between them. Ask yourself, "Have I not made this journey? Have you not made this journey?" I give one word of caution, that often these theories can give rise to beliefs in gods and divine beings and all mysterious practices. Therefore, be reminded there is but one God and He is the Father, the Creator and the Source of all things and His magic is there for your eyes to behold each day. Listen yourself to your own breath and perceive His miracle for what He has created is there for all to see, as it was in the beginning and is now. With this we shall leave Thomas no more dead. God bless you all.

44. Science and the afterlife.

Mollie: In these days of science we are taught to observe facts, draw conclusions from them and question anything that does not agree with the facts. For that reason, many people, myself included, cannot understand how anything of the person can survive death when nothing can be seen, heard or felt coming from the body at death or afterwards. Can you explain in a way that a scientifically-minded person can understand how the spirit survives death?

Stephen: The facts are there, if someone would wish to see. The fact that he thinks, the fact that he has emotions, the fact that time is an exact science, are all there to be investigated. That is, if the investigation would be willingly undertaken. Look then at these results that cannot be explained by using only limited facts or measurements: while you might measure water with a jug or a similar small vessel, you cannot measure the ocean with the same vessels. If we confine what we wish to know to what we already know we will have great difficulty. Be sure, then, that the limitation that is being used is not the limitation of want.

45. Resurrection of the body.

Michael: A New Zealand theologian believes that the bones of Jesus lie somewhere in Israel: what is the meaning of the story of the empty tomb? For it is, in fact, my belief that Christ's resurrected body was a spiritual body.

Stephen: The body that arose was indeed one that had cast off the casing that we would call our physical body. May I remind you also of the many bones, many Michaels, which might be scattered over the face of this globe and have no significance.

Chapter 6

The Cell, the Soul and "Reincarnation"

46. Discussion: Leslie Weatherhead on our subject.

[The renowned Rev. Dr Leslie D. Weatherhead (d.1979) makes a great number of interesting points in his book *The Christian Agnostic* (1965) regarding a Christian view of reincarnation. He remarks that Jesus is quick to correct error but his silence is noted when corrective speech would have been so easy on the occasion when our Lord Himself asked of His disciples: "Who do men say that the Son of Man is?" and they said, "some say John the Baptist, some say Elijah, and others Jeremiah or one of the prophets" [Mt 16:14, Mk 6:15, Lk 9:8-9] "Is it not extraordinary that He did not tell them not to talk nonsense?"

We can also note that: (1) Stephen says Joseph and Mary were Essenes; (2) as our Part Four study indicates, Stephen himself was an Essene too and (3) Josephus in *De bello Judaico* 2.8 wrote of the Essenes, "They say that all souls are incorruptible but that the souls of good men are only removed into other bodies."

Weatherhead writes, "Only in AD 553 did the Second Council of Constantinople reject it [reincarnation] and only then by a narrow majority. If some view of reincarnation had not been widely held in the early Church, it would have been pointless to have discussed it in a church council." [Quotations from pp 209-210].

I do agree with the points that Weatherhead is making. I must point out that Stephen himself is *not* discussing simple "reincarnation" which, as in Buddhism, has the soul migrating from one body to the next. It seems rather that Stephen is exploring the matter in relation to the "Communion of Saints", the communion of the living and the dead in Christ, where the experiences of all belong to the whole. This happens to be Weatherhead´s view, namely that if we are to have a Christian view of reincarnation we will need to see it in terms of the Body of Christ or the Communion of Saints.

It is a picture of souls inseparably part of the One, experiencing and acting through personalities and bodies and having access to the experience of all others. Is this not implied in the prayer of Jesus in John 17:21?: "I pray that they all may be one, as you Father are in me, and I in you, so they will be in Us" or in Ephesians 4:6: "One is God the Father of all, He who is above all, works through all and is to be found in all."]

47. The Continuous Self and "Reincarnation".

[If it were possible to perceive souls as entities, separate from each other, then Stephen here would be talking about reincarnation as commonly understood. But since there is no such separation, Stephen's teaching is more about the Communion of Saints, the unity of living and the so-called dead.]

Stephen: You have questions of course?

Michael: The question on our minds is the nature of what one could call the Continuous Self. Now to talk to you, is to talk to a person with feelings recognisably the same as my own, who experiences and reacts in ways that I might experience and react in. I think of you and then I think of myself, of how my continuous self has worn [other personalities] and myself and confusion begins to come to my mind, because I cannot, we cannot, quite formulate the question. Gerald, just now, to try and express his feeling, has drawn a wheel, with the continuous self as the hub of the wheel and each spoke, each part of the tread, covering fresh ground, rough or smooth, and there is choosing at the hub. Stephen, can you talk about this?

Stephen: I shall be delighted to.
Firstly let me again correct a misapprehension that we are all inclined to be under whilst we are in the physical body:
and that is the feeling of separateness.
You will find that you are thinking of separateness when we refer to Stephen, or to Michael and "Charles" [a supposed former incarnation of M's] as if they were truly separate.

Think of the wheel and the external perimeter of the wheel as the Whole continuously

With the spokes from the exterior going through the centre, being experiences of the Whole.

The experience of the spoke belongs to the Whole and is the experience of the Whole; the spoke itself is only the instrument of the Whole.*

Think of this concept now and ask your question again, at some other opportunity.

Michael: All right. But I think of "Charles" as dead. We have also been thinking of wholes. For instance, we have been thinking of what they call a natural theology that will embrace in one whole, animals, snakes (which someone said they did not like) and ourselves into the one Whole. So much of our thinking has so far simply involved the growth of the individual human soul. Can you speak of the Whole?

48. "Christian" being the name that defines the pursuit of what is Christ.

Stephen: You can see even whilst you are speaking
where your confusion is.
At one time, we ask a question
of the continuous self of an individual.
Now we ask the same question, but of the Whole.
Think again simply of the parable of the Gardener.
He did not make flowers or a border.
He made a *garden* where each of these parts are [make up] a garden.
The teaching of this you already have.

Let me again make this clearer, for it may answer another question. Many felt troubled when the question "What is a Christian?" was asked. You have even asked this, this night. Perhaps if I answered this question for you, it will answer many questions you may wish to ask.

"Christian" is the name that defines the pursuit of what is Christ. The example of the successful pursuit was in our Lord who indeed

---

* [In the *Upanishads*] "the totality of existence is compared to a wheel, and of this wheel the Lord is both the hub and the rim whereas individual 'selves' are the spokes that connect the two: they are inseparable from God but they are not identical with him." [Article on "Hinduism" in *Man, Myth and Magic*, p.1313]

was the Christ. Therefore, a Christian in the terms that you wish to think or, indeed, in the terms in which you *should* think, should be defined as:

"Any cell, each and any part of the continuous self, which acts in a like manner (in pursuit of what is Christ)"; whether it is called Christian, "yellow" or "rain" is immaterial.

For to be Christian is to be conscious
not of separateness but to be conscious as part of the Whole.

In the past, for joining of the Whole, parts of the Whole had experiences, continued to choose and gained further experiences in differing incarnations. This is the case with the part of the Whole with which we are blessed, called Michael. He is also a part of the Whole that gained the experience of "Charles". And backwards as it shall be forwards.

The knowledge of this part of the Whole (which is also called Michael) which was to be gained through experience was decided before the separateness of Michael was felt.

Therefore we can say that the experiences gained would be of the whole self of Michael, the choosing of the whole self of Michael.

But let this not go as far as to specify details of the incidents that occur to the body which the Whole, through Michael, is using.

For this body has a mind that has many functions.
This body has a mind that can be influenced
and this body was chosen by the Whole
through the whole self, the continuous self of Michael,
because of its situation
and because of the probability of the influences
that will be made to bear on the mind of that body
that we know as Michael.
Incidents will happen that were not planned
and yea even should not be planned;
but the total of the experience
of that part of the whole which is the whole self of Michael
(whilst that part is in the body)
was requiring that total experience,
not the separate incidents.

Should it be necessary for the "Charles"-Michael* to become a "George", then it will be decided at which stage the "George" should possess a body, where the body should be situated and also the time

---

* [Charles is a presumed former incarnation]

in evolution, when it would gain the experience that the part of the
whole (which the whole self of Michael) wishes to obtain.

  I need to feel and grasp this,
   and to grasp that I am Michael,
  that Michael is Stephen
  and that what I experience now
  is experience for the You which is also I.
  I need to feel and grasp that this is so,
  that I am but a part that could be described
  as a spoke in the "wheel" which is the Whole
  and that together at the outside perimeter
  we cannot be separated.

Michael: I get confused about this Whole. Are not you, Stephen,
also Bill and Olive and everyone else as well as Michael?

Stephen: We are all each other though we are not sharing at this
time the incidents of the separate bodies.

But the experience that we are sharing in these separate bodies belongs to us all.

* * *

["For to be Christian is to be conscious, not of separateness, but to be
conscious as part of the Whole." This is the starting point, in thinking about this Christian version of "reincarnation". No question of a
separated soul leaving a body, and then entering another. "I am but a
spoke in the wheel which is the Whole" and "at the outside perimeter
we cannot be separated." On the one hand, Stephen gave us reincarnation names that at first embarrassed us and then led us to self-centred
feelings of importance; then, on the other hand, he said that we are
all each other, including of course, you the reader. You could say that
Stephen was the cause of emotional disturbance for which we needed
prolonged counselling before we put things into proportion. Those of
us who were talking with Stephen were learning about our own spiritual selves but the message that we hope will be heard is that we are
all spokes in the wheel and most of what is said of us can be said of
everybody.]

49. I am called by an unwelcome name..

Stephen: You might recognize me as distinct from Thomas! You have questions?

Michael: I have questions and I am pleased that you are here to answer them. I am asking them because perhaps they are questions that trouble me more than the group. I was confused about an answer you gave to a former question. When I asked about mental disorders I heard you as saying "mental disorders are confused with spiritual orderliness". I thought it should have read "disorderliness".

Stephen: It would have been correct to have written "disorderliness" rather than "orderliness".

Michael: What is the distinction between a mental disorder and a spiritual disorder?

Stephen: Your questions, Michael, can be apparently simple. Try to imagine the concept that the physical mind is a manifestation of the physical body. Then with regard to our true self, or cell, should the body that is being used have physical or mental defects, it does not necessarily follow (in fact it is most improbable) that the cell which is part of the Whole would manifest any defect of a similar nature.

Michael: This is what I have felt on two or three occasions this week when, to my surprise, a service of worship went, what I felt, entirely right! It surprises me when things go completely right. On Sunday night we had ten people and it appeared to me that at least two of them were speaking with your voice or with the voice of the Source. We felt close to each other in love and caught up into the Whole. Although with our physical selves we might have disagreed, yet we felt one so I felt no disorder. And I felt this again on Wednesday, that there was no disorder when we had been bickering almost and yet underneath there was no disorder.

Stephen: And this surprises you, Michael?

Michael: Yes it does...Although, when I say that we felt caught up into God, of course then there can be no disorder...

Stephen: Pray continue.

Michael: Well, there are two things that would relate to this. Let us take Judas. Was there a disorder in him? In his cell?

Stephen: Again, you have asked two different questions. Was there a physical (and this includes mental) disorder within the person, or is there a disorder in the cell that was known as Judas? Now why each cell and soul has been separated from the Source and has come away as such...

Michael: As you have said, to correct a mis-arrangement, or disorder. Therefore, the cell is disordered.

Stephen: The word disorder is only the best concept available but you do have the correct concept. Do not confuse cell disorder as being the same concept as physical disorder*

Michael: We are not to think of "badness" or "sickness" with regard to the cell?

Stephen: That is correct... Judas.

Michael: What did you say?

Stephen: Judas, to continue; to answer your question. The re-arrangement that was necessary for the cell and the cell's choice in the purpose that it should serve in the body of Judas, though unconsciously so, and any disorders that the physical body of Judas may have had, can be considered two entirely separate discussions. Of the physical body that was Judas I know little.
Let us think about the experience and the guidance necessary to carry out the purpose, not only of the cell that was Judas, but also of many close cells that were in physical bodies near what was the body of our Lord:
I would have to start even before the birth of our Lord's body, and explain happenings which have neither been written down or in most cases even been remembered.

---

* Remember Stephen's words already quoted "the mis-arrangement of the self-consciousness, or cell, that acts as I have said, through the emotions, *taking and acting upon the emotions or the sense-consciousness of the body, and not of the spirit, or God-consciousness.*"

Therefore let it be sufficient to say that Judas the man, or the physical manifestation, may indeed have caused experiences that added in a minor degree to those things that needed correcting but the consciousness of the cell that chose and was assisted in doing those things that needed to be done, was the cause of other mis-arrangements being corrected.

On the one hand, we have the separateness of the life experience that was Judas.
It was not unique, it gained way and lost way,
as all of us do whilst we are in the physical body.
This was the pattern.
This was no more startling, in that it was Judas,
than it would be even in yourself.
The purpose and the usage for the Lord's purpose of the cell that was recognizable as Judas is another story which at some time you will know of.
Am I clear with this answer? For I wish to be.

Michael: I think when I hear it [*the recording of this conversation*] it may become clearer because as you speak my mind flits back to the name you called me by.

Stephen: We have again now, Michael, developed our separateness. If we did this of course the burden of Nero could fall heavily on a non-illustrious shoulder at some later time. Therefore do not be concerned for the burden that may be thought of as being Judas.. it would not rest upon you.

Michael: It sounds like saying that I was that cell but that we are yet one and share it.

Stephen: You have answered yourself well. We are but one and share it [the burden]. Is there clarity in the concept of the two actions that are now possible: that which is the mental-physical attitude and its actions and those actions that are required by the cell, from the cell to the group, to the group from the Source?

Michael: This feels clear to me. Now could I approach this question from a different angle? You - talking to me. It seems natural, and feels natural but is miraculous to my mental self.

Stephen: Indeed, it is miraculous. That Thomas should speak in the same manner is likewise. Let me explain more. Consider Thomas. For it is necessary that this time he is not with us. Let us consider the physical mind of Thomas.

Then we add to that the cell that has knowledge of what requires re-arranging. That knowledge must work in harmony with but with influence on the physical mind.

The cell chose that body which we see here now

for the probabilities in time, environment and many other things.

The experiences that happen to the physical mind

and how the influence of the cell can guide,

the influence the cell exerts on the physical mind

and the success or otherwise of that influence,

are the means by which that mis-arrangement may be corrected. Therefore, we have a mind that is completely free in choice to think and act as it wishes.

The exercise is then that the cell records experiences and gains knowledge on how to influence[23] [the physical mind]; the cell's success is measured and the mis-arrangements are corrected by the influence that the cell has on that mind, leaving it always, the physical mind, with its free will.

Michael: Just as you are having practice in doing now.

Stephen: Exactly. But whereas I the cell have the body of Thomas I am not hampered (poor word) by the physical mind which has choices of its own. It is the cell that activates. The cell, as you see, is (not to use another wrong word) as dexterous as the physical mind in manipulating the body. It can but physically stimulate some simple electrical impulses that operate the features and voice. When the physical mind is not currently attached, or present, (and again, please do not think that Thomas may be a distance away) when the physical mind is not attached as it normally would be the cell-mind can only operate limited bodily functions.

Michael: Hearing this makes me feel like a puppet; when I die is it that the strings are cut and I the puppet fall lifeless to the floor...and where am I? All my thinking is gone! Yet I guess, dear Stephen, that this will not be so.

Stephen: Michael, dear Michael, this is exactly what happens, of course. When the cell is rearranged or the body can no longer function for the purpose or becomes aged or is destroyed, then all that is left is the shell. The mind for a short time relatively speaking is still in a mind body and can gain further experience whilst the cell transcends finally out of its separateness to the Whole.

If there are further rearrangements to be made, then the cell does not transcend completely into oneness. It retains separateness until what has remained of the mind, such as personality, and I think you might say some character traits and some traits that will influence the shape of the physical features in a minor way, are then, with the cell, transferred into another physical body.

[Following on after his own previous words, after a break when we changed the tape and Stephen rested Thomas. He takes up the body of Thomas:]

Therefore, as we have just demonstrated, the whole process can begin again.

Michael: Might I ask, Stephen: you are here when we request that you talk to us, but what are you doing when we are not requesting? Because you have a life of your own. You cannot just be there, day after day, waiting for us to call you.

Stephen: I can explain this better. Michael. When you are not talking where are you? I do not have a life of my own but I have a life of our own. Where does Michael go when he is no longer conscious?

Michael: Where does the candle flame go when it is blown out?

Stephen: Michael delights me at times. For, Michael, you know your answers so well.

Michael: I don't know - to talk about the candle-flame only confuses my material mind. Because Stephen, you are me, I am Olive and Olive is you and so on. We are part of the tree and we are caught up into the whole when we receive and yet, surely, you said, I remember, you said to be you is like swimming in the ocean and to be a thousand miles away and to caress a friend.

Stephen: This is the conscious (or what is remaining of the conscious) mind of Stephen, not cell. Not the cell as such.

Michael: Yet the conscious mind of Stephen remains?

Stephen: In part. Think of it like this. I shall demonstrate. [*Lifts leg.*] In this body as a whole we have nerves that we can think of as the conscious mind of the individual person. We have in this body, muscles that we may think of as the cell and its conscious mind.

Therefore, if I move this body, my [Stephen's] conscious mind has activated the conscious mind of the cell (the muscles) which has moved the body. The feeling that has come to the conscious mind (of the individual) is the nerves. In the demonstration, the nerves represent the personality of Stephen, the muscle is the conscious mind of the cell.

Michael: I begin to understand, so... I think perhaps that we can experience this now, in the physical body. Would this be right?

Stephen: This would be correct.

Michael: Because when we had the experience of group receiving, the group all reported that they felt caught up into the spirit of God. Perhaps this is the muscle?

Stephen: This is very close to correct. Remember that I give the closest approximation that I am able, and that approximation that you have given is sufficient.

I must soon depart. Even I begin to talk of departing. I must return this body to Thomas.

[I see this session as containing some of Stephen's basic teaching. Remember his earlier words: "The knowledge of this part of the Whole (which is also called Michael) which was to be gained through experience was decided before the separateness of Michael was felt." We could substitute the name "Judas" here, or, in general, the name of the reader. "We are all each other" and, as we have noted from Stephen's parable of the Reflections in a pool, we are basically spiritual entities learning about ourselves and experiencing by immersing our consciousnesses in the pool, or in the physical.]

50. More about that unwelcome name.

Stephen: The atmosphere of inquiry! Therefore, let us inquire.

Michael: Are you aware of the conversation we have been having?

Stephen: Of parts only.

Michael: Would you speak of the drama, the part that Judas had to play in the drama?

Stephen: Your choice of the word "drama" does, I am afraid, cause amusement. But it is correct, nevertheless, for the events were dramatic. Two concepts you must have:
firstly, the conscious physical being that was Judas;
the second concept is the cell that must influence.
The cell being part of the Whole influences to a purpose.

Therefore, we are in a position when we must say two things of Judas: firstly, to use a concept that you often use, [from the point of view of the cell] Judas must have indeed been a saint! But were physical thinking beings to judge him a second time then surely Judas must be a sinner!

The cell that was influencing Judas of course was part of the Source and the purpose of that Source was achieved by the influence that was placed upon the physical Judas.
Can you not see how this can be so?
Let us not think of Judas, let us think even of "Geoffrey" [or the reader].
Let us consider the actions of Geoffrey, be they good, bad, or even ... questionable: the cell that bears influences on Geoffrey, influences for a purpose. That cell has (these words are not quite apt) corrections that itself must make. It does this by influencing the physical mind, causing probable noticeable actions of that physical mind and body. Success in doing this assists not only the Divine purpose but also the correction of that cell. But it will be sufficient to say that the cell that was influencing the physical Judas at that time was indeed successful in the purpose of the Source. It is known and must be realized that because the cell must continue exercising such influence through other incarnations, it follows that the cell did not

complete the correction of the mis-arrangements or disorder that was desired.

Therefore, we have the free and thinking will of the conscious mind that was Judas, we have the cell disorder that must be rearranged and we also have the purpose of the Source. The first two must and always will be subservient to the latter.

I must leave you with the concept here:

That you should think of yourself as the root of a plant which to grow has to experiment and explore to gain the food for the plant.

It does not sink into the soil with certainty. It senses and feels and instinct guides it.

Not all the roots are successful in their quest for the nourishment of the plant

but by spreading in all directions they enable the plant to remain upright in the ground.

Therefore, do not always expect that, before you undertake the mental search, you will be instructed.

The direction in which you are probing is not necessarily to bring the nourishment that you are seeking.

For remember that even the cell that influences you or your conscious mind must be subservient to the purpose of the Source.

But let us think more of what troubles you and that of which I feel you would have your mind eased.

The purpose, the Divine purpose, the purpose that is from the Source, the purpose of the actions of Judas at the time, that purpose has been fulfilled and therefore it would hardly be necessary to re-enact our drama even for practice!

Be not concerned, for should each conscious mind know of previous actions that it had taken, even though by its own free will, each conscious mind would prefer not to believe that it had been reincarnated. They would disassociate themselves very promptly from what had gone before. For that reason, it is not considered advisable for conscious minds to have knowledge of previous happenings and associations.

You can see why it is avoided except for a purpose which is generally the purpose of the Source. It is only when instruments such as ourselves are directed, and my receiving is such, that these things are disclosed. You will recall that when left to my own judgement, quite often I decline to satisfy curiosities such as this!

Michael: But when you spring Judas on me it arouses more curiosities.

Stephen: Unfortunately, but in your case I assure you, fortunately, what is, can never be sprung upon us! No more than I could disclaim what I know of my previous incarnations although well I may wish. But that is another story.

51. Stephen on Essenes now.
Michael: Tom wrote about the Essenes...

Stephen: We speak of the Essenes, for it is but a name of people who feel and believe in the same manner. Look around you - the Essenes are with us now and are very apparent! Not all believing all, but many believing part. God bless you all.

52. Stephen reminds us not to see our incarnations too concretely.
Stephen: We say many things that repeat themselves throughout the ages; they tell us the same thing. Is this surprising? For what we are, in truth, is no more than what we are. We may if we wish continue to clothe ourselves and seek for ourselves even finer garments than those which we originally had. But with the age [Aquarius] that we are in now, when we talk of ages, we shall find that with the water, the foundations of this clothing we have cast upon ourselves will be as firm as those of the house that was built on sand, and will wash away. For no matter how often we clothe ourselves, the [spiritual] garments, like the physical garments with which we clothe ourselves, can never be permanent. Even if we were to paint our skins it would not hide us for long. For we are there but we cannot feel the sun for often we are clothed. The helmet that we have upon our heads often has the visor covering the face and if we were to speak in such a position we would hear but echoes and we would hear the same thing again. We might say, "This is what I heard, echoes". The echo will continue until the helmet is lifted, for there will be no need to echo or no need to speak of what is, for we will see, feel the warmth, breathe in the air that is there, that has never gone, that can never be taken away.
There, that is serious, is it not!

Michael: Unfortunately, my helmet, dear Stephen, is still on my head therefore I have to ask questions.

Stephen: Therefore, dear Michael, I shall echo what you ask!

Michael: Well, you have spoken of the reincarnation thread with perhaps a hundred-thousand time-names, of the droplet of rain in the ocean. Can you give me an image which will combine these in my feelings?

Stephen: Rather that I should take away a little of the echo,
    for the image that we build
    [repeated] even a hundred thousand times,
    brings to mind the thread *that we seek.

[Elsewhere Stephen cautions against taking the thread image too seriously and also the tapestry made from the threads. The tapestry itself could be seen as a sheet of glass, even as an ocean]

    Your ocean I shall heat for you
    and it shall become steam and the steam shall vanish
    and become the whole of the universe.
    For you will not restrict me, Michael, to even an ocean!
    You have taken me now from a thread,
    to one that was stoned,
    and down through the ages until I, and we, Michael, were
first guilty of the separation [eating of the fruit of the tree of knowledge].
    I will not stay there; I will take you with my Stephen
    until now we are the universe.
    We often look from the sky invertedly,
    backwards, to dispel that whence Stephen comes.
    Turn and face the sky!
    The stories that we are shown,
    the teachings that we are given,
    and the things we had learnt,

---

* It is possible that, *in a certain sense*, some of the people in this book who are questioning Stephen, had *aspects* of themselves alive when Jesus was alive and were Essenes in contact with Jesus. The names of those *aspects* are changed, except that of Judas. When this *whole section* has been read, it will be plain that we are *not* dealing with "reincarnation" as commonly understood. There may be thousands of "Judases" alive today, their incarnational threads interwoven in an infinitely complex tapestry of other threads where ultimately *we are all each other*. None of us has the slightest memory of these ancient aspects of ourselves.

show us whence we came
so that we might know where to go.

Let us look at the elements of the Stephen; for which came first - the Stephen [or] the pool [or ocean] that became wet, that became heated, that became the steam?

So we might say, "In the beginning we were wet, then we became warm, now we are coming away - I know this because I have been there and I am travelling from there, not to there." It is this that we must know; we say this is the truth.

But when we have done this often enough in our mind we will see and be clear that it is a pointless journey, for we do not change; we have travelled nowhere.

Let us stop the movement and become what we are - all of these things. For we are neither separately the steam, nor the wetness, nor the invisible, not separateness but together, we are what is.

Therefore, Michael, and Thomas and all others, we do not go back to be Jacob or Judas; we go forward to what we are - where the vision must expand, as does the steam.

We might take care lest we even ascend the ladder of Jacob -to get nowhere! - lest we say and know "I am here" as with Thomas and his exercise when he, without his body, travelled across the room, to open his non-existent eyes and see what was there, what he knew was there, from a different angle. Needless to say, he did not succeed in his attempt to travel. For all that was there was Thomas. Without needing to use a mirror each of you look at yourselves. You can but see part of the Whole.

It is pointless to travel the journey, in which you might stand off to look at just who you are and then to have this knowledge. To stand off from yourself cannot be, for we are one: we cannot separate from each other, or be different. We may recognise parts of us but we cannot stand off to see all of us. Nor can we ask, "Should I be this, or this?" Or say, "That is good and the other is bad." Or ask, "Which is me?" Or say, "The good will balance the bad."

Should I perhaps say that when I speak like this I am speaking nonsense! For in this vision I have of me I create a falsehood that bears no relation to the truth. I am neither good nor bad, except as I would see myself in relation to this... or this.. [gesturing]

So the question becomes, "How should I look at myself?" The answer is, of course, "You cannot, for you are unable to." The limitations of what your physical body can see and know are the limitations that your search for knowledge imposes on yourself. These imaginings and judgements are the clothes by which you cover yourself.

Let them wash away.

As for me, I shall clothe myself in the clothes of a saint and depart, leaving Thomas with his body that he might be a saint also! God bless you all!

[*On another occasion*] Michael: I cannot frame this question correctly, because you are part of us. But if you were not using this body and if it were possible for you to think in separateness, would you be thinking in symbols?

Stephen: We even speak of *thought* as if it were a tangible and real thing.

For thought can only be the instrument
of the thing that conveys meaning to the mind.
Then the next instrument is the thought.
How can I separate myself from you or from the wind,
from what is there and all that is?
See how difficult it is to think of us as the Whole
when we can say in wonderment
and we can say with our mirror mind [The mind of our Earthly consciousness],
"How do I think when I am not me?
When even I am someone else?"
All that is "knowledge", is not knowing.
But knowing is all knowledge and all One.
We can understand Stephen at the beginning better as we thought we understood Michael and Thomas. It becomes less easy to understand Stephen as it becomes less easy to understand Michael. For the unreality of both is like a cloud.

Michael: I understand the unreality of distinctions. The time may come when I fully understand...but I do not yet.

I asked you this a long time ago and you laughed at me. I said "Do you know all things?" And you laughed. But you did not know about President Kennedy. So you are a centre of consciousness.

Stephen: For you asked me, "Do I know this thread?" But there is no thread.[24] Am I aware of the experience and of the consciousness of the Whole? That one can die and another can die in their bodies and the flesh of those bodies can rot. This I can be aware of. But this thread that we have visioned upon the sheet of glass, I would have to look into your mind and be your mind and be the mind of those threads that we have raised up.

53. Being reincarnate a thousandfold.

Michael: Olive was saying to me that she had the feeling that as Christ also spoke of himself as being a thousandfold, so too this could be said of Anne and Jacob. What do you think about that?

Olive: I am not going to give up!

Stephen: This answer is most difficult. The understanding of the phenomenon is sometimes beyond even myself but hear me now. Even as I speak through this body, I am Stephen and reincarnate possibly a thousandfold. The confusion is not in the reality of this. It is on in the concept of your conscious mind where it can but think of one body, where you are so mentally confined as to think of this [spirit being confined to one body]. Even with those you love, you still feel separated physically. You are conscious of the gap that is between you, yet you know and yet you feel that you can reach out and touch and caress the ones that you love be they a thousand miles away. Because of the physical function of the brain that has to associate, has to balance, has to move the limbs, has to operate the heart, lungs, the blood vessels, the antibodies, that has to compensate and balance the body when it moves and the million other physical things, the mind imposes upon the power of thought a confinement to that body. That poor physical mind. The innumerable duties that it needs to perform and yet always to serve the purpose we must ask more of it. Glad I am that I am not restricted forever in your body, Thomas, for the burden is very great and one I would feel myself unworthy to undertake at this time.

To return to the question: blame not your mind for feeling restricted in the body, understand that yourself are more and that when you come out of that body you will fully understand that what is you, Anne, is you in any form. For it is not logical that you could restrict the whole of you in one body for I cannot do that, not because it is impossible, but because it would take greater courage than that and only One has ever done it and will do so again. [The Cell of Jesus expresses itself in only one body, and will do so again...at the Second Coming?]

Olive: I know these things, Stephen; how do I know them?

Stephen: Bless you Olive. Would I but be able to take all of you out, Anne, I would, everybody that you may be. I would do it. Forgive this poor answer... You have other questions? (If you have the strength!) The strength is Thomas's.

Michael: I was going to ask what it was like to be you. But you have said it, as best as I think I can understand. I cannot understand that you can have a thousand consciousnesses, but in some ways I am glad that you are not just for us because that makes me feel more comfortable.

Stephen: My consciousness, as is your consciousness, is a thousand-fold, is not divided, it is the guest in many physical thoughts, brains, or what you think of as consciousnesses, the whole of me...

Michael: All right... now reading what you had said to Tom and Olive in their record and also looking at what I seem to have received myself, I seem to have had experience of what is called the group mind. Is the group mind myself in multiplicity?

Stephen: No. This is the short answer. I can explain it like this: Anne and I and many others are of a group. The consciousness that is in each of you may be separated in separate consciousnesses but they are part of the group, and even you will see this on the physical plane.*

Olive: The trouble is that we all belong to one another in the group. We cannot abdicate this.

---

* There is an interesting book by Michael Newton: *Journey of Souls*, [1998] in which he describes sessions under hypnosis where subjects are questioned about their state between incarnations. I do gain the impression that Newton's approach is serious and trustworthy. At pages 151-5 he relates a session dealing with multiple incarnation, then comments: "Most of my colleagues who work with past life clients have listened to overlapping chronologies from people living on Earth in two places at once. Occasionally, there are three or more parallel lives. Souls in almost any stage of development are capable of living multiple physical lives, but I don't see much of this in my cases."

Michael: We are all leaves on the one tree, if I understand you correctly. Stephen, was I present at the time of our Lord?

Stephen: You were present and therefore you are now present.

Michael: It is very good to speak to you like this. It gives me a feeling of being expanded to what I am, to what I was, what I shall be.

Stephen: Only, what I AM.

54. On being realistic about ourselves.

Michael: Your teaching Stephen, always feels true to me. Yet this very teaching, and more especially the knowledge of who some of us have been, becomes a burden and a source of anxiety for me, for I feel much responsibility and accountability to the Father for the use of what I know. I feel my own sinfulness and, indeed, a stagnation and a caught-upness in the events of my own past. I am also caught up in the imaginings that a great and glorious event must be wrought in the material world by an assemblage which includes Jacob and Anne, Judas and others, under the teaching of Stephen and somehow I have an important part to play in this happening. Might I add that I am talking about my imaginings... my thinking says, "Accept what comes, step by step, and be content with not knowing"... but my imaginings nevertheless often confuse me."

Stephen: The self-imposed discipline, of course, says that Michael should accept what comes without question but we are not made this way. That this assemblage of "great" persons should be gathered together with Stephen who is also "great", must have some "great" object is the question that is asked. Let us say this, and let the mind not be so disciplined, but let the mind say that at one time all of these "great" personages were in close proximity with the Lord Jesus for a great purpose, not under *noms de plume* or in diverse bodies, but there as they were and as they were created. At this time what were the "great" things *that they did themselves*? Think, Michael, then look at the things that these same personages are doing now, then explain to your reasoning the difference, if you can find one. Are their achievements "separated" again from what they have achieved before? Would their purpose be different? This is what we would expect; but your discipline is an advantage, that we should always listen, that the Father may, if it be His will, use any of us - His creation - as instruments for a purpose, in a particular way that may be needed. What we should do is to remain attentive, for the need may come that we be used in a particular way but let us not fail to recognise that we are now being used for the purposes of the Father in a way that we, as personages, have always been used.

Michael: Thank you Stephen. Another question which arose out of the last time, was the strand and the thread, a thousand - shall we say - Judases or Annes in one thread... I wonder whether the number of people who have Judas at one end of the strand increases as time goes on? Whether perhaps we should use the image of a tree. Could you perhaps give me a concept? And is there a limit to this? Does the number of strands become infinite or is there a time when there can no longer be more?

Stephen: First, let me take away the appendages that we have had. We shall speak of Judas, for that is the name of the time of that self which is still now. When we should speak of such a time to distinguish it from many parallel times or times of different threads we name that time and the time that we speak of and wonder of as the time of "Judas". Is that not clear to you?

Michael: That is clear.

Stephen: The time of that thread now is called "Michael", the length of that thread has many points of time, both incarnate and in other states and other places; each is recognised by its Time Name. That we be made aware of a Time Name is for the purpose always of partial recall of an experience that would be advantageous for the needs of the Time Name now. The question you ask, only the Father could answer, for you ask to come beyond and see the pattern and the texture of the whole of the tapestry.

55. Experiences are like ripples on a lake.
Bill: If I may be permitted, Stephen, do you recall at our last evening together, last Sunday - you mentioned about experiences and happenings occurring for the benefit of Us at a given moment of time, and you recommended that we do not hang on to those experiences too long, but take the meat out of them and use them, because in a few hours time, in a few days time, in a few weeks time, we are different people.

Stephen: To remember experiences is not harmful, but to attempt to retain that which is no longer is futile. We spoke of our continuous selves when we spoke of the non-retention of those experiences, therefore think of ourselves, our continuous selves as a body of water. Think of a disturbance caused in that water that creates ripples, such as you might have should a droplet of water fall upon the surface. Each of those expanding ripples is in itself an experience, and part of the lake; for the lake to attempt to be that experience in perpetuity as we know is futile, for the experience and the ripple is part of the lake, not the lake part of the ripple.

If we see Charles as a ripple, and the experience of that ripple still there on the lake, the oxygenation that was gained by the lake through the raising up of the ripple that was Charles and of the parallel ripples that have been many others - many other experiences - all contributed to the life of the lake. They all assisted in their time, and during that experience giving life and replenishing to the lake that which may have been evaporated from the lake. This is the purpose of the ripple. This is also, if you think well, what may be the purpose of us all, for often one law that governs one part of life is applicable to all others.

56. Previous lives- Reincarnation.

[The crying baby had been removed from the room]

Stephen: And did you really want to deprive Jonathan of my august company? [To Olive, the baby's mother.] ...Michael?

Michael: I am surprised that I take your presence so naturally.

Stephen: But it would be more surprising if my presence were unnatural. Then, I confess I would give fright to myself!

Michael: Would you speak on Reincarnation?

Stephen: Reincarnation? First then let us be clear in our mind about what is the truth. As always the truth is simpler than we can conceive. Let us take this one physical life of Michael. In this life that has worn this body of Michael, how many different beings has this Michael been? He has been as Jonathan, the babe. That Michael is no longer this babe, makes him different, but the same person. As a small boy in his school,

Michael was again a different person to that babe. As a young man with the experiences of that young man, again Michael changed and he was a different person. When he was first married and became a father, vastly different again to the babe, but yet the same person. This then is the truth of how we change.

Do not take from my words that in earlier lives we were less knowledgeable or not as well developed as we may be here. It comes almost to Olive's mind that maybe Jonathan is better developed or has a clearer sense of seeing than he might do as an adult. So it would be the case with the other Michaels in different lives. It is not as a school where one progresses as one learns more, for in truth the first time that we came as babes we had then with us all that we shall ever have. We have neither gained nor lost what the Father has given to us but we have merely used this in many ways for the purpose of each other and of all of us, and of Us. To attach to Michael's physical life a greater importance, to any one state, or any one of those physical Michaels would, as we can see, be a delusion and a mistake. We simply say of ourselves that I was younger and when I was younger I did many things in this manner and now that I am older I do the things in a different manner. Simply this. No more.

Then we look for a concept by which we might explain to others why this might be necessary, and, knowing that the truth is visible to all of us, we take an example from what is known and what can be seen in the physical realm and what is in the physical knowledge.

All of us might be compared to the cells which are the pattern of creation.[25] That then is sufficient. That gives an association.

It is not the whole knowledge that we would have difficulty in understanding, but be assured that whole knowledge and the whole of the pattern are similar.

Or like the whole of the universe and the whole of creation, this pattern and the method are always the same. The analysis of the details is often very different. But the purpose, the object and the final goal of all things are the same. We start to develop and finally to be exactly as everything is at this moment.

I have said that the journey that we have in our minds, the development and the concept of what we are, why we are here, often misleads.

Surely, as when we were babes, the pattern worked that we would be another, and older, as time went by. But at each time, as with this child now, it is what is.

We do ourselves less than justice when we imagine that our temporary existence is only *part* of the purpose, and in itself not important, for nothing of God's creation can be without importance.

Look about you: is not all this that we perceive of great importance, all important at all times as well as at this moment? So when we speak to others of reincarnation or of the continuance of the creation which is us, we speak also of the importance of being what we are as we are now. Not of the importance of what we were or what we might be.

If Judas, who in a previous life was one with great skill of hands but unimportant in his society, had known then of the importance that he would gain he would have stopped living as the one skilled with his hands and would have lost all that he might gain in the present.

So it is not always good - often I have shown a reluctance to do so - to tell someone of the memory which is theirs, for fear that they might lose what they have now and what they can gain for themselves in the future.

For it would be ridiculous if Michael now developed the personality of Michael the babe or even if he were to develop the personality of Michael the aged man.

When [Michael was Charles] that was the experience from which Charles-Judas-Michael gained. He could not gain from the experience of Michael for he would have to go beyond death to become aged, to become a babe and all would be confusion. Would we thus then put poor Charles in the position where he would have to live through death and through Michael? If we would not impose this on Charles let us not then impose Charles upon Michael.

Mention, as you will, the different lives that all of us may lead. Specify not the particular, for it might lead others to impose upon themselves what is no longer their experience. No gain would come to them from this, only the loss of what they truly are and what is offered to them now.

Let not the sun of this day be the strong wind and the discomfort of a little while ago, for each is necessary, as is the case now with the sun.

Use the concept that you know of this physical life and the cell, but make clear that this is a concept of the understanding, not a law by which we must live or divine instruction from the Father. Simply say this is how one of us understands what we call reincarnation.

Think of friends gathered talking about their past common life. When someone speaks to another of his days at school that brings into the mind of his listeners the days when they were at school. They cannot conceive or truly picture the teller's schooldays, but only their own.

Simply say that you have had your other lives in other bodies, as you have had other lives in this one body. They are to have, as we have, memories.

Chapter 7

The Trinity -
Source, Soul and the Created

57. The Trinity.

Mike Webb: Please help us in our understanding of the Trinity.

Stephen: The Son is the self of what was created, the Father is the
Source and the Spirit is the Cell of Influence [soul].
    Therefore, the Son takes upon himself
the burden of sin of the created;
the Spirit influences through the cell
the continuation of the refinement of the Father's love.
For only the body and the created
can accept the sin of the created.
Therefore the Son came.
And, indeed, when it is said that the Son
sits on the right hand of the Father,
it means that the created is now an extension of the Creator.
The Spirit, being of the Creator,
must also be part of the Trinity.
Therefore we have three in one.

58. Trinity: Spirit, Soul, and the Created.

Stephen: We have spoken of the interdependence on each other and
of ourselves.
    Let us see then if in our mind we can clarify the picture.
      Instead let us think of "three" - a trinity of things - rather than
of "two".

A writer, who may be known to some of you,
spoke of this Trinity as being: the spirit
  - or the God-consciousness,
the soul - or cell, being the self-consciousness,
and the created that is the body
  - being the sense-consciousness...

[...of both the incarnate **or** discarnate person. I consider Bohm's *"Implicate Order"* can be placed alongside Stephen's terms. cf. Karl Pibram who sees the brain as a microhologram being of the same pattern as the universe, also seen as a hologram. There is a confusing use of the word "spirit". Here "spirit" is defined as "God-consciousness" (or Source). In the previous session "spirit" means "Holy Spirit"= "soul" = "cell of influence". In this case "spirit" is the "projection" of the Source, *not* the Source]

This, then, gives us a very clear picture.
We shall take the two legs of the extreme [*polarities*]:
firstly, the created, which is the sense-consciousness and all the things that were created for the use of those senses.
We have a collection of created cells joined together in various forms

[See section 173 *Bohm's Gnosis*: "It will be ultimately misleading and indeed wrong to suppose... that each human being is an independent actuality who interacts with other human beings and with nature. Rather, all these are projections of a single totality."
" The individual is in total contact with the *Implicate Order*, the individual is part of the whole of humanity, and he is the 'focus for something beyond humanity'."]

but each complete unto itself.
We see a pattern; we see an inter-connection
between all things,
so that we might say that *all* that is created is *one*.
Secondly, we take the other leg, that is the Spirit - or the God-consciousness.
If that consciousness created what has been created,
how else would it create except in its own likeness,
and that pattern that is itself?

So that the Spirit, in the realms of the Spirit
and in God-consciousness,
is of the same interdependence
as that of the sense-consciousness that it created.
The interdependence each upon the other
 is where we often become confused
and has led us into mistaken thoughts
more often than any other concept we have been given.
I believe that in the early days a concept that I gave you may have
caused a little confusion and it would have helped you to think of
only "two", instead of "three". So then, let us look at the *self-consciousness* or the *cell of influence* or the *soul*.
This is the intermediary.
If we would say that the self-consciousness is
a "thought, created by the spirit
so that the spirit has communication
and communion with the created",
it would be a better concept
than that previously in your mind.

The mis-arrangement that we have spoken of previously
is the mis-arrangement of the self-consciousness, or cell,
that acts, as I have said, through the emotions,
taking and acting upon the emotions
or the sense-consciousness of the body,
and not of the *spirit* or God-consciousness.

We have often worried in our mind
about my words concerning "emotion".
I have said before that the emotion that comes from the Source
is the emotion of love and [is] the emotion that stirs
what can bring forth [re-]actions of the sense-conscious body[26]
to the Cell or Self-consciousness.
Arguments are now coming into our mind
about "good" and "evil",
that we cannot have one without the other
and that the spirit leads the sense-conscious emotions into the
cell,[27]
so that the contrast may be perceived by that cell,
or the soul, so that the soul may choose. This is *not* correct.

[If we look at Stephen's account of the "Seven skins" (later in this chapter) we could interpret "sense-consciousness" as the "non-physical senses" associated with the cell. Here it seems to refer to the senses associated with the physical mind.]

The Spirit - the Source, the God-consciousness - is what will
influence, beyond question, the *final outcome and emotions* that
each cell will receive and act upon, eventually. To do this, that cell
needs to be strengthened and to become unwavering by being exposed to the emotions from the sense-consciousness.

These are the concepts that would be easiest to understand, for it can help us to understand the usage of the cell - the self-consciousness - of different bodies, even in the same space in time.

We would complicate our thinking more
by breaking down [analyzing matters],
as we would in the physical
and then we would have a discussion about this trinity,
as we might have about the concept
of which we have been speaking,
of the many cells of all of creation that are joined together,
for they cannot be separate; and yet,
each part of that whole, which is creation,
is, in itself, a Whole.
Let us then go further and give examples of the emotions
or the battle of emotions
that we have when the sense-consciousness
puts forth emotions into the cell - the self-consciousness,
and [the] other emotions [which] come into that same cell
from the God consciousness, or the Spirit...[28]

[...the emotion of love, as Stephen says earlier.

Emotions such as anger, fear, desire to flee and aggression belong to the sense-consciousness.]

[See what Stephen has been saying a little previously about "misarrangements". Can one paraphrase Stephen a little and say that he is *denying* that God brings on physical experiences that cause pain to the soul so that the soul can learn?]

We might even have a case
where many wish others well

but they do not actually do anything for others,
even if they do nothing to hinder them.
This is because of the sense-consciousness
influence upon the cell.
The emotion of whatever may be uncomfortable or inconve-
nient to the sense-consciousness
then overrules and overrides [the emotion of love]
Even whilst the sense-consciousness
is overruling the emotion from the Spirit
the cell knows that it does not act
according to the influence of the Spirit.
We have a word to describe this –
the most apt of all words - it is "selfishness".
Think carefully on this word.
Think more of "sense-selfishness",
for no emotion[29] can come from the Spirit of the Whole,
for it is not like an animal –
if one part moves the whole must move.
For the Whole is,
and need not move, in the concept of Spirit.
[The concept of "Movement" belongs] only in the physical.
We can see very clearly that it cannot be valid reasoning to feel that
experiences [which are harmful and unpleasant] have been given, or
allowed to happen, by the Spirit, so that groups, small or large in number may gain experiences. The emotions that cause that hurtful thing
to happen can *only* be those of sense-selfishness.
Study these things that I have said:
remember clearly the three parts -
Spirit which is the God-consciousness, which is the Source;
the Cell or Soul, which is the Self-Consciousness;
and the Body which is the Sense-Consciousness. God bless
you all.

59. The Godhead.
[Tom had been saying that it must be nice to be Stephen "sitting on
a cloud" instead of facing the rigours of this mortal life!]

Stephen: Therefore Thomas, let you and me change places. You sit
on the cloud. Tell me one thing: does it relieve your discomfort? That
discomfort may be yours to keep and to nourish or you may give those

things that we find uncomfortable to the Bringer of Comfort. Rest there and decide.

How may I assist?

Olive: Tania would like to know about angels, fairies and nature spirits. Did she really see one?

Stephen: First we must understand many things:
That this God, as we have known or thought **of** Him,
is but a manifestation or a likeness of Himself.
This likeness comes firstly into the 'Head',
which we often call the Godhead[30] or, so be it, *the Christ*.
For in this 'Head' is the conception of all that we can see, feel, hear, and touch; [also] the likeness and manifestation of the Source of all things that came about.

60. God, the paint, and the picture.

You might say, as in your own heads,
when you wish to make a picture,
that the wish has come from "nowhere".
This "nowhere" is God.
In the [God]head that picture is made first as an idea.
Then from the Head
we must have instruments
that we call the Body of the Whole [All that is]
in order to create the picture
that the Mind and Head have conceived.

There are many parts in this Body. The picture and order of things that these parts have made and coloured are the things that we see, feel, taste and touch now.

But the instruments that are created through the Mind are the ones we might call angels, the smaller ones being those that would care for the finer details.

These then might well be called your angels, fairies, and those who put the care and touch into the colour and the form of these things.

When we perceive this caring
and those instruments of the Body
we perceive a little of what that Body is.
If what you saw felt unreal as compared to yourselves,

then indeed you did perceive the Truth.
For the picture might look at the painter
and say to another of itself, "Is the painter true like us?"
Therefore, to continue, we have the objet d'art that has been created
by the Body of the Source through the conception of the Head.
If hurt or disorder is apparent in the object created
who but that Head which conceived it, can correct that disorder?
No other person than the artist who is painting the picture,
can correct the mis-running of the paint.
Many might say that if there were another present,
another Artist,
could he not also correct the error?
That other person would have to be one
who had exactly the same conception
in his head as the original artist
as to how the picture should be.
An exercise for yourselves to practise:
One of you make a drawing of a pattern.
Decide in your mind what the pattern will be.
The others who have a like mind
observe and without speaking correct
any sin or error there is in the pattern as it is being created
with no knowledge of what the pattern is to be.
I suggest that you might find it difficult.
For only the one that has conceived the pattern in their mind, can
recognize the error and correct that error and thereby be Saviour of
the perfection of the pattern.

Olive: So we being pieces of paint on the picture often think we can
correct the errors ourselves.

Stephen: The paint may move and run but only the Conceiver or
Head or Christ can understand whether this movement is in accor-
dance with the pattern.
For often artists do pour paint so that it may run,
    and run it will,
    often according to the pattern
    that is in the mind of the conceiver.
But it is not only the Conceiver who, with his brush of love, can
divert the course from what might lead to the paint wasting away

from the canvas into oblivion.
> For it is a peculiar paint that we are;
> it is paint that understands that it is to
> be part of the pattern,
> paint that would most times run
> according to the conception of the pattern.

[Stephen is re-telling the story about the correction of mis-arrangements in the soul or cell of influence, where the influence of the Source can be diminished by the emotions and prejudices of the physical. The etymology of "Godhead" equates it with "Godhood" or divinity but Stephen uses the "-head" to mean a "head" which has the Whole to act as its instruments. He retells the story in such a way that we have a different feeling about "at-onement". God is seen as an Artist.]

For that paint has rules that it must follow,
> but often, in spite of the intention, it follows not the path.

> It then can appeal to the Conceiver for redirection.
> It can speak to the Artist and say,
> "I have marked where I should not have marked,
> [in Greek 'αμαρτια = hamartia = missing the mark]
and I have failed to mark in the places which I should have done. So save me from my error for only you can correct what I have wrongfully done."
> And through many instruments, other painters such as fairies and angels, or the elements and those who care, can pattern with the Conceiver to correct for you that course.

Olive: I cannot see how there could be errors in the first place.

Stephen: The paint is poured and the *paint* runs,
> not God, nor the Creator [*not because of God's action*];
> the pattern that the Creator lays is perfect
> and when the canvas is completed
> there might be paint that has spilled,
> but in these places where error is apparent
> it will be repainted, as is often done.
> Often new paint is added or paint is collected and replaced on the canvas. We might say that a blob of paint might be picked up

several times by the brush of the artist and be replaced on the canvas so that it might make a line and follow the path as it should.

When the painting is picked up and we see the canvas from a short distance we can see also where the paint has failed to be and the places it has been where it should not have travelled. The paint would want to return to the canvas and move along the line for it would indeed love the picture as much as the Conceiver and would also wish that the painting be the perfection that it will be.

Olive: I wish I could see that more right now.

Stephen: It would be nice, as paint upon the canvas, to step back, as the Artist might to view his work. But if we did, we would not be able to retrace our line. So then we must trust the Artist that he will know if we cry out, when we are lost from the line, that He will correct and save us from our sin.

Be careful that you do not come to conclusions about the painter as such, for it is only a concept. It is better to think that Christ knows the design which is pleasing to the Father. We are part of that pattern and we have been given guidance as to the line that we must follow. Should we stray from that line, understand that it is to our detriment and so call out and ask that our error be taken from us, that we might be repentant and thus be repainted.

Michael: We had a long talk last Sunday evening about the concept of the Father or the Source or Pure Being and we put this concept at the top of a triangle (just as a picture); then we agreed that the physical self was created. But would you say that the cell is created, or uncreated?

Stephen: The Cell, as you have mentioned, is a thought in [your concept of] the Source.
    And, as the thoughts of your own mind are created by that Mind, they remain part of what is your mind.
        They are of the Creator, for the created.
        You ask a question that I could only answer
            if I were to say that a river also has a source.
    Is then that trickle part of the ocean or part of the source?
    It belongs, and is the communicator

and is the instrument used by both, for both.
For the flow is from the Source that gives sustenance.
The flow from the created declines, or accepts,
or receives what is offered
and chooses for itself which of these fruits it shall have.

Michael: Is there a distinction between "Spirit" and "Holy Spirit"?

Stephen: If we wish to define what we call "Holy Spirit" we would be better to define it as the emotion of love as it reaches each one of you.

Michael: And "Spirit" is the "Whole"?

Stephen: The Spirit would be the Source, or the Father, or God.

We may often become confused, even as we have been confused here tonight by the concepts that many of us have put forward as being the truth. Receiving and common sense are the way to establish truth.

That is why we must receive with prayer and with guidance; why, when we look at another concept of others, we pray for guidance; we pray for wisdom; we pray for the ability to discern what we may understand.

We must never allow ourselves to think in terms of truth and falsehood for to do so would be to judge. Let us rather believe what we learn, hear and see and take from it all, whatever we can. Let us also understand that what we do not understand, as being the truth, should not be condemned as falsehood, misguided or lies.

I, and many of us, understand and feel the concepts that we have been given and understand them to convey to us the truth. Yet many who read these words may condemn them as false and misleading.

Let us not us fall into this error. When we have offered to us the feelings and understandings of another we should not judge what is good from it and what is bad from it.

Let us only say, "Those parts of the words here I understand. Those other words I understand not". Be regretful that you needed to leave them untasted; for much of our separation from each other is this misunderstanding of what is spoken, or laid out, by another for our enjoyment.

It is like the fruits of our giving - we are inclined to offer what we would desire to be accepted. But then, as with our tree again, Michael, only the fruits that are desired will be accepted. This does not mean, of course, that the remainder of the tree is bitter or unpalatable. You see, Michael, I use my tree well! Others may not like my tree or may discard the fruits that I have offered, for they would rather drink from the river.

61. The Void.

Stephen: The explosion which was to put me into the Void [through abandoning the personality of Stephen to become at one with the Whole, it has now come about that] I am now imploded! And once more together. In what way may I help?

Michael: Would you speak, Stephen, of the Void, and of the "explosion" which scared us a little the other night. We are very sorry that we lost part of your words because the tape was too short. So would you mind speaking to us again of your consciousness now?*

Stephen: Of course, my words are never lost. We invariably measure things in terms of the physical consciousness until we understand what it is that we are *being*. We still feel that there are changes which must come about in us, until we become part of something different - the void, if you wish.

Think in the other direction.

[Perhaps "Think in terms of awareness of what is, of what the Father is doing in us." Stephen then clarifies by describing in detail our relationship to the Source, describing the Seven Bodies or "Skins.]

62. The Seven Bodies [The "Trinity" described in greater detail]

Stephen: Once again I state that we are, all of us,
(1) *Being.*
(2) Then add to this *Being*, the first body of consciousness where we might become aware of separate things.
(3) Then add the body, if you would wish, of the senses
(I had better explain) the non-physical senses.
(4) Then add to this a particular kind of matter

which can be distinguished by the non- physical senses.

(5)Then add to this a separated recording of emotions
which we might call a personality.

For the personality reflects nothing more than the emotions that are felt by the non-physical senses, and later, by the physical senses.

(6)Then we add another skin [body]:
 It is one of mind, so that the senses
can coordinate the other bodies
and the senses of those other bodies
in relationship to the personality that we have grown.

(7) Then we give it flesh and we have then completed the instrument of total experience.

When this instrument has been used, it could well be cast aside until we are just *Being that is.*

The difficulty comes of course, because
each of the bodies [skins] that we have grown,
    must from necessity (until after the personality has been cast off)
    be taken away and cast aside with due consideration to that sensory body (i.e. 3) and [to] the personality and its recording of the emotions of these senses (i.e. 5).

When this is done, the [non-physical] senses are no longer needed
for the continuance of Being which is forever.

Our scriptures teach us that man must need to search for life eternal.

Our Lord has said very clearly that we might be as he is, with the Father. He tells us that we must learn and trust and know through His example and His casting off of His bodies, that we lose nothing: we have in fact gained the peace and the harmony of being.

It is understood that this is never easy. It is not even easy to give away or cast off what even we know is ultimately unimportant.

For the rich man to give and to cast away all his riches and all that he holds dear, this is the first lesson, and the first exercise of the shedding of the instrument that we need to learn.

Think then of the words that we might read that always tell in truth of what is important. You may peruse your books and find all that I have told you now is written there plainly that you may see.

The consciousness of Stephen that you would know of should be understood as a stage of casting off. Stephen still has the [non-physical] senses and is very close to [what Stephen calls the "tent" of] the personality - for the senses enjoy the personality of Stephen.

But still my Lord says to me, if you would follow me, cast away what is dear to you and come and be with me.

It is not a Void that we must explode into. It is [a matter of] a barrier that we must shed.

The sweet fruit often has what might be judged to be a bitter skin.

Do ask more questions.

Michael: To clarify one of the points that you have made so far, Stephen, you speak of the *first body of consciousness of separate things*. Could you speak about this please?

Stephen: [It is] the refinement of the things of which we are conscious now, the awareness of the order of what is created, of the first awareness that we might have from an inverted viewpoint.

We might even say, would it not be wonderful if we were aware of the whole of that order and feel all things.

The wonder is when we are no longer aware. For all that has been created has been created for the [non-physical] senses of that body. The continued creation is what is first sensed.

Michael: To go back behind that, almost sounds as if this barrier, which is not a barrier - to go beyond this barrier, would be to lack consciousness at all.

Stephen: Consciousness, as I have said, is for the bodies. The feet may be conscious for the shoes are tight. In your mind imagine the comfort of neither tight shoes nor feet that may be hurt.

Michael: But it is not nothingness?*
Stephen: One with aching feet might say it would be Heaven!
Think on these things. God bless you all.

63. Healing.

Stephen: When we talk of healing and the power that we send out,

think not that the power is what grows within the physical
but that the power comes from what is truly us,
then comes in to be diverted
or redirected with love as the projector.
Love is the best motive force
that the physical can use to transport these powers.
Where then, you might ask, do I find me?
Come back along the line through each of these bodies
until the time arrives when you cast them off.
You must first then start with that body
which each of us now wears.

---

* [In my words to Stephen, I have in mind the Void. In subatomic physics this would be the vacuum of space. Dana Zohar (*The Quantum Self*, 1990, p.225) writes: "The quantum vacuum is very inappropriately named because it is not empty. Rather, it is the basic, fundamental, and underlying reality of which everything in this universe – including ourselves – is an expression. As British physicist Tony Hey and his colleague Patrick Walters express it, (continue on page 110) *Instead of a place where nothing happens, the 'empty' box should now be regarded as a bubbling 'soup' of virtual particle/antiparticle pairs.* Or, in the words of American Physicist David Finkelstein, *A general theory of the vacuum is thus a theory of everything.*"

Space forbids going into detail with regard to Zohar's picture of consciousness as characterising *bosons* i.e. photons, virtual photons, gluons and gravitons(?), as opposed to *fermions* which, unlike bosons which are waves, have the nature of particles. These are seen as arising out of the 'soup' of the vacuum of space. At p.78 Zohar speaks of the "problem of the unity of consciousness, the distinctive indivisibility of our thoughts, perceptions, and feelings". She describes the work of Herbert Fröhlich demonstrating a process by which molecules in the cell walls of living tissue "pull themselves into the most ordered form of condensed phase possible – a Bose-Einstein condensate." In this process unitary consciousness becomes possible. Add to this thinking, the "everywhereness" of quantum particles as seen in the Einstein-Podolski-Rosen experiment, (which I have described in other footnotes) then we have a concept of consciousness transcending bodies and brains.]

In our consciousness know that this is a projection
that is made for your use,
not you for its use.
And the same with each body.
Recognize the limitations of that.
Do not say to yourself, "If I understand more,
I could give out power"
when you [are] think[ing] of yourself as your body.
For the power is indeed truly yours
if you with your consciousness would reach back
to where each projection of yourself has come from.
For here begins the [im]pulse
that moves not only the physical but also all others.
For I found myself when I lost all of these bodies.
It was not a fruitless or frivolous message
that our Lord gave us,
"If you would follow me to where I am,
you must give up all this that you treasure,
for the treasures that you have here in the body,
with which now you listen to these words,
are but treasures of the moment
and cannot bring you more than a passing pleasure.
But if you would have the power
and the light of love that is yours,
come away in your consciousness back to who you are."
And He did tell us how we must do this: He said,
"While you are furthest away from yourselves,
and you possess what you feel and touch and taste,
practise this giving of all you have and of all you hold dear.
For these are your chains, these are the things that hold you
from yourselves.
They are the experiences that you enjoy,
the loves that you feel are yours,
and also your pleasant memories."

These things that are taught are not just nice things
that it would be pleasant to do.
They are useless, uselessly done,
if we do them so that others may recognize that we are good,
for we have changed one set of possessions for another...

we have changed wealth for the admiration of another,
or the imagined admiration.
If we give love so that it may be returned to us,
better that we had not given that love,
for we have exchanged part of our reflection
for another part that we wish to grow as ourselves;
until often we end in an experience of giving up
what we hold dear of ourselves,
so that we might receive the love of another,
only to find that what we receive was not worth
the exchange of what we had already,
but we are left still with love that was never given,
but only returned to us unsatisfied.
When we give these things, we give that they might be taken,
for we want not their return.
We use them as vehicles of us,
that each time we send out these vehicles
we are drawn back to ourselves,
beyond the pull of our imagined gravity
that holds us to these things:
the [im]pulse of greed, the [im]pulse of possessiveness,
the [im]pulse of coveting, that pushes along discomfort.

Chapter 8

Is there development in the realm of Spirit?

64. Is there development in the realm of Spirit?

Michael: In the material world we have a time of past, present and future. In the world of which you are a part, which I suppose is related to this world, are there a past and a present and a future? Is there development? There must be development.

Stephen: Take your mind into the ocean. Can you define there, time? ... Yes there is development. There are currents, and there is light [and] evolution.

Yet, does it really change? (No.) This is the closest parallel in the physical. Only when you yourself have physically travelled into space, will you gain a closer parallel. Seen from the perspective of outer space the world appears to remain the same, as does the ocean. Suppose you are in a cave, back from the mouth. It is as if what you can see through the mouth of the cave is the present moment. But if you move forward to the mouth your angle of vision becomes greater and you can see then both what has come before and what is to come.

[This brings to mind Plato's Allegory of the Cave (Republic VII). Renée Weber, in an essay, *Field Consciousness and Field Ethics*[31], with reference to Bohm, writes: "When pressed, Bohm agrees to the correlation between Plato's cave with the explicate order, and Plato's metaphor of the light with Bohm's implicate order. Both Plato's light (sun) and Bohm's implicate order can be apprehended only through insight, both lie beyond language and both are inaccessible except to those willing to undergo strenuous and single-minded change". I understand Stephen to equate "world seen from outer space", "ocean", and the reference to seeing the past, present and future all at once. I would also equate these with "light" and with "the implicate world" and Plato's world of "ideal forms." Stephen's picture of the cage has us in the physical looking out, whereas Plato has prisoners looking at shadows on a wall.]

If you *feel*, it is much better than being able to hold with the physical mind. For as some insight comes in, other insight may begin to escape you.

[It seems that Bohm believes that insight is "inaccessible except to those willing to undergo strenuous and single-minded change". If we remember some of the intuitions which come spontaneously to many of us, shall we say that we correctly intuit the death of a person on the other side of the world or we have some life-changing dream, then "strenous" and "striving" might seem inappropriate words. The intuitions just arrive. But no doubt, unless there is a true wish to respond to the Cell of influence, the coming of isolated intuitions will have limited significance in our lives.]

Feel within; *recall* the knowledge, which you have.
Call upon the reserves, probe, recall to mind
and pray for the right questions,
as I pray that my answer will be right,
as I probe long back into a consciousness
with physical restriction
to give you an answer in relationship;
as I probe into Thomas's mind, into his experience.

Michael: Do we have an expanding God?

Stephen: We talk of expanding and that God must expand, because, for instance, the population increases and the universe gets larger. But then again we would lose the truth that all that there has ever been was always there. Do not think that I speak against anything that has been spoken for; if the conversation had continued, you would have come to a conclusion, each of you separately, and as a result of that conclusion you would have stopped learning any more on this subject.

[Refer to the previous chapter: "This knowledge is brought to your consciousness, not as a gift, but as a recall. I have said on many occasions that nothing I say is unknown to you. Fear not your questions, for what you ask is what you know. I assist as your memory, only in so much as that I help the decision as to when you might recall." Our cells, souls, belong to the ocean, to the light. It is certainly a question of letting go the exertions of the mind because mind, thought, reason and striving cannot bring insight. Meister Eckhart asserts that "there is nothing in the universe so much like God as silence". But for Bohm and even more for Stephen, beyond silence there is the consciousness of the One "a paradigm of a unified field of being, a self-conscious universe realising itself to be integrally whole and interconnected". [Weber, op.cit. p. 42]]

Olive: Is it necessary to learn any more?

Stephen: If by "learn" it is meant "Do you pass tests, do you have a record of achievements of learning", then we have never started. Do you have specific questions?
To understand what is,
in the way that you have been given to understand
and the way that it becomes easier for you to understand,
is the way that you should understand.
The way that you feel, motivates you into the [helps bring about the?] experiences.

If you have these experiences,
know that these experiences are needed for you.
This is the childlike simplicity - the jacket you wear is your jacket, simply because you have that jacket. It is the one that you have need of. What you have is what you need. All may like the concept that your needs will be supplied to you.

Olive: Is there any sense in which we supply the need? I mean this: Is it possible in this physical to sow a seed in what we might call the spiritual and the harvest of which I reap? I sow an angry thought, a destructive thought and reap that harvest?

Stephen: You will recognise a harvest that you reap as being the results of your angry thoughts.

This does not necessarily mean that you have your needs supplied [by others]. Most of these needs are supplied by you. But they are supplied, nevertheless, with all these other things that we choose to produce.'

65. God the Babe.

[In meditation I had the image of God as a babe coming to consciousness in this universe. Immediately the phone rang and a friend invited me to visit her. As she prepared the refreshments, I took a book she had indicated, and immediately found a passage where God was suggested as being a babe. This seemed too much of a coincidence, so I asked Stephen about it.]

Stephen: As the length of the question would indicate the brevity of the answer, I am tempted only to say "yes!" But I see that this might not be equally satisfying, so we shall go back to the beginning of the question - the beginning that was only partly recognised - "Why is it that when I need God most, I cannot pray?" and "What is prayer?"

We nearly had the answer when we spoke of the passion of our Lord and the sacrifice; because prayer is a sacrifice. It is a sacrifice of self and of self-will, and of the consciousness of that physical self - and I speak now of the physical consciousness.

When we once, in our minds, renounce all will of our own accord - when we give the destiny of our physical self and our physical well-being away to another - then this is the sacrifice; this is the thing that we must all give. As our Lord has taught us, to give is to receive; to give up all that you feel is yours in the physical.

This not only means giving up the physical objects of our desire – [but also giving up] unhappiness, [seeing this] in the form of a punishment. For punishment is an entirely physical concept.

So, our prayer then, is a sacrifice.

We must jump suddenly now to the concept of the babe, as it becomes conscious of itself. We had much argument, saying that the image of what is cannot be a consciousness. But we did not go far enough with the babe, for we did not let it grow and mature. We left it at the stage of development where it was discovering its various parts and limbs, and becoming conscious of those parts. Truly the babe is conscious of those parts.

Each part that it becomes aware of, that it becomes conscious of, is a new experience that is recorded, recorded for the time when the babe uses these parts, and [acquires] the ability, flexibility and mobility of these parts, unconsciously. It is a recording of experience.

So, let the [babe grow into a] child [and in turn let the child] grow, as you have done in your story where my answer could have been 'yes'.

But we would have left a significant gap that could confuse, as it did, and it required much thought, many more concepts to join them together. So, for your reader, save them this exercise, for I fear many might tire; close that gap and let the child grow, simply, as a child. Therefore my answer to your question must be 'yes' [*God can be seen as such a babe.*].

Chapter 9

Love and Faith

66. Love and Faith.

Stephen: recognize the love of the Father that is being given to you.

Does mystery alone bring faith?

Should it not be what you can see, what you feel,
even what you breathe and taste.

Should not this be the means of the satisfying faith that you desire?

Michael: So frequently faith comes to me when I pray rather than when I reason.

Stephen: When each of you prays or looks within yourself,
when you are at peace with yourself,
you are quiet,
and you take your mind above
the things that are generally accepted
that would give you comfort,
then indeed you do know comfort.
It is good to pray, for faith is also a gift;
it cannot be grown, only accepted.
And for those who would seek faith,
then ask often that faith
which is a seed among you all,
would receive each time the nourishment

by which it grows.
No magic or manifestation
that even the Lord Jesus gave,
gave faith to all those who witnessed.
Your previous self, who witnessed more wondrous things
than you will ever witness in this body,
did not have the growth of faith that you desired even then.
For when you look from without for what you require within
you will be empty within and dissatisfied without.

Michael: Faith is a gift and those amongst whom I move and I keep awaiting it; a great deal of the time I feel now that I have it but I always look to see how I might stand by others as they await that gift.

Stephen: Let me then ask you this, that they may be asked too.
What is it that you wish to have faith in? When you have answered this question yourself you will find your search much easier for it is very close
and each of you has felt what you are seeking.
It is like when you asked about the baptism in the spirit
and the answer was that to be baptized in the spirit
is to recognize the love of the Father that is being given to you.
Faith may not be unlike this.
It is also similar to the question given to you for the children, when you were to ask them what would make them happy. For if the answers are the same perhaps then the questions may be the same also. We are indeed learning much of ourselves. God bless you all.

67. Against those who teach a wrathful God.

The Voice of Christ: My son, would a father give to a son who asked for bread, stone to eat? Or to a babe that thirsts, sour wine in the place of milk? Neither would the Father give thus unto them who are his children.

Be at peace; be not disturbed by hypocrites or those who use the word of the Father to separate Him from thee and thee from Him. For they are people whose ears are full of thorns, whose inward self is black with the curtain of darkness and even from their eyes no love can penetrate. From their mouths pour forth vile abominations instead of the seed of love, which the Word has planted. For it is with your heart, not with your eyes, that you will read the love which comes from the Father.

Remember that I have been criticized for the breaking of the law on the Sabbath. Each child that learns on the Sabbath, can be seen as the breaking the law, each act of mercy and display of love can be interpreted as the breaking of the law.

Let not this evil penetrate into your minds, and into your heart. Cast it out. Feel, know me now.

[He blessed us.]

68. The sacrilege of suggesting that God is not Love.

Stephen: I think perhaps that one time I mentioned that I might be called a devil! You have questions to ask, child?

Olive: We have been helped immensely but would like further knowledge about the Bible - especially Reincarnation. This does not seem to be very clear in the Bible.

Stephen: Sufficient to say that there are many things not mentioned in detail, only in concept. As you, Thomas, so aptly put it, it does it not mention your aircraft either nor does it mention all the birds nor all the animals; but we see, we know of their existence.

The evil would be if we said a being other than the Father created these things that are not mentioned in the Bible. Recognise evil when you see it and when you hear evil teachings. Our adversary is cleverer than even you would conceive.

I give you a better concept.

What better way to separate you two here as individuals from your God than to have you believe that the God of the Bible is evil, harsh and vindictive and one that could bear malice.

If the words taken as they were given to you, were accepted by you as truly being the concept of God [given the previous evening by a visitor] you would answer as you have answered, if this be God then I want not to be part of Him.

Therefore this cannot be God,

this abomination that is created from evil,

by using the seeds of truth.

For these words destroy love, they destroy pity

and they destroy forgiveness.

He demands joy, He demands laughter,

and He demands all things that are beautiful.

He abhors what is ugly, what is painful and what is evil.

For by the same law and by the same interpretation
I was stoned and the Lord Jesus was crucified.
You will often hear these words.
Know them for what they are.
In the wilderness these words and more
and the seeds of vile sacrilege were planted
and they will continue to be planted.

It is on the day of judgement that the planters of the seed will know them and understand how they, through their own words, separated themselves from God.

They have asked for the god that is close to their own hearts and minds; *therefore, they shall be given what they asked for.*

For the Father of Love, the creator of all beautiful things, tells us to accept no other God than He: *not because he will punish you, but because you will be given what you ask.*

That someone should suggest that the Father would withhold his protection from you because you have not grown enough to be the same as our Lord Jesus, is to mouth foul lies. May the Lord God forgive them.

Read the book yourselves and feel [for yourselves], for indeed the beauty is in the eye of the beholder. God bless you both.

69. Paying our debts, with love.

Olive: I have some questions tonight, Stephen. The first one is: would you please give us more understanding on asking God for forgiveness for our sins, in connection with Karma? [The necessity of recompense for the wrong we have done.]

Stephen: Is it your intention that you ask: Does the Father take away your Karma?

Olive: Perhaps, yes.

Stephen:Then let us ask ourselves: What is our Karma?
Our Karma, if we would allow it,
would condition us to judge - maybe not even consciously - our own sin, to decide what is a suitable recompense for that sin and to sentence ourselves to that. This is, in fact, what we often do.

When we confess to the Father, we pray that the responsibility of this judgement be taken from ourselves

and what needs to be corrected in ourselves
[may] be corrected through the guidance and love
which is the Father's.

The two methods can not be confused, for the results are greatly different. If we ourselves judge ourselves we would be harsher than would be the Father. What we do in our judgement, from our own will and by our own choice, need not necessarily be the will of the Father. That is what we must learn.

We have spoken before of these things and we have said that it is the desire of the Father that we raise ourselves above the Karma.

Let us not then decide at the other extreme that by confessing we alleviate any necessity to pay a debt that our actions may have caused; for that debt should and will be paid with guidance and with love.

Think each of you of what you have judged to be your own indebtedness. As an exercise even now decide, in your own wisdom, what you would have considered to be the correct recompense or payment in return for what you have done wrong.

At the same time, look at what you do now, and the many things that you have done that would balance those things that you have done wrong, the opportunities where, through love, and feelings of love, you have done kindly deeds.

Do not judge that because you harm or do injustice to a particular person that the payment that the Father will have you give through love, shall necessarily recompense that same person. Often their recompense comes from elsewhere - from another who pays a debt.

But always these debts are paid with love, not with duty. These debts are paid in grace and not in duty. We pray for forgiveness and know that, through the love of the Father, we shall pay this debt - a debt that shall become a joy for us to pay, that shall bring love to another.

Never revenge, for someone to give another satisfaction for a harm caused them can often lead the one thus paid into sin - the sin of satisfied revenge.

Therefore, I say that it is better that you pray for forgiveness and allow the Father to help you pay what you might owe. Only He can judge, only He has the strength by which you can repay.

Always, with love, you pay a greater price than what you took without love.

Do not believe that your way to salvation is by judging yourselves and repaying what you consider to be sufficient payment. Most often the payment which you return will fall short of what is deserved, it will be paid more often to the wrong recipient and lead the recipient into a debt of their own.

70. Love.

Stephen: The first thing you must ask about love is,
What is the nature of love?
And we have felt that love and God are the same.
Therefore it must be true that we cannot ourselves give love
but be used as the instrument that allows love to flow.
We have decided for ourselves and in our minds
that I, Stephen or Thomas or Michael,
or some other one of us, shall give love to this person,
or love somebody who is good,
then we shall proceed to give our love to this one.
We decided this time, in which direction the love,
that should be flowing through us, must go.
Like when we point water at a flower
we direct and give it to that one flower.
But as good husbandmen we know
that if we did not direct the water also to all other plants
they would wither and die for they needed this water.
Therefore should any of us decide
that we ourselves must give love,
to be correct, we must be sure
that we could nourish all that require that love.
We can see that, should this be the case,
we would faint and were we the giver of love
 many would be denied that love.
Let love flow through us from the Source
in the direction that is designated by the Gardener
who can see the entire garden.
This is not that we do not realize our full potential,
for our full potential is that we are a part of the Father,
never that the Father is a part of us,
for we are a part of the Whole and the Whole is the Father.
To realize our full potential let us be that part that we are.
Let us never assume [ourselves to be] a part that we are not
for the little that we can give of our own
can be only unsatisfying both to ourselves

124

as givers and limited by those who receive.
For why else would the Lord say
that we should love our neighbour as ourselves,
when we know that if each of us were
to attempt ourselves to love all our neighbours
with the love that we can give, we could not succeed.
And if we did not succeed
we would feel that we had failed
and cease even to be a channel of love to ourselves.
We would indeed feel ashamed;
we would indeed doubt our ability to be loved by the Father.
For each of us now can think of many
whom we have had great difficulty in loving.
When this happens it is usually because
we have decided that love is ours to give.
Think now of these ones that you cannot love.
Ask yourself, "Are they denied love simply
because you are unable to give them love,
your love? Do they lack sunshine?
Does the Father not care for and love them?"
You must say to yourself, "The Father
has chosen me as an instrument to love these
and I am pleased that I am an instrument
and that the love of the Father flows
from me to these and I feel the love I have given."
Do not admonish the Father and say,
"Father, why am not I the instrument for your love
to go to these that I feel no love for?" or
"Father, why am I not the parent of all children;
why do you slight me?"
This then, is the nature of love.
Be your instrument to allow what comes
from the Father to flow through you.
Do not give yourself the unhappiness
that a finger might feel if it wanted to see.
Know that you do have potential and
do not judge what that potential must be.
God bless you all.

71. Love that is the flood.

Olive: Now I have received [intuited] quite a bit on UFOs and be-ings from outer space coming soon to help humanity. Others in the group have received this too. So is this true or is it just something we are imagining?

Stephen: Should we be surprised that in the whole of
    creation,
    the whole of that creation that is the parched land,
    love is the flood
    that shall make the parched land fertile.
    As the parching becomes more
    than the flood from the whole of creation
    which is the well of love,
    and the well of love should not increase,
    then from the depths, and from the sides of the well,
    Love will flow forth.
    We are in danger often of minimizing our vision of many of
    these things as man has always done.
    These things that we see and hear in these days,
    in days when I would need not to use Thomas
    [when I was on earth]
    would have seemed stranger
    than these [present days] that cause you wonder.
    There are many things yet
    that physical man will need to experience
    and will need to know;
    the greater the need, the greater the parching,
    the greater the growth,
    or the greater the flood of love that will come,
    and it will come from greater depths,
    from all that has been created.
    We might, as a particle on the parched land,
    look at that one drop of water and say
    that this has come from a great distance to help humanity,
    where in truth we have only become a little moist.
    The flood that will come
    to quench the thirst of us all
    is yet to come,
    and there will be no misconceptions at this time
    for we will not be in need just then

for we will be moist and fertile.
It does not always need the water
from a distant part of the world
 to moisten or dampen us,
for close to us, each day of our lives,
there is moisture enough that we might breathe and not crack.
Maybe we think it is that the moisture
that comes from the place furthest away
will dampen us better,
therefore we forget what is nearest
and look for that which is distant,
when all we need to know is that
when the well springs forth
and growth has come and we are saturated,
we ourselves will blossom forth.
I say this: neither deny that moisture
that comes from a distance
nor attach to it greater wetness than what is yours already,
for both are for the same purpose
and none greater than the other.
If we stop drinking what keeps us from cracking,
in order that we might wait for the distant droplet,
then we will shrivel and become hard.
For in the distance is the imagined sweetness
which we already have in sufficient quantity.
For when the flood is come,
all that love from the distant and the close will be with us;
we will not lose one to gain the other,
nor gain one to lose the other.
Take what we have.
Should the other droplet come to us
then be glad that the well of life is the same
and comes undisguised
when the need for growth is the greatest.
I have said to Michael:
Be a good husbandman and sow your seed.
Do not be concerned that it will perish
through the lack of the flood of the Saviour.
We are here now and we plant our seed for growth.
The soil is open, that it might receive the seed,

AFTERLIFE TEACHING FROM STEPHEN THE MARTYR

and the flood of living water will come upon that seed.
If we have planted well
in truth it will flourish and the growth
which we came away from the Source to achieve,
will be great.
For as you can see that each thing that was created,
it was created in the image of what truly is.

As man is in that image, and represents what is the Father, so all things represent and are in the image of what is.

Each day, before our eyes, each month, each year, each season, unfolds the story of the order of things.

We can see when we plant our seeds, we have the sun that dries, the water that nourishes and makes to thrive. We know that to feed ourselves in order that we might grow we must care for and plant our seeds well and till that soil. This then is the order of what we must do for the Father does not leave us without a book of reference.

He does not leave us with a great mystery that is insoluble. He teaches us that wherever and whenever we rest, having everything with no effort, what is remains.

But with our so-called achieving, what we call "knowledge" has created barren land which nevertheless the Father can use to make the garden, that was indeed perfect, much larger, so in the end we have not one garden of restricted boundaries but a continuing one that will flourish.

Chapter 10

Other Questions and Answers

72. Abortion.

Olive: I have a question which has been bothering a few of us women. That is abortion - the rights and wrongs of it - could you say something about it please?

Could you explain more? The taking away of the foetus, when it is very tiny, when it is unwanted.

Stephen: What is the question?

Olive: Some people think it is almost murder. We would like some guidance. There is a lot of controversy about it.

Stephen: I can but guide you in this manner: That it would be wrong to impose this termination on a mother that would not wish it, as it would be equally wrong to impose on a non-mother a conception that she would not wish.

We give ourselves many concerns, We must look closely at the stage of development at which we judge that we might be killing a child. Always this judgement is based on what constitutes a child, and in nearly all cases, we use the size of that developing child as a guide. The potentiality of physical life exists much before the seed is implanted in the mother. Therefore, if we wished we would have to judge whether either contraception or abortion are wrong terminations of potential physical life, and which ways the physical must manifest. This I believe would pose a problem without providing the wisdom for the solving of that problem.

So let us go to what we are taught concerning Sin.

If two people conceive a child while both are in separation from the Father, then the conception is of Sin. If for the convenience of this separation [from the Father] and of this sin, in the minds of those that choose, the life is prevented and destroyed, then the purpose and the sin would be known to both.

If, on the other hand, this conception is caused by the love of one, giving consideration to the other, and the termination of that physical life becomes necessary, then this is not sin. But in each and every case we must judge and feel that it would be wrong, as wrong as imposing a conception on an unwilling mother, as the forbidding of a conception was imposed on another. Each would surely know if they had sinned. It can harm and lead another into sin, or the feeling of having sinned, were we to forbid by some law, the conception, either before or after the seed and egg become fertile.

But I say this, that many of those who would forbid, judge only on the size of the form of life which has been produced. [How much the foetus has developed] The sin (or maybe lack of sin) has been committed long before. The size does not have any significance whatsoever. For as the Lord taught us it is not only what you do, but what you *think* of doing.

Lest I be interpreted wrongly, when the child is born, and the body is separated from the body of the parent, this then is the time when it would be right to speak of murder. Before this the term cannot be used, unless all should be judged in the knowledge that can only come from the Father. For each time a conception is terminated let him judge if he will, but he will be judging himself at the same time. For each of us, in some life, and in some way, has terminated such conceptions. Advise, comfort, understand and love, but do not judge.

73. Ethics of Abortion.

[*At a later date*] Michael: We have been discussing in the group what happened on a Friday evening, and one or two questions have arisen from that. One was the reference to the continuous self and the foetus, and the baby. At which stage would it be right to say that the continuous self would become associated with the physical form?

Stephen: The continuous self may have been indeed the influence of the conception or the mating. Let us not confuse, in our minds, the necessary reasons for the experience that the continuous self wishes to have, for many a child is still-born. The continuous self that chose that experience would have been present at the time of conception, in fact, and even before conception. But this is not the question, nor the answer that you wish to have. The question was "How can it not be a sin, if the cell of influence was connected with the child, as some might say, the soul, or the trinity of creation, were together." For this you must understand completely that you do not kill that soul. Any experienced injury or as you might put it, karma for the action would be borne by the parents, or those who cause the termination. Do not think that when an individual physical body is destroyed by some means other than by natural causes, that the self - or cell of influence - of that body is either harmed nor destroyed. This is the main confusion in the mind of those that would judge murder. You can but murder an individual body, you cannot murder a limb or part of that body. Is this clear in your mind?

Olive: It seems to be clear in my mind.

Stephen: The question still causes some distress. I then say again, that even though the continuous self - if I may use your term - and a cell of influence combined, be present in the conceived to-be being, or individual, that the destruction or termination of that being in itself as an action, does not constitute a sin. Other factors before and during the conception, and the state of mind of those who are confederates in this action, these things only can determine the state of wrong doing, if there be any wrong doing at all. For if they share a responsibility for the wrongdoing they must also share the joy of the blessing when these actions are done for the good and in love.

74. Astrology.
Simon: Could you speak of the symbolic interpretations of the planets?

Stephen: The symbolic interpretation of the planets is purely physical. Be not misled, for in seeking explanations of concepts that are not easily grasped by the physical mind, the physical mind will often, through observation, come to conclusions that quite often are so far from the fact, that it can be harmful.

Remember that this planet that you walk on was even at a time when I was in a physical body, considered a disc. Now we say that it is a separate ball. [In fact, however,] it is separate as the teeth in your head, as the breath that you breathe. It may be spherical in shape, but so are your eyes, but they are part of your hands, for your hands are part of your tongue.

Simon: Are we to understand that the planets in any way represent the mind, the functions of the mind?

Stephen: There is a similarity, for all things of the Source, must of necessity operate in a manner that is of that design. Think rather of the works of an artist that works with paints. From the same source, namely the artist, one can always detect the technique. But be cautious, for though the technique may be the same, the picture or pictures may be very different. Some may be of a landscape, while the same technique creates a picture of the face of a woman. Therefore we cannot say that both are a landscape, or that both are women. Simply because of the technique being the same, or the brush strokes being made by the same hand... with those words of confusion, I will depart! God bless you. Be peaceful Michael.

[Perhaps Stephen is implying that although everything is part of everything else, and although the hand of God is to be seen in everything, we cannot assume that mental and physical things are connected in such a regular and predictable way as astrologers make out.]

75. Authors of the Apocalypse and John's Gospel .

Stephen: As we have been talking with much seriousness this night, let me also be serious: this moment we share is the most important moment that each of us will ever experience. And it always was, and it always *will be*. Now, Michael I have finished my jest.

Olive: One of us is asking another question: The author of the Apocalypse was John the Apostle, or John the Elder?

Stephen: The actual writer of the book was of course neither. The combination of ideas came from John the Apostle, and prophecies of that one [John the Elder], and things that were shown to him. [All this] together with the ideas of others, unknown to you, and the conclusions they drew from what they heard, saw, felt, or judged.

76. Who wrote the John's Gospel?

Stephen: I can but say the Father, for in the Gospel lies the truth, that Michael or Stephen knew. Who grew the tree? Who was the gardener who dug the soil, the nurseryman who nourished the seedling?

Ask yourselves, who made Michael?

I Michael, am Michael, is it I who am I?

Is it I who knows?

It is a combination of all that you have been given in your knowledge, and in your understanding from the point of view from which you look: and that point of view was given to you, from the Father, and from many sources.

Michael: The point of view, many of us feel, in the St John's Gospel, is as free from distortion as one could meet in the New Testament.

Stephen: Depending on the reader. I wonder how many of those you would call Buddhists would agree as to the clarity and the truth? I wonder how many of those who would choose not to believe in the Father, but only in themselves. Would they agree? And how many of us might agree?

It might be a good exercise to read and discuss together those truths that you perceive in the Gospel. See whether they might agree with the truths that you write, or John writes, or Thomas writes. You see according to what you understand. You understand according to what you have experienced, and are yet to experience.

For what has been given to you, has been given because it will hold you in good stead for what you are to experience. Think now each of you, of these things that you have been given in what you term 'receiving', and experiences that have followed that giving, and accept them. Did not what you have received assist in the experience that was to come?

Michael: It intensified it immensely.

Stephen: Then I shall give you a lesson: I was not speaking of the receiving this week, but of what you received from your mother and father! As an example of drawing conclusions! This applies to all receiving. If it were prophecy, you have received for a purpose, for your use.

For us truth is relative to our experience.

77. Creations of the mind.

Michael: It is good to see you again, Stephen.

Stephen: The term "see" is unique!

Michael: Well, experience! We have been enjoying ourselves, and we thought we would like to invite you.

We have been talking about feeling and experiencing. I have been investigating that this week. It seems to be important to me at the moment. And I have been thinking about what somebody said, that as you think, so it becomes, at a certain level.

Stephen: If you conceive anything in thought, it can be said that this is creation. For what is conceived in your minds has come into being. Then it is truly created as an example. Should you create in your mind the thought of a grand dwelling in all of which there is beauty and comfort, can you not at that time, even though it be for a moment, feel that comfort, and feel the possession of that grand dwelling? You may never physically create in stone, this dwelling, for your physical body to rest in; but you did with your mind, and your mind dwelt in beauty and comfort. Then should you not have, as I do not have, a body, and I did thus create [a dwelling with my mind], were I to desire such a dwelling, then I also could dwell [in such a dwelling].

Michael: That would be nice for you. But if you without the body got into a depressive state of mind, as I sometimes do, and say to yourself that the only place fit for you would be an old rabbit warren, or perhaps a tumble down shed, lo and behold, there you would be! What if, like me, your moods were changeable, one moment you would be in your palace, and another you would be in a tumble down hovel! Is there permanency in these constructions?

Stephen: May I suggest that you imagine a small palace in the warren? I do not say this in jest, or only partly so.

Michael: I find this a little hard to take in, for it makes me think of a surrealist world where everything is changed and altered by the feeling of the imaginer!

Stephen: I shall cease to tease, and explain. Who judged that you should be at times only fit for the hole of the rabbit? Who judged that at the other time you should be fit for the palace?

Michael: I judged, but my judgement reflected my imagination concerning how other people judged me.

Stephen: Not only did you judge yourself then, but also you judged how others would judge you! You can see how you can create what you would wish for yourself. Not only would you create a palace or a hole for yourself, but you would also create the opinions that others would have of you. You create in your mind; therefore it can be so. You consider that others think little of you, therefore you judge that they would put you in the hole. All this you have created, for you have even judged what they would feel for you. It would be very humorous to discuss the situations we could lead ourselves into, if it were not so serious, and if it were not one of the greatest evils that one could bring on oneself. For to judge yourself, or to judge what you may deserve, with so little knowledge could only bring disaster. At the risk of repeating myself, I would say this, that should you be in doubt as to your place, be it a palace or a hole, then say to yourself,
"What would my Father have for me?" And then your answer must be "All that he has to give."
You must start *living* your love for the Father.
The gifts that he bestowed upon you,
the joys that he has for you can be like a beautiful instrument hung upon the wall for all to admire, that is never played,
for fear that you might drop the instrument or in other ways soil it.
For your true motives are known to the Father if not to yourselves. Try; take down this instrument that others might hear.

God bless you.

78. The flea and the ass.
Stephen: On listening to your conversations tonight, I am reminded of the story of the flea that was on the ass, when it spoke often to its neighbours on other animals. Often the flea was heard to say that he had difficulty with the rest of himself, and that at times all he could make the whole self do, was to rub against a tree, and scratch.
Often we are like the flea, for in our consciousnesses we feel, that we would like the whole of us to conform and to do many great things.

Often, maybe the whole of ourself would rub against the tree, to relieve the itch. But I jest! In what way may I help?

Mike Webb: Your analogy of the flea has helped, it gives comfort. One thought that I've been thinking, which you will be aware of, is communication with us in this group. Purely curious, I know, if it were suitable that we know the answer. Do they [the consciousnesses] communicate with one another, and then push our mortal bodies into communicating along those same lines, with the same thoughts and ideas. You see what I am seeking, Stephen?

Stephen: Perhaps I should use the ass and the flea once more: Then the ass might say "the flea itches! But he is difficult to scratch, for he keeps moving".

Your talk this evening almost made me feel that I may be unnecessary. Almost! It is good that you should feel and that you should explore. Do not lose always the simplicity; look inward often for the answer, for it is as close as your breath. The distance is the cause of the answer.

79. The furthest sun is closer to you than your tongue.

Simon: Could I ask how we are to understand our relationship to the planets in our solar system?

Stephen: Again, just as it is only an illusion that you are separated even in your physical bodies, for even your science tells that matter is not separate, that it is one, then the distance or the apparent distance apart is only relative to your own dimensions,

therefore the furthest sun from you is as close as the seat in which you now rest.

For to move a finger is to touch that sun.

The physical impulses from that furthest sun affect even the hair on your head at this moment. I speak of course of physical relationship and physical manifestation. Beyond the physical relationship then we will say that the furthest sun is closer to you than your tongue.

[These words spoken in 1973, are in line with Bell's Theorem, propounded by the physicist J.S. Bell, which states that we either discard the mathematics of quantum mechanics, (which the Clausner Freedman experiments forbid us to do) or that we drop the idea of local causation, and see physical reality as one indivisible whole. This theorem was put forward on the basis of the Einstein-Podolski-Rosen experiment which demonstrates that energy particles which have been together, continue instantaneously to influence each other, regardless of distance and time. There is a popular exposition of the above work in The *Dancing Wu-Li Masters*,(1979) by Gary Zukav, in the last chapter. Theoretical physicist David Bohm, draws out some of the implications of this in his book *Wholeness and the Implicate Order*, 1980.

Biologist, Rupert Sheldrake, in a whole series of books, draws out further implications of this work as regards mind, instinct and natural law. Here is not the place to discuss such complex matters, but the enquiring reader should be advised to look up these names in library catalogues to obtain references for further study. The reader should also take note of the work of Alain Aspect, of the Institute of Optics, Paris, whose experiments were vital in confirming the indications of the EPR experiment. A Google search will uncover many interesting references under the names of these scientists.]

80. Healing.

Stephen: Again to Thomas I say, that one catches a cold, as one catches a fish, by doing all the things necessary to catch that fish!

Michael: Healing... on the one hand. And magic.

Stephen: Magic is what in the physical state, is what is not normal for you to perceive, things which you are not normally aware of. You will find that magic, (and I do not like the term), is usually confined to mind-power, doing things of the mind, and using the mind in such a way that unusual phenomena [occur]. Also magic, so-called magic, may be the witnessing of phenomena which are non-physical, caused by non-physical persons.

All of this magic which you may perceive or hear, or have spoken is very ordinary in comparison. For there is no magic yet that can circulate blood where blood does not circulate, to divide your foods into the necessary fuels for the many parts of the body. If there be a magic, let us recognise what is, and what is not.

Do you have some particular magic in mind?

Michael: With reference to healing: I am in a little confusion of mind because I recognise that it maybe is the will of the Father for that person to be healed, and I can see on the one hand that we can collaborate with the Father, in love and in prayer, but on the other hand it seems to me that we can attempt to influence the Father by different ways of holding our hands over people's heads, that we should hold hands in a group, with the idea of increasing the healing power, and this worries me, for on the one hand it may increase the love - I can see that that would be helpful, but I can also see that it could be done for other motives.

Stephen: The main help that could come from such a situation, the influence would be upon the one we would help. We cannot influence the Father, for let us not lose the concept of the Father that is the Whole, and that is the Source.
Most ills, like Thomas's cold, are well caught!

Michael: What do you mean by that?

Stephen: That they are well chosen. Do you find this difficult to believe that someone would rather choose illness than to be well? Nevertheless this is so. Each of us has a picture in our mind of ourselves, and what we are, and how we are, according to the way in which we choose to act.

Michael: If a person has this picture, should we attempt to alter their picture?

Stephen: You might have some success. You may have little. We have many methods of rectifying these malfunctionings of the body; the more successful of these methods are the ones that are the most usual: for it is expected that they will be successful. You have experienced yourself a tooth which ached; this ache will stop immediately this tooth is removed, not because there has been continual pain in the tooth, but one time only, did your tooth remind your brain that it was there, and that it needed attention. Receive that signal, and the pain and the mind continue together to continue that signal.

Michael: This suggests to me that our pictures of ourselves are very important.

Stephen: Most important.

Michael: And they may largely be unconscious to the physical mind.

Stephen: There are all sorts of conditioning which causes you to form these pictures of yourself. You may have a parent or friends, that if they were to tell you that a certain malady was yours, certain hereditary illnesses belonged to you.. each time this is suggested, your mind, deep in your mind these suggestions are recorded, and acted upon. Were it to be suggested to Thomas enough times by many different sources that he could no longer (I think you use the term) "sink" into a trance, then he would not do so. That if we continually spoke to Thomas of a withered arm, his arm would wither; if we continued to speak to anyone of a condition, and if the mind of the listener accepts and believes, then not only would the arm wither, but the arm might be straightened again.

Our Lord was an expert at choosing these circumstances, for he did but say to the woman who touched his garments that her faith had healed her, and she believed that this was so. And she was healed. Magic?

No, rather a miracle of perception on the part of the Lord, that he knew the time and the place and the mind, and the receptivity of that mind to which he spoke.

Michael: I can see that this perception would be most important. One must know that to which one would speak. With some of my friends, I feel that they have perceptions of themselves that would make life uncomfortable for them and would appear to interfere with the flow of love amongst us. I find it not easy to suggest to those people that they might perceive themselves otherwise. I must know the condition to which I speak.

Stephen: There is one thing that could be helpful to you, with a group of friends, who might become disappointed with their healing, or their powers, and stop loving because of this. This is always the danger with those who collect together for what they might term healing, and they are unsuccessful. A simple method to test the effectiveness of a group is to have one of you bleed, then if that group can stop the flow of blood, all will have faith, and many ills will be cured. But if that group could not stop the flow of blood, then the faith in that group and the trust in each other would not be there, and you would have danger that the simple and the ordinary be neglected, for the sake of the exercise. Then this could be harmful.

81. Activation of healing through prayer.

Michael: I forget in which context, but once you spoke of the "activation of healing" through prayer. Would you comment on that?

Stephen: I will speak as many of your great healers often speak. That many diseases or disorders of the body, more than is realized, are caused through the state of mind. If that state of mind through prayer, and through good reception, be put in peace and love, then disorders and sicknesses that are apparent, will cease to be so. Arguments against prayer, even by great healers themselves, are often that the correction of that which was wrong, was correction of the mind only. We can but agree, for what the Father has made the Father has made perfect. The perfection that we are able to accept is often like the readers of your book, acceptance with reluctance! And in part, with mistrust!

I say to all here now, that all disorders that are even in this room and beyond, that the mind and our free will have caused, our hearts and minds may cease to... Often when we fail in this task, we create even more sickness by our judgement upon ourselves. This is why we pray, for we must know that only in prayer, can the Father reach to us. And when the Father reaches he is accepted, then disorders can no longer be apparent. What we pray for is not that we be remodelled, or corrected, but that we become into a consciousness and to be at one with the Father. When we are at one with the Father then we are at one with all that is perfect. That we may often try with the mind to pray, and not apparently succeed, may worry and discourage from prayer. But I say this, that each prayer is answered, each time prayers is made with the heart. For we know when we truly pray. Those times that we allow the Father to come close to us perfection is very near. We worry often that limbs may be torn, and that our bones may disintegrate, that the whole body must groan.. when we truly pray it is also possible that these things also may be corrected and find perfection.

82 A heavenly game with pawns.

[The group had been discussing synchronous happenings, and saying it was a like a chess game with higher powers moving the pieces.]

Stephen: A heavenly game with pawns. I find the concept amusing. Worry not, I feel that laughter and happiness are often the greatest gift of God. But still.. Know that [Spirit] often comes when the laughter comes from the happiness in the heart.

83. What about the Mission of the Church?

Michael: Stephen, what about the Mission of the Church?

Stephen: About the Church as a whole?
  You ask the most surprising questions!
  First, let us define the Church as a collection of people of a Christian belief, who follows this belief in its particular way.
  In your case, the particular group of people is Anglican.
  The mission of the church (and it is a good question),
  should be, and quite often is,
  is to assist each other and those
  that they come into contact with,
  to develop into the eventual path of their own salvation
  with the Lord Jesus Christ.
  To follow the teachings of the Lord,
  to give water to them that thirst,
  to clothe him that has no clothes,
  to give bread to them that hunger,
  to love them that appear to be unlovable,
  this is the mission of your church.
  Also to receive those that come to you,
  but not despise those that do not come to you,
  for there are many ways to salvation.
  Think not that God would abandon any soul or any child or creature through the lack of understanding of your church, or through nonconforming with the rules of your church.

84. Offering our gifts.

Stephen: Before you would ask your questions, let me make one thing quite clear for you, concerning our discussion on the sharing with those in need. We speak all the time, of what we may choose that we should give to them; the uses that those that we would give to would make of those gifts of ours.

This is not what the Lord has taught us. The Lord has taught us that we offer all that we have, so that they whom we would wish to receive from us, would take what they desire.

There is often a great difference between what we would give and what would be received. Until we offer all that we have, as a tree would offer us its fruits so that those who would receive may take from the tree (which is us) those things that they would receive, we cannot share.

If this tree would offer you only what the tree decided must be given, would we ourselves be available to receive just that? May we not decline to accept? We must also be these trees. We must also display the fruit that the Father has given us, for this fruit has grown, not as our decoration, but as an offering to those who would need. When a hand reaches, give freely what the hand reaches for. Offer not the substitute.

There are many stories that have been told or could be told about what happens between parents and children: should a child wish love, and we give things other than love, does this suffice? Does this satisfy the child?

85. The Point of Unfolding..

Stephen: In what way may I best assist?

Michael: The point of unfolding, in each of us.

Stephen: The unfolding, and the point of unfolding [in each of us]: how can I best describe the seed in the ground,
 which will grow into a great tree?
Each stage of the unfolding is essential for the tree.
The object of unfolding is the tree. Each stage in itself is of the greatest importance at the time of that stage.
Is it your wish to know the stage of unfolding
 at which you have arrived?
Would a seed, as the first sprout reaches from the ground, from inside the earth, and sees the light and feels the heat of the sun for the first time, not say to itself, "Is this the object, or is there a further purpose?"
Would it not maybe recognise or perhaps associate with other trees, from what it can sense, what it can feel of the vibrations that come to it, and say, "This is what I wish to achieve, this is what I feel I should achieve."
The concept of unfolding is [in] the now of this moment.
The importance of knowing what was before for that seed
 is only of relative importance for the understanding
of what is *now*:
not what it may be, nor what it shall be,
nor understanding the desires or the instincts.
The salmon that returns to the same spot
 from which it had come away as a fingerling,

that is the object. Each mile of the journey is of importance.

Is there something that you can ask through my mind that will help me to make this clearer, Jeremy? Feel and probe...

Jeremy has nothing to say yet.

Has this in itself prompted a question, or are there other questions that will help me make it clearer? Feel my difficulty, if you please. How can a leaf tell, through the branch, the seed that is yet to come, of the unfolding after it arrives and it has fallen to the ground?

Even though the leaf knows, what concept for a comparison can it use to explain to the seed yet to come, except

when the seed begins to come, to tell it that it is a seed,

and as the seed begins to grow to say,

"Do not worry seed, you are progressing well."

When the seed is due to fall, to say to the seed,

"You will live again, do not worry, you shall unfold."

Can you see my problem?

You can say to the seed, "You shall one day be as the tree."

Believe this, for each thing that happens to you

is for that object.

Each belief that you have ever heard, and ever seen,

or can ever conceive, has the same object.

Each seed has been told this object even before it was a seed.

To explain whilst things are happening, what is happening,

becomes a simple task for the leaf

that has been through these experiences

and then finds itself only a part.

The concept, even though experienced, and the unfolding,

even though the leaf came about through this unfolding,

are hardly explainable.

But the leaf does know that it is a part of the tree,

that it was a part of the seed,

that it did unfold, as the coming seed will unfold.

In this way only can I help, to say,

"Think of yourself as this seed.

The stage of the seed is immaterial.

Unfolding you may be, as is the case with what I am

and what I am connected to has unfolded in a manner,

has unfolded not to become the tree but to produce the seed, which produces the tree."

86. Prayer.

Michael: Quite a long time back I said "Stephen, I pray, but even I need to be taught about prayer." Now, at that point you gave us a pattern of prayer that you yourself followed, but when we came to type the transcript this was inaudible. I do have an impression of the pattern in my mind but could you say it again please?

Stephen: The occasion of the asking for the prayer was...?

Michael: We were talking about Anglican worship and Olive was thinking about her dealing with cross feelings, I remember, and we were talking about prayer in the group - whether it would be right or wrong to have prayer in the group.

Stephen: we speak of what we feel and how we should feel...

87. Prophecy.

[Stephen has been pictured as wearing a space suit since he comes into another dimension.]

Stephen: The suit does not leak, therefore, I feel secure! In what way might I assist?

Mike McGaw: [A young American, present at a few sessions] Just to say hello, I guess, talk a bit, maybe ask and answer a few questions. Any questions I have to ask, I just don't seem to like asking. Perhaps just a chance to talk?

Stephen: You have a question Michael.

Mike McGaw: Yes, there may be perhaps thousands of questions in my mind, but they just don't seem worth asking when you are here. This one comes from when I first met Tom and was introduced to you; it is about trance receiving. I'm interested in this, and I'm going to say thanks for your help. I've found myself able to go into a trance state fairly easily now, but I'm not aware if or of anything that comes. I was wondering if you know if it is possible that I could receive in a trance state.

Stephen: It is possible always that what you call a trance is an openness in a particular way, that is peculiar to a small number of people.

What we say in this state, "I am open, I have made an invitation, would those who wish, use it as they wish?" This of course may sometimes not be advantageous to the one so used, depending on those who would accept the invitation to use. Not only should the invitation be extended, but also, the protection demanded, for it is your right. Not always would you be conscious of the use for the invitation is an open one. And the invitation says, "Use, if you will, as you would". Usage is often for experience by one who needs to learn. Therefore openness can always be of service, either to you, or to another.

Mike McGaw: I was packing some books; one presented itself to me and the subject upon which it was written was prophecy. Then several events surrounding prophecy had been coming up. The subject as I said, has presented itself, and I was wondering what you could tell us about prophecy.

Stephen: Prophecy is the recognition of what is bound to happen. Much is made of foreknowledge and recognition of a turn or event, but if a purpose is not clear for an obvious reason, then the foreknowledge is but a phenomenon of memory.

The prophecies are well recorded: it will be shown that not only were the events to become known, but the purpose of those events, and the reasons for those events were quite clear.

Those who spoke those prophecies spoke in full knowledge of the purpose of the foresight, for they had been given insight. It is important thus to know that this foresight of prophecies is useful only when the knowledge of the purpose, the full message is given with it at the same time so that no mistake can be made.

Most of us at some time have glimpsed at happenings yet to come but we have glimpsed without any need for the foretelling of these events. There would be little gain in relating these events, just as little as if they had happened in the past, for the past, present and future, in terms of time, have the same relevance.

It would mean nothing to you if I said that certain flowers exist if you had no conscious need for the flowers. Only if you needed them would the words I speak have importance. Therefore, prophecy given to someone that has no need of it can be pointless.

So let this be your guide to judge the usefulness of my prophecy: "If what I tell you can be of use, be it of the past, of the present or future, then it is of value. If what I tell you has no use or meaning, it is but noise."

You will hear in the not too distant future of events yet to come. Judge their worth and the usefulness, decide if it is just noise, how true it may be, and whether it is of use. To say the fire burns now or in one year would be of little use unless we know that the fire burns for the purpose of cooking, heating, or disposing. Remember then this prophecy, for it will be often!

Mike McGaw: There is only one more question that I have written here, which I was wondering about. How do you perceive us? We perceive you about us, at least I do, as a sense of good being, of happiness, of just wanting to close my eyes and be very contented. But, how is it that you perceive us?

Stephen: When I am with you, I perceive a warm feeling, contentment and love also. For this is what we are in truth, and we cannot separate ourselves from ourselves. Remember this, for this is what you are. God bless you.

88. Sacrifice.

Michael: Thank you very much for your help. I had numbers of questions to ask you, and in a way you have answered them. Except that we had been talking about depression, and today a few of us were feeling a little depressed, and I had tired myself by my writing, and I was feeling irritable, and thinking 'when I have discovered what God, the Whole, is like, wherever else is there to go?' I want to know where I am going, and what the drama is to be, and it just seems to me that I am staying wherever I was.

Stephen: Bless you for the question, for I would have prayed that you had asked.

For then I must give you the theology that you know so well, that you must continue to 'sacrifice' - you must continue to pray.

How many things I could speak that you have heard so often coming from the lips of our Lord. He did not speak idle words. He did not speak without meaning. He did not speak of Love simply because love is nice and makes us feel good. He spoke of Love because it is essential - for it is all giving, all sacrifice, all sharing.

We should hold before us the goal, that our wishes and desires might be directed to the situation where 'ourselves', through our sacrificial self, becomes truly 'Ourself.'

If we must do what we would want to do, if we must, and wish and will, that ourselves - our sacrificial self - becomes truly Ourself. It is the non-physical that makes us all one. In the non-physical we must love, we must pray, we must sacrifice, we must give up those things which hinder us - those things which are solely ours, in our minds, those things, that indeed do possess the real us, rather than we possessing them. We want no part of them. We only want what they have taught us.

What must we do? The instruction was clearly given by one who experienced and sacrificed all that we could possibly have as our physical possessions. Sacrificed the whole of what physical mind would believe to be the ultimate of their possessions. This then is John's prayer, and the lesson of sacrifice - the lesson of love - the lesson of giving - or casting off.

When we give to another what is dearest in our mind, our greatest possession, then this is Love, the Love of which our Lord spoke - the greater love of him who could lay down this last barrier of possessiveness, a physical self, a life, for another. For this is the sacrifice, this is the ultimate recognition, of what we need to give before we can have the consciousness; before we can give even that consciousness, and truly be.

Michael: That explains why it was in meditation two or three days ago, I was asking myself 'What do I need to go higher, to make the leap of consciousness?' All I saw was forbidding rock, and all that was horrible. But now I understand that this was my physical self, not wishing to give itself up.

Stephen: Think, all of us, of the burden that we feel in times of stress, of our bodies, of our circumstances, and of the unhappiness experienced in those circumstances, of the negativity, of our wallowing in self-pity. Think of the times when we would gladly and willingly - or we say we would - give up what is the body. But think, do we really want to leave the body, or only wish to cast off the circumstances that we have placed the body in?

Therefore self-destruction, is always futile, for it is the last[ing] regret that we have taken away what is most dear to us. To remove - Thomas joins me in saying that we might take away our nose, to cut off our noses that our face might be unhappy. This is not the sacrifice. The sacrifice is to be fixed to this body, to have it taken from us as, and when, it desires for another, or by another - either a person or a circumstance - because that is what we would wish and will. Our Lord did this so well. Then pray, for this is good sacrificial practice! God bless you all.

Michael: God bless you Stephen.

89. "Sanity".

Michael: I have always had an antipathy to magic, to the idea that we can manipulate God. With you I think I am finding sanity.

Stephen: What is sane, and in relationship to what is sanity? Think now, the sane, in humankind, the things that have been done in the name of sanity. Then we would weep for sanity.

90. Spiritual discipline

Michael: Sometimes when our group meets, we forget to listen to each other; we sometimes follow byways of speculation and complexity, perhaps not picking up the signals that come form the Source of the signals.

I, or some other within the group, could with loud voice, ask that the group should follow the path of receiving and action which appears right to myself. Plainly however, it would be desirable that the path should become apparent to the group as a whole, and that they follow what they have discovered for themselves.

Discipline in following a path can come from external authority, or it can come from within.

I am asking therefore, whether you would suggest some simple guidelines for such self-discipline in our group, which will help us to put the minimum barriers to co-operating with each other and with the Source.

Stephen: What happens of course, when you meet together, is that there are many thoughts and many conclusions that have been drawn, which we wish to share, and to pass on, which we feel might enlighten.

Or we might ask questions on what we have perceived ourselves, in the hope of enlightenment.

But we ask a different thing. We ask for discipline that will guide us into a particular path. Let me then carry on with the words that I have been speaking. For much is applicable to your question.

The discipline (if I may again refer to you as "paint" and as "colours")[32] is that the paint does wish to travel the path according to the conceiving "from the Godhead". The conception of a small part of that path does come to us, and is often given to us. The discipline that we must look for, is the discipline that would have understand a little of the direction of travel.

It would be helpful, if each time that these friends meet, if they look firstly at the inevitable guide in things that we know and do, should we wish to follow the path. These guides may be considered by various members of the group to be ancient and no longer applicable. That they are "ancient" in those minds is because those minds are themselves so young.

Remember that the pattern was first conceived in the Head of the body and it has not changed simply because of the newness of the paint or because of the differences in the materials. So then let those who meet speak then of themselves and their conceptions of what might be, but let them relate to these ancient guidelines, for that is the pattern which is being followed.

If one of the group should relate an experience or a receiving that has been perceived, listen well and then, for understanding turn to the book which has the guidelines and plan of the pattern. Relate their experience that has been spoken of to an experience that is the same [in that book]. See what came before in that ancient experience.

See what would come after and then you might know yourself in which way it would advantageous to act. Then your discipline would be the voicing of an experience, the study of a comparison from the books, the enlightenment of how the pattern follows the course.

There are other things that you can do which will afford much love and contentment: your songs are good, your prayers also. But do not each time attempt to give each other so many experiences that you need to stay together to study the whole book each time that you meet. Take one or maybe two, look for the parallel. Discuss and then [pray?].

It is always best that when groups meet together they depart at least as happy as when they arrive. Always finish with what has made us happy during that meeting, whether it be song or a prayer or even the humour which is a mirror of the love that is often felt.

Each should have their turn if they so wish. The questions that need to be asked will often become apparent and the assistance with your questions will be as always readily available as you will have recognised from your questions this day.

Michael: It is my feeling, after hearing many theories and receiving of others, that it is best to be simple. Sometimes when we interpret the Bible, we can "discover" secret meanings; we feel that the Bible should be interpreted by certain regular methods of interpretation [as if it were in code]. For instance, concerning the *Book of the Revelation of St John*, or the book of *Genesis*, it is felt that the teaching of the Bible is largely secret, except for the illumined.

Stephen: If only the words of the books and the experiences laid out therein are taken literally, you can find the parallels to the experiences related by the one who relates his experience. Do not initially look for the mysterious. Look at what has gone before. The action and the experience are parallel with the results of action and the experience. Do discuss, and then let those who will, think on, and study deeper the lesson that they have learnt. They much reason, look then in the books for a parallel, for another who was asked to make a sacrifice, when there seemed to be little reason.

91. The Virgin Birth.

Stephen: Is it inconceivable in your mind that a creation of so simple a biological happening can happen when it is required that it happen! The wonder is not in the conception.

It is the sign of the conception that should be noted for what was received and what was previously told as a sign that others would recognise made this form of conception necessary for some.

In truth, it mattered not in which way the child was conceived; only in the recognition of that child would the conception be of importance.

Often we base our arguments, our discussions, on points of a nature that could be trivial but for the importance that many, who would think negatively, attach to these manifestations.

We should look rather at the child: who the child was, and is, and what is done, and what is to be done because of that child. Details such as whether the fingers of that child should be short or long, or whether the mother had a blemish on her face, these could only have significance if they had been foretold. If they were foretold it would have been by the will of the Father, and given as a sign.

Chapter 11

Intuitional Receiving – Guidance

92. The process of receiving spiritual guidance.

[I have mentioned an informal group of changing composition present at many of the times when we questioned Stephen. Our questions often arose from a striking synchronicity that we had experienced, or from dreams, or intuitions of various kinds. I myself had been receiving spiritual guidance for many months prior to my encounter with Stephen, often through consulting what some people call "The Library Angel"; in my case this involved asking a question in prayer, and waiting to be referred to a particular book, page and line. Others had different ways of intuitional "receiving". Trance receiving of the teaching of Stephen through the usually entranced Tom Ashman was of course one of many possible modes of spiritual guidance.

Readers will of course be most interested in Stephen's teaching but it will help to understand a little of the context in which it was "received". And the context in fact was much of the "receiving" that I have been describing.]

93. A very strange episode.

How to describe the situation though? Seventeen times at least during between May and August 1973 before I came on the scene Olive had been both questioning Stephen and transcribing the conversations that had been recorded on tape. There is much of interest from this period, that Olive relates in *her* book, *Communion with a Saint*.[33] It includes a number of parables using imagery derived from the culture of the ancient Near East, and key happenings in their developing relationship with Stephen and sometimes, with Jesus.

It would have been in July, 1973 that there was a very strange episode not so long before I first spoke with Stephen. It seems that a conscious Thomas was asking God the Unseen questions, hearing answers in his mind (as I have reported doing myself) and recording his answers on tape. Then however, it seems that Thomas went into a trance, and a being whom Olive understood to be "St Peter" continued the answers, in the same vein. Next "St Peter" was displaced, and it was then "St Stephen" who continued. (I put the names in quotation marks not to beg the question of their identity).

Whatever are we to make of all that? It is very confusing, and for that very reason I could skip this story. But there are pressing questions: "What is going on when we talk to Stephen? And what are we to make of hearing a continuous teaching coming through first Thomas, then "St. Peter" and then "St. Stephen"? Are we hearing from separate personalities or from a wider dimension of mind or spirit? I am inclined to believe the latter since the Giver of all gifts is the Unseen (the Father if you like). There is no reason at all why the gifts cannot come in several ways either at once, or after each other. We need to be clear that ultimately it is a Wider dimension of Spirit rather than Stephen who is giver of the gifts we receive. If we can bear this in mind, what follows will not seem so strange.

Here is a transcript of this strange session:

94. Spiritual and physical, like two legs operating jointly..

[Thomas himself asked:] "I would like to be clear about the interaction between the spiritual and carnal planes of mind and how they may interfere with each other. I have to become incarnate on the physical plane in order to correct my disordered relationship to the Source, so on what level of myself do received words originate?"

[An answer, I gather, that Thomas consciously heard dictated in his head:] No, no, no! You are only thinking outward from the physical and so come up with an illusory distinction. Both physical and spiritual are God-created; therefore both are of equal importance. There is no contradiction in the co-existing of minds [spiritual and physical] unless the contradiction is self-created. Try to think in terms of joint co-operation! Just as your two legs operate jointly. To walk on one leg all its parts must work in co-operation with the other leg: neither is the tool of the other. Both are necessary.

But again, do not get the confused idea that the physical mind is part of the physical body. What we think of as the physical mind in fact needs to continue and to survive the death and discarding of successive physical bodies. This physical mind continuing in this manner might be termed the "continuous self".

To become very old [physically] is of no advantage to this continuous self, as age must restrict the experience of the physical mind, or continuous self because an aged body is not able to give the mind sufficient variety of experience.

[Then Thomas goes into trance and "St Peter" communicates:] Therefore the message must continue that incarnations must come about because of the wearing of bodies. So let drop from your mind any idea that the continuous self and the physical mind are two different affairs. They are the one and same.

You may sometimes worry that you are having delusions of grandeur when you allow yourself to receive such extended teaching from the Lord our God and to pass it on in His name. But it is not profitable to speculate why God should use you in particular. You could equally well, and more profitably, ask why He should not use you. You do not know why or why not He should use you. But if the Lord God sees an instrument He must use, He will use the instrument.

Now the Lord God using an instrument may aptly be compared to your mind using parts of the body. Your mind uses your legs or lips when you walk or talk. They are yours and you are theirs, and if you must walk then you must move your legs. The leg does not know where it is going. Only your mind needs to know; for your mind would not lead your legs into danger purposively. And God, in all His wisdom, would not guide nor lead you, or operate you as legs, unless it were for a purpose.

If you are to be used to teach, then first you will be taught. For what you need is already *there* waiting to be known and used.

We are to be used to teach. And before we teach, we have to recall some of the knowledge we left behind when we incarnated.

It is much better to take each day as it comes. Concentrate on that. And I should say, follow the signals that come from the Source of the signals. For if opportunities and invitations present themselves assume they are of a purpose, for nothing in this realm can be accidental.

[I don't know how Olive had the impression that it was St Peter speaking but I readily understand the characteristic manner of Stephen would have been recognizable when he now speaks:]

> Stephen: There will be simultaneous receiving by several people and by several methods. The usefulness of this multi-communication will be obvious. You will really attend to it; also you will each attempt each method of receiving, for your mutual advantage.[34]
>
> Do not worry or be concerned about these things. Be content to be the legs for the moment, and to be guided along the path. Step forward boldly, do not be concerned; be at peace with yourself, for things are going well.

[To continue with our story: The day after the above session, Olive met me and gave me a transcript of it. I was fascinated with the whole thing, willing to accept that it was truly Stephen who had spoken. But I was uneasy about "St Peter". I could see that the teaching hung together as one narrative regardless of the speaker, but I did wish to check whether the receiving of information had become contaminated.

I should explain one of my methods of spiritual intuition. At that time I had the custom of typing down the words I used in my prayers for guidance, and then listening to answering words in my head, and typing the answers in turn. Sometimes the words in my head referred me to books that I had never read, mentioning the page and line that I should consult for the answer. So I sat down and typed my question:

"Now, Father, in the face of what you have explicitly said through the being whom I believe to be Stephen, it seems most presumptuous to cast doubts on Stephen's words, when he clearly says that St Peter was communicating through Tom. But I do doubt."

My intuited book receiving was, *"Browning ii p.8 col. i, line 15"*. And lines 15ff turned out to read:

> "And don't you deal in poetry, make-believe
> And the white lies it sounds like?
> Yes and no!
> From the book yes; whence bit by bit I dug
> The lingot[35] truth, that memorable day,
> Assayed and knew my piecemeal gain was gold, -

Yes: but from something else surpassing that,
Something of mine which, mixed up with the mass,
Made it bear hammer and be firm to file."

My typewritten prayer continued:

"I know even for the past four years I have had to mine for the truth among the books, and to find bit by bit the gold. I will indeed continue to mine, for my inner feeling tells me that there is some dross even in the words spoken by Stephen. I ask again... what about St Peter? Did he speak?"

The intuited reference was *"Browning vol. ii 217 line 13"* which read:

"Come into court, Formosus, thou lost wretch,
That claimest to be late Pope as even I!
And at a word the great door of the church
Flew wide, and in they brought Formosus' self,
The body of him, dead, even as embalmed
And duly buried in the Vatican
Eight months before, exhumed for the nonce
They set it, that dead body of a Pope,
Clothed in pontific vesture now again,
Upright on Peter's chair as if alive."

I then typed: "If I may say so, Father, that does sound like a some-what overly forceful agreement that the entranced Thomas was not being used as an instrument by St Peter." .

Some days later I was to tell Thomas about the latter book receiving, and he asked me to show him the passage in the book. We both began to read the text together, when Thomas noticed that the quote was preceded by the words *"and Stephen said:"*! "And Stephen said, 'Come into court, Formosus, thou lost wretch,' etc."

On this Saturday came the great event: I spoke with Stephen. I was awed, but even so all prepared to challenge him because of my Tuesday receiving. Other people I am sure, when believing they are truly speaking with the spirit of a Christian saint, would not go all prepared to make their very first words with this saint, a challenge to the truth of what he had been reported as saying. Thinking about it, I am very surprised at myself.]

95. Michael's first encounter with Stephen.
[It was arranged that I should meet with Thomas and Olive in a room in our church hall. We offered prayer and spent some time in meditation. Then I saw a change come over Thomas. The white, almost dead-looking face, the drawn lines on the face, the little jerk in the body as if at that point taken over by Stephen, then the half-raised hands and the smile that I later came to associate with Stephen.]

Stephen: There are of course many questions that you wish to ask.

Michael: The things that you have said to Thomas appeared to be really good and true. But when I asked God about Peter last Tuesday it seemed from my receiving that my answer was, "No, it was not Peter, this was error". Would you speak about this, please?

96. Contradictions.
Stephen: Let me first ask you all a question. If either method of communication gave you a definite answer on Peter, each of them continually disagreed with one another; assuming that you are students, what would be the logical course of action?

You are quite right in assuming that the things that have been said, have been said for a reason, and to show you how you must teach. And in the communications received you find a disagreement. So what conclusions will you draw from this disagreement? This, that only the truth can have no contradiction; and on the other hand, what is untrue will have contradiction, and must be disregarded.

Take an example from chemistry: you wish to demonstrate that two chemicals put together will produce a certain effect. You put the two chemicals together and the effect is not produced. So what do you do? Do you try to separate the chemicals to see what went wrong? To see whether one of them was the wrong chemical? Or do you first make sure that you have the right chemicals, and then try again?

In spiritual receiving we always tend to say that because there is some good in it, the good should be extracted and used. But this is wasted effort, and it is better to disregard the whole. In making sure that is true, only accept what has no contradiction. Of course you should make quite sure that the contradiction is truly there. But if it is there, then you should discard either the part or the whole in which you have found the contradiction.

Michael: I suspected that you put in this contradiction in order that we might be taught. Should a contradiction come in other circumstances, could you speak about the source of the contradiction? Does it come from a misunderstanding soul or mind or does it come from a source, which is not divine?

Stephen: It often happens that there is a duplication. Accept this fact, for you will find in your source of truth and from your unknowing that this duplication is well recorded.
[cf. Romans 7:22-23: "For in my inner being I delight in God's law; but I see another law at work in me, waging war against the law of my mind and making me a prisoner of the law of sin at work within me." (*Today's New International Version*)]
Therefore your method of learning and of teaching is always to look for an obvious contradiction. Examine it closely. If the contradiction remains in the information it should be disregarded.[36] This method will be taught to all; you will always find that by using your source of known indisputable proofs, what can be confirmed and what can be rejected because of a discrepancy between the receivings.

[I went on to tell Stephen about the visit from the evangelist who had felt guided to come five miles across Christchurch to tell me what to do with my life. He had said to me that it was plain that the Lord God was working in me to teach me to receive better, and to help others to receive so that they in turn might help others. This was where my life should be concentrated. In fact, he said he had "received" that he should come to me; he too based his life on receiving, and felt that this should be the basis for the living of our lives.]

Stephen: Firstly, each and every soul does (your word) 'receive'... you will help, and your task will be to help others recognize what is reception, and what are receivings. You have helped in this way innumerable times in your ministry.
Receiving is basically the awareness and the feeling of God within you, as you are within Him.
Finer receiving becomes aware of detail from the Source, so that the guidance becomes clear and even clearer.

The reception in all souls is only hindered by themselves in *"duplication"* [as in our Romans quote] otherwise it would be apparent.

Even in the organised churches, and I use the word in your terms, there are such "duplications" which have misled both before and after the coming of the Lord.

With this confusion from "duplications", together with the nature of physical man, it is hard for receiving to be recognized.

Therefore you will find that the Father will use souls like yourself, who have begun to recognize receiving using many different methods, to collect together in many places. From their own recognition of receiving through differing ways, speak to others, and tell them of their methods. Then others will listen and the seed will be planted, and they will be able to recognize in turn, their receiving.

In all souls, receiving is only hindered by the distortions caused by the physical mind. Without the distortions, the receiving would be apparent. What we must teach others is to recognize their own receiving and to distinguish what is of the truth, from what is from "duplication".

You will even recognize yourself how in your ministry you could have helped many souls by helping them to recognize their receiving[37]. Each one when we feel love is receiving. Let us recognize this receiving from whence it comes...your task is to teach people to recognize.

Earlier, Thomas and Olive, it was said to you that your ministry will be to teach and to heal disturbances of the spirit. This again will help people to recognize their own receiving, to discern what is of the truth, and what is not. In this way, the Lord will be well served.

You will each have gifts other than the gift of being able to recognize your own receiving. There will be gifts of prophecy, of healing, and most important of all, the gift of discernment. Each of these gifts will enable others to trust you.

Michael, what your friend told you, can be confirmed in your own heart. For what I have told you, is not news to you, and now you begin to recognize that you have always known this.

Think on these things, and may the Lord bless and keep you. Pray for me.

97. In an early conversation, I asked whether I was hearing from God, or from Stephen? He replied:

Stephen: The answers categorically come from God. Think of the telephone when you answer it. You do not say, "Hello telephone". If we were taken to a strange planet, and shown a strange instrument of receiving, we might shy away from it. Yet when we are helping people to recognize their own receiving, we must see to it, that they recognize that there are many instruments of receiving. If a blind man received visions he would know he was receiving, and if a deaf man were to hear words he would be more convinced that he was receiving. The personality and instrument of receiving is particular to each person.

When statements of truth, firm guidance and deep comfort are required, then the instrument for them is the Lord Jesus. When rational explanations, humour and conversation is needed, then I Stephen will talk.

As for the Lord, he once said, "I speak for my Father, when my Father speaks, I speak."

Receiving is always from the Source, even though the Source used instruments in conveying what is received. If we were to receive from the Source through a telephone, when it rang, and we recognized the speaker's voice, we would not think to say, "Hello telephone!" Similarly Stephen is an instrument, but we hear from the Source.

When we are helping people to recognize their own receiving, we must see to it that they recognize that there are many instruments of receiving. Some instruments seem quite foreign, out of this world, so much so that we might well reject the very idea that they could be channels of receiving from the Source. But it is not wise to reject anything as a possible channel or instrument of receiving, but rather you better always be open to what may come.

[Stephen concluded by saying:]

> If we want to ask a question now, use Michael's method of receiving.

[So I said, "Stephen I would be grateful if you would use a book reference to show your work, so that it may be more mine, the belief that you communicate." And to my mind came the reference *"Ephesians 4.8-16"* which turned out to read:]

"Each of us has received his gift, his due portion of Christ's bounty. Therefore Scripture says "He ascended into the heights with captives in his train, he gave gifts to men." Now the word "ascended" implies that he also descended to the lowest level, down to the very earth. He who descended is no other than he who ascended far above all heavens, so that he might fill the universe.

And these were his gifts: some to be apostles, some prophets, some evangelists, some pastors and teachers, to equip God's people for work in his service, to the building up of the body of Christ. So shall we all at last attain to the unity inherent in our faith and our knowledge of the Son of God - mature manhood, measured by nothing less than the full stature of Christ. We are no longer to be children, tossed by the waves and whirled about by every fresh gust of teaching, dupes of crafty rogues and their deceitful schemes. No, let us speak the truth in love, so shall we fully grow up into Christ.

He is the head, and on Him the whole body depends. Bonded and knit together by every constituent joint, the whole frame grows through the due activity of each part, and builds itself up in love."

[Indeed, I had "received" a scriptural passage that repeated and amplified what Stephen had just been saying. To the sceptical reader, I should say that I am not one of those Christians who carry around numerous scripture references in my head to be recited at appropriate occasions. I did not know to what words such a scripture reference would refer. The passage contains the essence of the Stephen experience, both in his teaching, and in experiences of synchronicity. The part, "ascended into heaven with captives in his train" seems particularly to express what our experience of Christ, of Stephen, is doing to us. Our consciousness is step by step lifted to a wider realm where spirit is plainly seen as connected, where all is one.]

[The next session marks the beginning of a journey lasting very many years, in which we are very slowly brought from our individualistic consciousness to that of the One.]

98. When the sheep are scattered in the field, and the darkness and the night-time come.

[On this occasion, Thomas, Olive, and myself were present. This was my second conversation with Stephen. The previous sessions had contained words that needed to be thought about again and again, and their implications unpacked. Now this session was portentous, for...

The hand is raised in blessing: the voice loud: it is Christ who speaks.]

Christ: Sic ecclesia Spiritus Sanctus.* When the sheep are scattered in the in the field and the darkness and the night-time come, they gather together to receive comfort and warmth and the knowing that together there is security and there is the care of the shepherd. This you should do also.[38]

Awe holds us silent. The hand raised in blessing is lowered. There is a long silence, then the two raised and welcoming hands, and the smile of Stephen. "You have questions to ask?" I did not feel able to refer directly to the words of Christ, so I said: "I am concerned about numbers of people who seem to have begun to receive from Spirit. I am walking a path I don't remember travelling before, and I want help as to how best to support people who are beginning to respond to their receiving."

Stephen: Firstly, as you have heard from the Word, let each of these our sheep, if they will, be gathered together. Because as you know, your strength and your learning are coming because of your joining together and hearing from others what you have heard also.[39]

Michael: I still cannot understand how Christ might relate as an individual to many millions of people - it seemed that he spoke to me and took my hand[40]. Much as we may be all one, it seemed that he spoke to this little ripple on the water. But there are millions of ripples, and I cannot understand how he can speak in an individual way to each.

Stephen: The words of our Lord Jesus and the speaking of our Lord Jesus are forever with us. One individual at that time heard these words, took the hand, yet the communication of our Lord is continuous and non-ceasing.

It is there for each one of us, if we would but hear, at any time. If we can regard ourselves as radio-receivers, it could be said that the Lord could communicate when we are "turned on". The one who speaks is always there and can communicate with all of you what you would receive.

Therefore, the communication depends as much on the active openness of the receiver, as on the speaking of Christ.

---

* "Thus, in the church, is the Holy Spirit" "The Holy Spirit is acting in the church, in this way"]

The communication is, for each of us to hear
what is always present.
You have had many instances where you have heard,
where you have seen, where you have felt.
Not at those times when you are occupied with other things. But when you truly need, and want,
and set aside your time to listen, you do receive.
For all that is there to receive is always there - often we are not [there].

99. In the dimensions in which Stephen dwells, how does one come by knowledge? [41]

Michael: Bryan has asked about your knowing [I referred to an incident where Stephen seemed to be aware of details that I had read in a book.] I wondered how you did it. Bryan is wondering whether s you go through a library to procure knowledge. We wonder about the limits of your knowledge. Are you omniscient, are you at that stage? [Stephen laughs] You laugh, but we do not know, and we wanted to know whether we could ask you about matters which have nothing to do with religion (I don't like that word), and the development of the self. If we were to ask you about atomic physics, for instance could you answer? We are asking about the reality of things.

Stephen: To answer the first part of the question first: to credit me with these abilities is most flattering. I do not, as you put it, scan, or pre-know these books. The knowledge is there, and I am directed, as you are directed, to this knowledge, because this knowledge is there.

The physical plane, or the physical manifestation of this knowledge which you feel is hidden, is even less hidden to you than your thoughts and the thoughts of others.

It is there in a physical form and there are written words. To feel and know these words and the availability of these words, surely this is as simple a matter as knowing the hairs and their number on each one's head. The knowledge is there and it is used.

All knowledge comes from one place,
and what has been said has been *given*, and has been *received*.
Therefore do not read difficulties into a task that would be, if you were not in a physical state, a matter of simplicity.
How can I therefore give you an example

of this simplicity for yourself?
The keys to your door. Do you know where they are?
The brush for your hair, the blades for your face?
Think then now of at least four hundred things
that you know where their place of rest is.
Do you find the concept so difficult to think
that you yourself in the confines
of your own physical mind
should be able to know these things?
Is it difficult to imagine that if you did not have the confinement of this physical body, that you should know the place of many more?
It is very difficult I know for you to understand this concept of the openness and availability of these things.
These are the only comparisons that I can give you, namely the things that are available, and the knowledge that is available in your own minds of other things.
The second part of the question:
I must not be misinterpreted here, but all knowledge [is] only one [and] has one source. The source is not religion.
The source is the Creator, God.
The knowledge of these things that you wish to ask
is His to answer.
For these things He created,
and the knowledge of these things He created,
and the learning of humans of the knowledge of these things,
have been created and have been fed to him.
Therefore ask the question,
but take the answer from whence it comes,
if the answer comes.
For it is His to give,
and the knowledge is only given
for the use and not for the possession.[42]

100. Jeremy's receiving.

Michael: Thank you Stephen. Every time you speak, I want to ask you twenty more questions, and if I have the chance, I probably will... Jeremy wishes to know in what manner he may continue receiving when he returns to his home in England. He has begun to receive very well here, but what have you to say?

Stephen: Jeremy, do not think that I am being frivolous.
Receiving, think of the word,
one receives what one is given.
You do not have special ways to receive, you will receive.
Think of an anniversary day when people bring you gifts.
Do you first ask yourself which is the best way
to receive the gifts,
without knowing that you are to receive these gifts,
and in what form these gifts will be?
I know this is a serious question.
The gifts will come and you will receive.

Michael: I am beginning to think that we should change the word "receiving" to another word, and talk about "God's giving."

Stephen: Receiving is a good word, it describes accurately [what occurs].

Olive: I feel the type of question we ask is very important; can you advise about this?

Stephen: Ask all questions that puzzle you, or confuse you;
ask when in doubt or in need of comfort
and you will receive answers, reassurance and comfort.
Ask a barren question and you will receive a barren answer. We have asked many like this.
When you have asked this type of question, the answer does not satisfy.

Olive: Why do we feel we have to know so much about everything? Why do not we just accept things as they are?

Stephen: A blind man would stumble if he did not ask what lies six paces in front of him. Read the Lord's Prayer - the Shepherd likes to hear our cries for he knows we are following him.

[In the Christian context of our Stephen conversations, the following conversation is important for better understanding him.]

101. Universal theology underlying all religions.

Michael: Can there be a universal theology which might embrace Buddhism, Hinduism, Christianity, Islam and whatever else one might introduce into our thinking? You have almost done this, I think, but would you like to speak about it?

Stephen: There is the thought, learning and teaching in each of those you have mentioned ... *should understand what has been said.* .[...is consistent with a universal theology?] Again we tend to separate, and this time [we do this] not even by physical bodies, but by words alone. [It is the words that] make us separate. If it were not for the sadness, I believe that we could spoof with this.

Michael: Would you please repeat that?

Stephen: Joke maybe, with this. Again, whilst our minds separate by words, or [we] feel that we are separate because of the words, how difficult for us to feel as one, when we can be separated by a body also. We must try to study more the word of the Lord to see what the Lord Jesus said many times on the same dilemmas. That some were separated for they ate one meat that the other one could not eat. That they were separated through the lack of an operation on parts of their body. Even now we are separated through an accidental pigment in each other's skins. The Lord never separated, he joined together. And he said, "Become as me, become as a child, be born again," for a child when it has quickened in the womb of its mother does not understand separateness. It has no words. It would not know which was mother and which was child. And throughout the separateness, such as Christian and Buddhist, would be ridiculous for the child. Therefore in our thoughts we must be born again, put our minds back in the womb of that which is the Whole and then we know that we are part of the Whole. I am sorry, I preach.

102. "if your choice be wise, you will indeed see the fire from my eyes".

Christ speaks: *Sic ecclesia Spiritus Sanctus:* The task of your servant Stephen is that of messenger and he speaks with great authority. The task of yourselves is the decision as to which way you choose to use what comes. I say this to you, that if your choice be wise, you will indeed see the fire from my eyes, you will indeed recognise the feet that are of burnished bronze. Wonder not, but proceed with courage, for thus far we are well pleased.

Stephen: I believe that we have had a visitor. May I help?

Michael: You were right in suggesting that when Christ came, we would not have the courage to ask him about the Second Coming. I felt very much in awe. But when... do you know what he said?

Stephen: I am aware of the message.

Michael: So when he spoke of, "seeing the eyes of fire, and the feet that are of burnished bronze," was he referring to the Second Coming in this material order?

Stephen: That is the correct interpretation. May I suggest that you fully read the passage from the Bible with the references to the church to which he gave the same indications of his appearance. You may find it enlightening. You know it of course?

Michael: The Letters to the Seven Churches.

Stephen: Each angel of each church was given a recognition.

Michael: You are speaking in riddles, but I think, dear Stephen, I hope that when I read, I shall understand.
[Stephen has been comparing us to the church of Thyatira *Revelations*: 2:13]

Stephen: I am sure you will. Again may I explain that it is not a plan on my part to confuse you. I aim only to conserve some of the energy of Thomas. For where it is written, and it is written clearly, then perhaps it might be better...

Michael: Thank you Stephen.. Are you aware also about our conversation about you in relationship to our group?

Stephen: Can I first explain about my awareness?

Michael: That question was also in my mind!

Stephen: You need have no concern as to my knowing all of your thoughts or all of your actions. To say the least, this would be impertinent on my behalf. The things that are necessary for me to know to be able to help you, are given to me, in knowing. It is similar to what you are now being given. And this also comes from the Source. There is only One who knows all that is in our hearts, and in our minds. And it is for Him alone to use.

Michael: Well.. I do not like some of the thoughts that I have, but I do trust you. In my knowing of you, you have given me sufficient reassurance that you are with me.

Stephen: If it is any consolation to you, it is only your thoughts on spiritual matters, and questions in your own mind to do with the development and the service of the Lord, that it has been my privilege to know.

Michael: That is a relief! But I am hopeful that the outside of me may eventually fall away or become transformed. I think it is best not to fight these thoughts but to receive.

Stephen: You will find that the mind that is fully occupied behaves like hands that are fully occupied; it becomes useful if occupied with the right things. I believe there is a saying...

Michael: .. that Satan finds mischief for idle hands to do!

Stephen:... therefore one would be blessed indeed if all the mind's work were taken with higher spiritual matters! Do not think that I am laughing at you, but rather with you, for I love you all indeed.

Michael: No I have not felt that you are laughing at us. And I have felt your love. ... Stephen, about our group and worship: it is my responsibility as a minister to be involved in the ordering of worship. It is my feeling that worship in where you had part in ordering it, would be a better worship than it might otherwise be.

Stephen: That is praise indeed for my work, and I thank you for it. I am but a servant for each of you, and if there is any way I might serve, then I will do so gladly.

My worship generally takes the form of prayers, not unlike your own, with a terminology much the same; for I believe that the Lord our God is also our Father, therefore I speak to him as I would my Father, for I know that he does know me, he does understand me, he knows each fault in my mind; therefore the words that are not mine would cause him maybe even to smile.

It is better for worship connected with this group where you have freedom from dogma, should be in the form of individual prayer so that each of you should benefit by knowing that your Father sees. For no person's prayer which they could offer to the Lord our God could ever come from their mouth as a false emotion. Therefore to hear another soul, to hear their heart and to know their mind; when you hear the heart of a person speaking to their God, then surely you can only love them. You see love. You see the willingness to do that which is the will of God. Therefore be privileged to hear the prayers of each other, know that this which is in each of your own hearts in your prayer, and you will find that each of you knowing this about his neighbour, with garments washed white in the eyes of each other, therefore all will become blessed.

Michael: Some of this I have begun to experience. This feels very right, and I feel that it will be very helpful to the group to hear you say this. The important thing will be for them to experience this for themselves.

Stephen: It would be better if this were to come about by their own wishes. Unfortunately for you three here, you hear my suggestion, and have the agreement from each [of you]. It would avoid embarrassment for those who at this time are not able to pray, who would like to, but unfortunately do not have the courage to pray.

Olive: I pray, but I do need to be taught about prayer.

Stephen: About feeling at one with people, and loving them: it is a gift, a tremendous gift from God....When one is able to do this! This is not easy, except as in all endeavours, one must practise to learn. I shall speak further this at another time, for much needs to be spoken, and explained.

Olive: I have so many likes and dislikes; is it so terribly wrong?

Stephen: I of course have never experienced dislikes!

Olive: You seem to know what to do with them!

Stephen: I shall leave the explanation if I may. The Anglican service: the prayers as such have deep and good thoughts, and are good for the purpose of arousing feeling and emotion. Therefore if at times they may fail for one or two souls, this is unavoidable for they are good. But like all general things they only act in a general way. They take all minds into consideration. Therefore the saying of these prayers must be assisted by listening.

Olive: Why do I always agree with what you say? But I do genuinely feel the truth of what you say.

Stephen:: Would you perhaps, as Olive thinks, agree that I am perfect? [laughter]

Olive: Stephen you have advanced much further on the way...

Stephen: ... and also during these times, I must be on my best behaviour! As you are too, no doubt!

Olive: True I am on my best behaviour... but as I get to know you, I find that you are human, whatever that means. Would it not be true that whatever it is that is human in music and creativity and joy should only be intensified as a person progresses?

Stephen: May I put this a more simply? That each of God's creation is able to recognise God in other creation, irrespective of the state the other creation may be. Is this perhaps what you might recognise?

Olive: Yes, it seems to me that even with the most annoying male or female, curiously I can be glad of them, and find that there is God there, even at their outward self I might feel angry, and feel like hitting them, yet even there, one can sense, surprisingly, God at work.

Michael: Stephen, did you know that I have been feeling angry, and as if my head would split, most of today. Did you know that?

Stephen: No I did not.

Michael: Well I now tell you. I have felt at odds with my family [*true at the time, but not these days!*]. I have felt that they were not turned on to the Spirit; and I wished I could talk to them, and I felt frustrated and angry, and had constantly to remind myself of their very many good points.

Stephen: It will improve with time. But before you condemn your-selves, wait for further explanations. To answer you Michael, as I must, when you say that you can get impatient and angry with those you love, when they fail to understand or to recognise that which you know. If it be any consolation to you, think of the Lord Jesus himself when he was in his physical body, when his father, his brothers and his mother did not understand. When those he loved most first denied and then betrayed him.

Olive: Hmm. A good answer.

Stephen: One that I cannot take the credit for. But I must leave.

Michael: Thank you for being with us.

Stephen: I must first say this, Thomas, that he was regained his sense of humour, and that the man did bang his head! [..on a brick wall] God bless you. [Stephen is jokingly referring to something Tom had said prior to falling into trance.]

[P.S. With reference to the words of Christ with which the session began:

On inspection of the second chapter of the book of *Revelation*, we find these words at verses 18ff: "To the angel of the church at Thyatira write: 'These are the words of the Son of God, whose eyes flame like fire, and whose feet gleam like burnished brass: I know all your ways, your love and faithfulness, your good service and your fortitude, and of late you have done even better than at first.']

103. Christ speaks: The two witnesses of Love and Sacrifice, the main teachings are simple.
[Tom has the strong feeling that the whole basis of our group should be receiving. All that we accept should come from receiving, and all

receiving should be treated as lies, or at least suspect, until there is check-receiving]

The voice of Christ: Sic *ecclesia Spiritus Sanctus*: verily I say unto you Thomas, that should you extend your hand, you would feel into the wound. My word is the word of my Father.

[The previous evening a visitor to Tom and Olive's had been stressing the wrath of God, and His punishing of sinners.]

The voice of Christ: Sic *ecclesia Spiritus Sanctus*. For what you hear must not be misinterpreted as has been before. You have been told that evil, and the benefits of evil, have no lasting effect; for that which causes a temporary joy will also cause the greater hardship. The way to your God is through two things alone, and these things are your witnesses: love and sacrifice. For these are the lances of the Lord. For love to pierce your heart, and the sacrifice to come into your heart are what is needed; for you must sacrifice the lesser for the greater. At all times your ears, your mind and your eyes are assaulted with half truths and blasphemies. Believe this, that you are commanded, and the most important commandment is to love the Lord thy God with all thy heart, with all thy mind, and with all thy soul, and that thou shalt love thy neighbour as thyself. For this is your duty, for this that which your God does only. Punishment and retribution are not his. If you accept what evil gives you, then you will accept the full rewards of that evil. If you accept love and sacrifice what is evil, then your reward will be love.

104. What do we mean by the term "Receiving"?

[Interchangeable Synonyms: Recall, Intuition, Knowledge, Memory, Guidance, Holy Spirit.]

[Discussion: Knowledge, memory, belong to the Whole, to the Father, to the cells emanating from the Father. Knowledge is one unity. Some QM physicists theorise that memory is in fact a dimension of general reality.

You can usefully compare this Knowledge to "Cyberspace" [43] and the Internet. You have access to cyberspace knowledge, available to everyone.

It could be said that we could see our experience of Stephen as implying that we live in a Information Universe (a very modern idea,) where all that has ever happened is remembered, where the DNA of all things has originated, and is recorded. Rupert Sheldrake and others think that the complicated instinctive behaviour of animals, birds and insects is guided from this unified memory.

But be a little wary of my explanations: remember the contrast between the dry information as is stored in books, and the living information and knowledge underlying true love, ecstatic experience, wonder and marvel, underlying the experience of the holy. Unfortunately analogies can get in the way of the living experience. So while we may accept that we live in an information universe, let us be open to the living experience, which is where St Stephen leads us. He emphasises this with the following words:]

105. Stephen talks of Receiving in simple language.

Stephen: Firstly, each and every soul does receive. Each one, when we feel love, is receiving. We all receive every second of the day and night, God's love, sunshine, rain, food for the body, the mind, the soul, the love of others and much more. I receive also; I receive from you, I feel the willingness here with myself, to serve the Lord. To receive this feeling from others is a gift that comes to me from yourselves. Receiving is basically the awareness and feeling of God within you as you are within Him.

When a child dresses itself, when a child eats, when a child plays with its toys, it does so in acceptance, not in wonder. For a child knows that these things are there as a right of love, by the grace and love of its father. Therefore these thing can be enjoyed simply and without question by the child.

Now take another child, one that does not know its father, one for instance that lives with other children in a home for orphans. The child is told, "These are gifts to you from this or that organisation, this was given for our use from yet another organisation and a kind person has supplied you with this." Each child, the one who knows its father and the one who does not, has the same things. But the one who knows his father, has what can be received by no other!

So our first step in being able to receive is to know that there are not diverse organizations throughout the universe, not some mysterious union or club that supply us with these things. These thing come from our personal Father. We should ask for grace to receive from the Father, for without this true concept of our Father, we become lost and we have not received.

[Everything without exception is *received* from the Father. The whole of the present moment is received. Knowledge, intuition, guidance are only aspects of what is received.

Knowledge or memory was left behind when each of us incarnated. When we are ready for the *recall* of some of this knowledge, then we receive that recall: we remember, in differing ways, at different times.

About the word, "Father": Stephen is using the traditional term for God, hence his analogy with a human father. But we ourselves can use our own term, like "Parent" in understanding Stephen's words.]

Stephen: The cell influences the extension of the Father, for the Father knows all and the cell of which it is part, knows all. The influence of this knowledge has been with yourselves a long time. Not everyone needs the same method, [trance], for this recall. Not everyone has that knowledge to recall.

A helpful friend once spoke to you saying, "If the answer were not yours, then the question cannot be asked". Fear not your questions, for what you ask is yours to know. I assist as your memory only in so much as I help the decision as to when you might recall. I even assist when I tell you that to progress further in conversation sometimes confuses. Be at peace with yourselves, for you know in your emotions what you should be and how you should be. Never let the mind persuade you against emotions in these things. I will depart now. God bless you all".

106. Ways of receiving knowledge, or recovering our memories.

Stephen: Guidance and answers to questions are received in many ways: visions, intuition, instinct, symbols, images, dreams, the spoken word, the written word and trance. These are but a few of them. Spend time quietly by yourself, eyes closed, and pray for guidance. Some may call this contemplation, and we are often told that we must make our minds become blank. This is a mistake! We should let our minds act, let our minds receive, let our minds understand and let thoughts come and go. Allow an answer to arise from a question you have asked; you may be surprised at the wisdom it brings. For we can learn much from our thinking. Ideas that come into our thoughts are our receiving if we would just allow ourselves to accept what comes.

After contemplation, check and confirm your answer, for a true answer must satisfy the question. Confirmation does not necessarily have to come in words. The truth of what comes is either felt or not felt. If confirmation comes in like words, then what is felt when these words are seen or heard, is the confirmation, not the words themselves. Words help; they are seeds and these seeds when planted, will grow. They grow, not in thoughts, but in emotions and feelings.

Words, and what words convey, are very minor and crude tools, feelings and emotions give us a greater range of expression and receiving.

Remain open to receive, for you know that it is only at these times when you have remained open with no preconceived ideas, that what you receive is the most satisfying. Achieve this consciousness of openness and you will receive. Ask and you shall receive. One receiving or word or sentence in itself, is insufficient. Each true receiving or true purpose, must be the truth. The guide to truth is that there must not be any contradictions.

So receive parallel to the receiving and check for errors. To follow just one instance of receiving, would not be wise. Remember, the message is the important part of receiving. What medium or instrument is used, [books, trance, painting, visions], is of little consequence.

107. Trance Receiving.

Stephen: The ability depends solely on the function of your own physical body and the one who is able to use it. What you call trance, is openness in a particular way that is peculiar to a small number of people. What we say to bring about this state is: I am open, I have made an invitation, to those who would wish, to use as they wish.

This of course may sometimes not be advantageous to the one so used, depending on who accepts the invitation. Not only should the invitation be extended, but protection should be demanded, for it is your right. Also, you would not always be conscious of the use, for the invitation is an open one. The invitation says, use as you will. Usage is often for an experience by the one who needs to learn, therefore, openness can always be of service, either to yourself or to others.

At this moment, Thomas sleeps like a child. He has done nothing except pray, be quiet and let his mind wander and drift on thoughts, and I have been able to come into the body of Thomas to use it. The words that I use through Thomas, are not my words. I did not create them, they are from his mind; I only activate those words.

For myself, I do not speak this language and I never have. I activate these words that are in Thomas's memory and are known to him.

Occasionally there is a little 'magic', when I join together sounds and symbols that are in Thomas's mind so that words may be spoken that are not known to Thomas. [e.g. Thracian Greek]

Even though Thomas is so willing, so open and his help is a great blessing, the tool is crude because the language is restricted and I cannot speak the emotions that I wish you to feel. I can only plant seeds with words. This is why I say: confirm all that you hear!

We often say that the language that Stephen speaks is his language when I do not have a language. For language is but sound and sound needs a throat, a tongue and an ear with which to listen. Of these things I have none. Would the gift be of use to us if the language could not be understood and when the words were spoken, there was no emotion felt?

We use our bodies as one might an instrument to catch what we must feel. That the mind that I use, [Thomas's], has a store of sounds that can be used and understood by the ear, makes the instrument useful, for words by themselves when they are spoken or written separately mean little, but together, [when Stephen speaks], with what is in our hearts, what has been previously in our minds and in our thoughts since we last spoke; these sounds for the ear can reach the heart.

108. Why has trance been used to communicate with us?

Stephen: Simply so that you may understand what is being given. The methods which were communicated to you both, [e.g. book receiving, dreams etc.], were not of sufficient impact. Think not of this as faults in yourselves, but rather of your needing, like instruments, to be tuned to a particular pitch before you can be played. Your own desire for the extraordinary is understandable and this type of communication was allowed.

You have noticed though, that the contents of your trance receiving are not the same as that of many others who receive by the same method. What you receive, is the same as many such receivings as you can read about in the Bible, and it is for the same purpose."

Michael You are talking to me. It seems natural and feels natural, but miraculous to my mental self.

Stephen: Indeed, it is miraculous. Let me explain more. Consider Thomas, (for it is necessary at this time that he is not with us), let us consider the physical mind of Thomas; we add to this mind, the cell that has the knowledge of what requires rearranging. That knowledge must work in harmony, but with influence on, the physical mind. The cell chooses the body which we see here now, for the probabilities [of experience] in the time environment, and many other factors.

109. Strange parallel coincidences.

[Once again we had been questioning Stephen about how he knows things, how he learns about things. How would he go about answering a question such as that about the strange parallel coincidences between the circumstances surrounding the assassinations of US presidents, Lincoln and Kennedy? He answered:]

Stephen: I do not delve into a store of knowledge nor do I look into great books, where this knowledge is recorded and written, as we might imagine.

The mirror concept is good: I have to think back, and become a mirror image stretching back. You have given me four mirror images. These images I must pick up: I will see in the minds of these images, and I will hear the words, the words that are ordained, but then [consider] the coincidences of mind.

I may then become the second assassin; [I had asked about the assassinations of Lincoln and Kennedy] I am sure I am this assassin, for the coincidence told me so. Now I will assassinate. For this is the image that my mind has created, this is the truth that I have accepted, this is the knowledge that I have partly received. This is what my mind will believe.

This I recognise from my own receiving with others. I look along their thread and I feel this.

Michael: But you used the word, "I". "I notice", "I look."

Stephen: I am the assassin. I have become the image. I have then become Stephen or Michael. For we spoke of the *centre of consciousness*. In the centre of consciousness I cannot answer this question about the assassin, because it was but experience. Can you yourself distinguish between one breath and another? Remember one breath from but a day? Tell me about the breath that was breathed at that time, the length and the duration, the sweetness or otherwise of that breath. You would have to use the imaginative powers of thought to bring back the experience of that breath.

Michael: My mind is grasping little bits. But here am I. I say "I" and I have my own consciousness. In my receiving, I have the consciousness of the other, concerning what belongs to the mind of the other. It is as if I travel from where I am, (and I know this is wrong) to where they are. It is as if a whole number of points of consciousness were moving from one point to another. I cannot make the word "I" ascend high enough (the wrong word) to become the Father, or to become the Source.

Stephen: "I" is the wrong word, the wrong concept. I shall leave you with this, for I feel that you will be helped. Do not be too troubled with your images, but *lose* them, for, as they are *not* Michael, neither is Michael the image. Take those things that you receive, all things; enjoy them for it is *love* that you receive. Accept that love often, for when you do, you recognise what you have accepted, for you feel the warmth of that love. God bless you.

110. Questions about receiving.

Stephen: I assure you, Thomas, that the aircraft is easily avoided! Perhaps I should explain. The humorous thought came to Thomas that I had better take care with much [air] traffic. Perhaps I might come from a different direction! Thank you for your invitation. In what way may I help?

Michael: Many questions tonight, Stephen, which have to do with "receiving".

Stephen: You have one question which will help, that I [should] answer.

Michael: I feel baffled, Stephen.

Stephen: The question that is here, is the indirectness. "Why does not the receiving come direct?"

Michael: Yes, of course. That is correct.

Stephen: Will you now enlarge on the question?

Michael: [I had prepared written questions before I came. And I read my question:] "You, Stephen, are the loved instrument through

which the Source has been communicating to us. We have also received through vision, and through book-references. [We think] that
you Stephen, the vision, and the book-references are channels used
by the Source. Now, to test my understanding of the truth, would you
please comment on this suggestion?

Stephen: Firstly, we must look closely at what we feel. What is it we
feel? It is difficult! Each of us does receive, in the majority of cases directly
from the Source. What happens now is indirect, and in the minority.

We mistakenly prefer, through our own choice, that the communication were indirect and a little extraordinary.
  Each [person] does receive,
  each does know that what is received is the truth.
  Each of us knows that in the place where we are now,
  under the circumstances in which we are,
  that is the truth. It must be, for we are here.
  The place where we are, is the place that we have received. This
is the direct communication. For it can only be the truth.
  You hear, touch, see and feel, direct.
  For what you see, what you hear, and what you touch
  is the direct communication, and is the language of the Father.
  Not words. For the Father speaks not with the tongue,
  nor with limited vocabulary.
  What the Father is, is not separate from All that Is,
  but is what is.
  For it is common that when we receive direct,
  we take what we would choose to have,
  and ignore what we choose not to have.
  Therefore, often, it is easier to receive with words,
  in a limited vocabulary, from outside.
  Does it surprise us that we feel then, that the Father,
  the Source, does not communicate
  when our choice is the indirectness?
  Now we shall answer the question.
  You will again now, if it please you, ask your first question.

Michael: May we compare the Source, the Father, with a giant computer, with many channels, into which we may make a connection?
Through them information was fed into the computer, and through

them information may be received from the computer. It would not be meaningful to speak of the computer, or the Source, without channels, [of the Internet as a whole] for the computer consists of the wholeness of these channels and their inter-connection. We have to understand that love, and creativity are part of the information being conveyed through these channels - all of which make up the whole.

Stephen: This question can help greatly for clarity. You speak of your computer. Feel that the computer is what is created. Think not now mystically; think truly of the computer that you know and can touch. Think of that man who created that computer. The computer is a product of the man, and has the knowledge of the man; can analyze and answer the questions of the man. No question that computer answers, is beyond the knowledge of that man. The man has feelings; his computer that he created, cannot compute these feelings.

Therefore, *we* are the computer, and the Father is the *man*.

Michael: Thank you Stephen. That clarifies.

Stephen: This is then your answer, when you would receive indirectly: the answer there for you is what is pre-stored.

But [we must] know what we ask, before we understand the answer that is truth - we ask three alternatives, knowing which one would be the answer, for [as] I have said, without knowledge of the answer, the question cannot be asked.

The computer calculates, draws forth from the mind the choice of feelings - do not confuse - I say again, draws from the mind the choice of the feeling, the feeling that *does* know the answer, and can bring forth the answer that is known. If a person, with a computer, wanted to test that computer, it would be of little use asking a question for which an answer is not known.

First the answer would [have to] be known, then the question asked, and the answer compared with what is known. The test is greater and more evidential if alternative answers are suggested. This then, is how the test is arranged. For we say to Stephen we have an answer that we know and have felt. To be sure again that we are not mistaken, we use *you*, "Stephen-computer," giving three alternatives, to tell us what is the answer; and Stephen will dutifully answer.

Learn this lesson well. For every part of the computer must, for its own functioning, be able to draw [receive] from all other parts. We say then that the way that we choose to draw might be indirectly from the Source, but we ask ourselves the answer that we know - whence does it all come?

[It does come] from the Creator of the computer, who put there the answers we know. The directness of the communication then becomes apparent.

Would we rather that the Father speak to us from the outside, separated, and in a loud voice of authority?

111. Each moment is a gift of the Father.

Stephen: Let us not forget also, that when we are the arm, it is difficult to understand what the leg feels! Or, it can be imagined that were the legs to converse and argue with each other and explain to each other what the ear hears, it might indeed be an interesting conversation! Such as we have had together.

We are of one body, but the Father's gift to each of us, is the function or part that we play in that body.. Do not confuse your mind more than this; say rather, as John [Pope] has often taught you, that this is what I am, and say, "Thank you Father."

Michael: Before I first met you, you had said, "It is much better to take each day as it comes. Concentrate on this: follow the signals that come from the Source of the signals. If opportunity and invitation present themselves, this is purposive, for nothing in this realm can be accidental". Would you comment on this please?

Stephen: I will simplify what was said:

Each moment as it is there, you [have no choice, but] to take that moment for the experience that it brings. Often the mistakes and the hardship that we cause ourselves, are because we often give thought to those moments that are yet to come. We say to ourselves, as many of us here this night have been saying for several days, "If we but know what is to come, then we will judge what our actions would be, we would not under certain circumstances leave our shells or our homes; [or] for three days, we would go to such and such a place."

Harmless we may think, but by this we can lose our way for the moment. For when that moment, with its experience arrives, we will have predetermined - judged, what experience we shall receive. We have closed our ears, eyes, and mind to the experience that is offered. (We have, again, exercised our free choice [with harmful result]).

But ask yourself this, should you know what is to happen in the next year, where would there be the joy of the surprise? Would not the new manifestation of love, that is your gift from your Father, which is prepared for you, be diminished?

This is why this was said, "Live and experience each moment as it comes, for each moment, like the breath you breathe, is a gift of the Father." He cares, and He knows. This then is my comment.

112. The gates ... can only be opened by perception.

Michael: Sometimes when I have received, it is after I have almost battered against the gates of heaven! Other times, I receive clearly, easily, and with much feeling; other times yet again, I receive easily and without much feeling; and I wonder whether I fall victim to superstitions about receiving, because I do not understand why one and not the other. Would you comment?

Stephen: A picturesque term, "battering at the gates of heaven"! I picture that in your mind you climb laboriously and with great effort to these gates, and laboriously and with great effort, you beat upon these gates. You do all these things, and yet do not receive; for, like planning for the future, you have said at this moment, "I shall try to receive, and I shall choose this as my instrument of receiving, now I shall receive." At other times you are relaxed, but you receive.

We are not taking what [in fact] is already given; we [should just] recognize the gift that we receive. If we are to open this gift, then the gates to this gift can only be opened by perception.

What is to happen will happen even in spite of resistance.[It will] in one of many ways. To help achieve your object, remain open to these suggestions and to the guidance and inspiration [that are] for your use. In itself, it will unfold. Do we not see that there is nothing that we need to do for this to happen, there is only that we must *not* do, that we must avoid. The things that are to happen will happen. They are changed only by the things we do to *stop* them happening. Think not in terms of doing and achieving. In fact, the opposite is [necessary]. Generally when we do, it delays, deviates, and detours a happening. Accept guidance, truly receive, think of terms not of words, not of messages, not for confirmation of what you already know, but think of "receive" and "truly receive" and "allow."

Perhaps it is better if I say again, "Do not *do* things to receive. Just receive." This is the best I can help you. Do not make an effort; just follow and remain open. For you know that it is only at the times that you have remained open with no preconceived ideas, that what you have received has been the most satisfying. You yourself know this. Achieve this consciousness of openness, and you will receive. Ask, and you shall receive.

Malcolm: A friend of mine received a verbal warning, and I would like to ask whether this was of true receiving, true inspiration.

Stephen: Intuition, instinct, visions, all of these things are receiving. Judge the usefulness of the receiving. Mentally follow it to a conclusion. Firstly say: "If a receiving had not come, what would be the possible consequences?" Then you ask, "If the warning is heeded, what consequences will be avoided?" Above all, check for error, always. Even in what I say now. Even in this receiving error is possible. One receiving, word, or sentence in itself is insufficient.

Each true receiving or true purpose must be the truth, therefore the guide to the truth is that there is no contradiction; so you receive parallel to the one receiving, or in many parallels, and check for errors.

To follow one instance of receiving would not be wise. Receiving it was, but its value should be checked. You are able yourself to give a parallel check.

I must leave now, the body is tired. We shall meet at other times. Bless you all.

113. Receiving of Jeremy.

[Some of those questioning Stephen, were questioning also the deeper Self by intuiting book-references. (Someone has called this "Questioning the Library Angel") In this case Jeremy is satisfying himself that there is Someone listening "at the other end of the telephone."]

Jeremy: If you are there, and I know you are, and ready to commune, please do.

[Intuition:] 1 *Corinthians.* 2:6-7 [...which turns out to read:] "And yet I do speak words of wisdom to those who are ripe for it. I speak God's hidden wisdom."

Jeremy: Please, one more time. Make your presence known.

[Intuition:] *Exodus* 4.8 [which reads:] "now said the Lord, if they do not believe you and accept the evidence of the first sign, they may accept the evidence of the second."

Jeremy: Make this the deciding quote. No cryptic comment. Make me believe.

[Intuition] *Galatians* 6.12 "You see these big letters. I am now writing to you in my own hand."

114. A little about the way Spirit was operating in our group.

[What brought us together was the pull of Spirit, and our desire to grow in Spirit. We were indeed questioning Stephen and listening to his answers, but we were also actively nourishing our intuitional selves in other ways. Malcolm was doing this partly through meditation and visioning, Robert through his art, Jeremy, as we have noted, through what we have called "book receiving". A woman called Shirley Obbard, who joined us later, was a talented woman in art, sculpture, dress-making, and much besides. One of her methods of receiving from Spirit was to play with words in a most illogical way, draw the most illogical conclusions, then exasperatingly hit an intuitive bulls-eye. More than many, she seemed to respond to important movements of Spirit within the group.

Much more time was spent talking amongst ourselves, than in listening to Stephen. We would talk about our dreams, compare intuitions, and especially note when the same intuitions came to several of us, quite independently of place and the spoken word. We would speculate on possible more precise meanings for our intuitions, and what they might imply for the present and for the future. No doubt we spoke and thought some rubbish. But there was plainly much that was gold. Occasional specimens of this gold are presented in this account of our conversations with Stephen.

As I said, we talked a great deal amongst ourselves, both face to face and over the telephone. In all this we felt caught up in something much greater than ourselves. We awaited excitedly the next developments in the spiritual teaching that apparently were unfolding. That was the context of our conversations with Stephen. Those years of conversations were heady years, and our hopes were high for a great dénouement, maybe even for the Second Coming itself.]

115. Olive: How is receiving to be distinguished from guidance by the Holy Spirit as spoken of by the Church?

Stephen: [The events you call] "receiving" are gifts of God, great gifts, but there are no gifts that are greater than others.

Each gift is a wondrous gift indeed,
and a great gift of God is receiving the Holy Spirit.
But the operative word of course is "receiving".
Each person receives, each person feels.
Do not think too narrowly about the methods of this receiving
and how it may come about.
Only recognize that it comes.

116. Baptism of the Holy Spirit.

Olive: Could you, Stephen, explain the baptism of the Holy Spirit?

Stephen: It is very simple. The baptism of the Holy Spirit is to recognize the love of our Lord's gift to each of us. For the Holy Spirit *is*
God's love. We might complicate and try to search for meanings that
are abstract, whereas [in fact] the Holy Spirit is God's spirit - God's
spirit of love, simply this.

Olive: Well then, I could perhaps ask you more about the apostles
at Pentecost.

Stephen: They, through God's love, or the Holy Spirit, were given
strength and responsibilities for what they must do. As I have said we
can add in our minds mysticism and all of what could confuse us; but
in truth, only the simplicity of God's love can be your answer.

Ask yourselves now, children, when the baptism in the Holy Spirit
came upon the disciples, what works manifested through them? What
did it produce but love? Love of God, love of their neighbour, healing,
understanding.

Now I believe you do know the answer; but first let me be sure: does
this answer satisfy you?

Olive: Yes, although there is still one that worries me, and that is
"speaking in tongues."

Stephen: For many that feel in this way, it is good. Might I remind you, perhaps, of [how it was when] you yourself had deep
feelings, and were lifted above cares, when you had many; did you
not dance?

Ask yourself this, would not others have considered it strange that
you should praise the Lord in this manner? Are you surprised that you

might think it strange that others praise the Lord in manners that they themselves feel ?

I will speak further - if the others who would think your dancing strange, were to be in your company long and often enough, they too might catch the dancing; for your dancing was with such joy it became contagious.

That the tongues' praise should be a little contagious is not surprising.

Olive: Why don't we feel like that? Why don't we feel we belong there? We feel so *lacking*! We are like parts of the body, receiving and acting in different ways.

Stephen: It is hard for me to answer this and not praise yourselves, for to love God as you do, you can be a little jealous that others might do so as well.

You criticise yourselves a little. I think our Lord has said to you - "Give what you have to offer", for always when you compare yourselves with others you will find some are greater than you, and some are less than you, if you would care to judge.

Think then of the dangers of saying, "Why do I not feel in this manner?" for the Lord God has given you his love, your own feelings.

Do you doubt that you love much? Think also how those that speak in tongues would feel estranged if they were here. Would they not perhaps think, were they to believe, that what they see and hear is the truth, and comes from the Source of all truth. If they then believe this and it was not manifest to them in the same manner, would they not also feel that *they* might be lacking? We are [all] different.

I shall speak further, and maybe your eyes may open just a little more to the truth of yourselves.

The Lord said, "Blessed are the meek".

When you, my friends, search in others for what you might lack, then this manifests meekness.

Think now of the world that you are in.

If each separate body and mind were to look upon their fellow and say, "in them is so much good that I can gain from"

we would all indeed be blessed,

for this is truly what you are doing -

looking to others that you cannot feel akin to,

and saying that they are good, and that you do love them,
in spite of your differences,
and you wish to see more clearly the good that is in them.
Maybe your lack, or feeling of lack,
is because at this time they fall a little short of your expectations;
for you are searchers, of this be in no doubt,
you search for feelings everywhere
and joy comes each time you find these feelings.
Can I say more that might help?
These other friends we might [think of] as the hands of the body,
and ourselves as the mouth of the body.

I think you will recognize similarities
in the separate physical behaviour;
the differences [of experience] when the hand touches something that is soft and pleasant, it is pleased, and the whole body has pleasure;
while the mouth, on the other hand, does not feel the softness in itself; but when the mouth takes in what is sweet and warm and pleasant to taste, the whole body [again] finds pleasure;
the hands cannot taste the sweetness of the mouth, nor can the mouth feel the softness that the hands feel.

Although you all are of one body,
experiences are different in the feeling.
We should not expect the hands to taste,
nor the mouth to do what the hands do better;
but the mouth must learn to feel with the whole body
the pleasure of what the hands hold,
as the hands must learn with the whole body
to feel the pleasure of what the mouth does taste.
For I cannot say that we are separate, only different.
If I might talk a little of myself,
we could liken me to the eyes, that I can see and anticipate what the hands touch, that it is soft.

And I can see and anticipate
the sweetness my mouth is going to taste.
I am not speaking in parables and examples
for frivolous reasons.
It is the best way that you might understand
and still grow in the spirit.
You perhaps have other questions?. . . I am pleased.

Olive: Michael sent a question too. Is there something we lack in our group meetings?

Stephen: I shall say this for it will help your work – each part of the whole lacks in itself a little of something.

We should, as the mouth, try to appreciate the sense of touch, also the sense of smell and many other senses, some of whom you have contacted; others are yet to come.

Each of these things has something to offer the other, and each one has something to gain from all others.

The choice of what you would take must be yours, for I cannot say, "Take this from these, and that from these others," for only you will know what you must take, and only you will take that into yourselves. When you have taken it in, it is there in you with the other things that you have collected, and then you can share with others if they also choose to take.

117. Receivings about earthly destruction in the near future.
Olive: What is the meaning of all this?

Stephen: You are back to *Revelation*. Premonitions, prior knowledge, come often, distortions come more often. The message that comes to so many in so many different places, as has come to each of you, has been checked with others and with the Word.

Therefore, it can be accepted, but each form is interpreted differently, none of which is completely correct, except only the concept.

You have asked before of the return of our Lord, Jesus Christ, and I have said that soon His return would become apparent. The Lord Jesus spoke of this and he said, "No man will know the day or the month", therefore, neither will Stephen... [*tape indistinct*] May I just say this, there are very few who have *not* received a similar message. For this is a recall of our memory and the knowledge that we have, that is very strong.

For it is a message of promise and help, of hope, of love and joy. It is a message that even the great physical barrier can never completely suppress.

Your message, and the message of others, is the message of joy, love, hope and gladness that we should all pray in more wondrous ways than you can yet conceive.

Rest easy in your mind, for what you see and what you have received is the very opposite of disaster, one thousand times more opposite. I dream a little, and long often, for this time.

Give this message to anyone who speaks of these things to you:
say to them that had they looked more closely they might have felt
for one brief moment the great joy and love that will be. We would
verily speak in tongues, and give praise for this.

When this time comes we shall step together with much good
humour. Thomas has given me the thoughts of Michael; I give you,
Michael, the words that have gone before. God bless you all.

118. On not coming to conclusions.

[Tom had been speaking of how the previous day he and Olive had
been high up on a hill looking down towards the seashore. He felt that
Stephen with his level of consciousness would have more of a vision of
the Whole, yet he would also have the ability to visit the particular.]

Stephen: From my elevated position where Thomas has put me,
I shall come down and get a little wet!
The idea was good, Thomas, but beware that you might
fasten upon a concept that still gives us no peace,
for next you would go to a higher mountain,
and then to a star,
and still you could not get high enough;
but the feeling you felt was good.
There are many things that are to be asked,
and many answers that can be given.
If it were your wish, may I speak about them?
(Please.)
There are many things that cause us wonder,
and perhaps cause a little excitement;
there are many things that we may hear, or see,
that would show to us things that are known
to be true and good.
But as always, even in these words that I speak,
 they must be looked at with the greatest of care,
for if I were a deceiver I would not tell you
of what you know to be untrue.
I would take time, and tell you with confidence
of things that are good and true,
and then, when you had trusted me,
with this very truth I could deceive you.
For man, in the body, or without such a body,

believes many things in himself.
The conclusions that he has drawn
he fits into things that are true.
He explains them to himself, and would be apt to say:
"I know these things that I have concluded are true,
for are not these words here written
a confirmation of that truth?
Does not this that I do, speak with truth?
Do not my figures join together,
and some of those figures agree with my equation?
Therefore the truth is mine, that I might give to another.
Then I perceive these others, and I say to myself:
'They are mistaken; they see the same things that I see,
but their additions are incorrect.
Therefore, I shall take them back
through what they have heard,
and what they have known to be true, and,
from the point of view that I have learned my answer,
I have drawn my conclusions, I shall adjust their arithmetic'."
Could we then thus blame, or judge, people who, believing that
they have the truth, offer this truth as a gift to others?
Yet, we have been taught that to draw such conclusions
would be to stop learning.
To lead others, to draw the believers' conclusions,
would be to stop them from learning also;
but not from hate, or deception, but from love.
This is why the Father needs to watch over
what we should do.
Pretend that Stephen, on the mountaintop where Thomas has
placed him, decides that the conclusions that he has drawn show
that to increase the wetness, we must bury ourselves deeply into the
sand. He could then teach others that they must bury themselves in
the sand if they would follow him. It is for this reason that the Father has given each person the will to decide, and to listen for the
truth, and to feel what is the truth, for them.
But not alone, for the Hand is outstretched,
the Hand is always outstretched that we might grasp - each one
of us for ourselves.

119. "Knowing" and 'learning' things.

Stephen: This conversation has reminded me of a time when people had discussed many things with Jesus, disagreed violently and said, "Does this mean that all we have learnt we must give away?" They took him from the place, and they threw stones.

Let me say this that what you have learned, and what you know, you must surely need to depart from. For when you "know" any subject at all, then you have lost the truth.

Part Two
The Five Fives Puzzle

120. What happened at Berlins.

[For much of the day, I had been travelling to stay with Thomas and Olive at Berlins, on the West Coast of New Zealand. Berlins was near Inangahua Junction, the scene of a devastating earthquake some years before. The area contains some of the most beautiful scenery in the country, with deep river valleys, alternating with lush pasturage, rain forest, and ever-changing vistas. There is dairy farming, and opencast coal mining in the area. In the Berlins district there was absolutely nothing save the hotel.

Thomas and Olive were beset with worries, for they were trying to buy the hotel as a Christian centre, but finance was not working out. That was one thing. But there had been another thing which had disturbed Thomas: while he had been travelling the 200 km from Blenheim to Inangahua Junction, a bright light had settled over his car, interfered with its functions, and there had been a buzzing noise. He had been really scared of the thing. The question was, was it a UFO?

Thomas, Olive and I talked about many things, while seated in the public dining room. Then late in the evening, when the last guest had left the hotel, we asked Thomas if he would go into a trance, so that we could put some questions to Stephen. Thomas was always a little unwilling to do so, and increasingly unwilling from that time on. There seemed to be several reasons for this: he did not like his conscious personality being put to one side, his normal self being unconscious, while Stephen answered questions which did not relate to Thomas's major concerns. Furthermore what Stephen said was not always in tune with the views and beliefs that Thomas expressed with his waking mind. And there was his disappointment when people found Stephen's words hard to take in. So I think Thomas found it difficult to see where the whole exercise was leading.

On this evening we had been expressing uncertainty about the paths we personally were following, uncertainty about the future.]

121. Gestalten.

Stephen: Where things in our lives are confused, and there is no clear pathway before us, what must we do? Must we cut a path? Must we blaze our trail? Or shall we be like the wise traveller lost in a physical wilderness, who will sit and think, look and heed? For there must be a path. But when we rush backward and forward and in circles, we get further and further lost, and the sweat comes into our eyes. When the path does show, we are not be able to see, in spite of the impending doom, the approach of darkness and the cold that comes, and in spite of our mind telling us, "Surely if I do not find a way soon I must suffer, I must die". This is the time when the wise traveller is calm, and contemplates, and looks with both eyes, in all directions. For there is a path, there is a truth, and that path often is very close, and in a direction that our preconceptions might have caused us to overlook.

Michael: Thomas is still curious about the light above his car. I do not know the full details, but perhaps you do.

Stephen: To the best of my knowledge the light was a discharge of electrical power from a "vehicle". Not a vehicle which is a physical machine, and yet not of another dimension. It was of this dimension, but of a different substance. It is not an uncommon occurrence. To Thomas personally it was of no particular significance other than that he was there.

Michael: I want to ask about patterns. There is a German word *Gestalten:* If you look between two heads facing each other, noses three inches from other, you can see the space between as a vase. If you look from the "Vase" you will see the faces. It depends on the focus. Now it sometimes seems to me, if we look at each other, that it is almost the pattern between us that is important, rather than we ourselves.

It is almost as if we represent the thought of the One Thinker, and that these patterns reproduce themselves over and over again.

Stephen: You have described very accurately the description of the dimension in the previous question: the vehicle was the "pattern between" the two physical [bodies]. A simple way to put it would be: take this universe: instead of speaking of bodies existing in the void of space, we might speak of the bodies as holes in the void. We could say that the void, or the pattern between, is of greater substance than what we feel to be solid, that we form the outline of what is, and this is why our shape, or the shape of the happenings, and of our purpose, does not seem to fit our puzzle. It makes space for that puzzle.

[Stephen seems to prepare the ground for the puzzle of the Fives which he is about to set.].
Stephen: Take this into your everyday life; look at the void, the pieces we feel are not filled, and ascribe to that the substance. [On the other hand] regard what has been filled, like the past, and our history, as making place for the substance. It is a difficult concept to grasp.

Michael: But it seems necessary, this thought, to explain the interlockings, the patternings.

[It was only two or three days before, that I had discovered interlockings, synchronicity, happening in four other locations, during the same night that I was talking with Stephen. It was after that that we saw clearly that there had been a Thought, a Something in the Space Between us that we were all touching, all surrounding with our minds and actions.]

Michael: I get the impression from the interlockings of meaningful coincidence. Sometimes it feels as if my consciousness lies between you and me, or between Olive and me, or between the fireplace and me.

[Dana Zohar, ibid, p.145 "Viewed quantum mechanically, I am my relationships – my relationships to the subselves in my own self and my relationships to others, my living relationships to my own past through quantum memory and to my future through my possibilities. Without relationship I am nothing".]

Michael: But I can only infer this, for to me my consciousness feels mainly in my head. When my body dies will my consciousness fit into the space between? Or will I have no consciousness?

Stephen: We forget that there are two parts of us, this that thinks, and has bodies, and this that is of the Creator, which is the space maker.

But the pattern is determined by the Creator, and these lives that we find so confusing and so unsatisfying, we are told by the Lord, are necessary, so that the space and emptiness can be created and experienced, to enable what has substance, the true Substance, to be placed there.

Michael: Can you give me a clear example? If I were trying to say this to someone else, all I can do is to point out the meaningful coinciding as I see it. But is there a simple way of talking about the "Space Between" to some other person?

Stephen: Think of it like this, that we look upon the land, the dry land between the seas, as the substance. We look at the shape of the earth, with a picture in our mind of the different shapes of our land, where the greater part, and the substance of what is the surface of our planet, is Water.

The greater amount of life, the greater amount of wealth, even measured in carnal or human terms, is in the greater part, and what we *call* substance, the land, has less of this wealth and life, and only fills the outline.

Michael: That makes a very good picture.

Stephen: Now think in terms of our lives: instead of the physical we shall see the mental as the full substance. [But the mental] is the outline only, and does but have one tenth of the nourishment and wealth of the Void (the Space Between).

Then Stephen spoke the following words:
Iácho me, phaíno sé, phrontithe [phrontízesthe?]
In Greek characters:
Ιαχω ᾽με θαινω σε φροντιζεσθε
........*five* Greek words
"I proclaim myself, I reveal thee, consider ye (this)"

194

[I did not comment, for I had not understood. Work with a lexicon was required. In a subsequent session there was doubt that these were Greek words. But the first four words do mean, "I proclaim myself, I reveal thee" in Attic Greek. The fifth word sounded like phrontithe, based on phrontizo, "I consider". Phrontithe has no meaning, but perhaps a "zes", as in phrontiZESthe, was not heard; that word does mean "consider ye.."]

Michael: Before I spoke to you last time, I had been writing in my book about Jacob's Ladder not being something to be climbed, then I come here, and straight away you talked about Jacob's Ladder not being something to be climbed. Were you aware that I had written this in my book? Or was it simply given to you by the Father?

Stephen: As with all things, I gave my knowledge (this is not a good word) I gave the knowing, for I dwell in the Space Between the minds and the experience. (Oh!) Therefore the hole that your thought has made, or the contour the concave of your thought is the convex in the true substance of thought, which is the Void.

You remember one time, when I spoke of those coming from distant planets being closer than the breath of the tongue in your mouth. Even though as with other things they maybe either on the other side of the sea, or the pond.

Now you can see that if they are but the outline of what is the true Substance, then indeed they are very close, for like you and your experiences, they touch always what is Substance.

That is why I often correct when people say that you must look within yourself. In one direction that is correct, if the Self you look into is the Creator, or Substance. But looking into the created, is to look into what is merely the outline of What Is.

Michael: Norman [Kjome] and I, from across different sides of the world, have sometimes picked up or outlined the thought which is the real thing; such as when I saw the UFO film [Spielberg's *Close Encounters*], which was set in Wyoming, and I knew that the following morning Norman (being interested in UFOs, and living in Wyoming) would supply me with a coincidence. In one sense that is mad thinking, In terms of the physical, it was mad thinking. but it worked out. Norman did supply me with a coincidence, I did hear from him, when his gift of a book, Jacob Needleman's *A sense of the Cosmos*, arrived in the post.

So I suppose that both Norman and I were aware of the thought that Reality is *one* regardless of manifestations.

Stephen: Provided that we recognise that Reality, the Substance *does* have an outline, and do not confuse reality with what is without Substance, and appears to us in the physical.

Think then of this, that if the mind that was the contour, whether [or not] it be at the opposite side of the Substance is immaterial, that if it were to touch the outline, then they touched the Substance, and then of course the thoughts coincided.

It cannot be surprising that this is the case. For touch one of my ears (I should say, "Touch one of Thomas' ears") then the other ear would be aware. Not the space or air which surrounds Thomas, but the ear has been touched, and *all* that "Substance" is aware.

Things that you have in the true void or *non*-Substance [i.e. physical reality] are of no value other than they are an outline.

These things that our Lord spoke of, when he spoke of the camel, and using the camel as the thread to the needle, [contrasting] Substance, and non-Substance. For it would be easier to use the camel as the thread, than to turn what is nothing into something.

The Lord performed miracles, when all that was [required] was [for] the knowledge of Substance to alter the outline of what is non-Substance. To touch from Substance [Spirit] and change the image, would [cause] someone dealing with non-Substance, [Physical] thinking non-Substance to be real, to cry "Miracle!" for it has been changed!

Your scientists often speak of the non-solidity of what we call "non-Substance." [Atoms are largely empty space associated with patterns of energy.] Solidity is between these minute particles of energy.[Quantum vacuum].

Michael: I ask about the role of the ego, or physical self, the contour: Why is it needed, if reality is in the Space Between?

Stephen: The ego is a product of your mind and its concepts. That mind, that body, and those concepts, must belong to the Whole. Is this not so? For nothing can exist that is not part of the Whole. You have spoken of the dissipation of the ego (considering that it separates us from our true selves in the Space Between), but you have not yet considered that it *also* is an instrument of the Whole.

We have spoken about the recording of experiences that are necessary for the Whole.

[Your body is essential for this process.] Each part of your body, being part of the Whole, is unique. The workings of the Whole require the workings of each part of the body for its uniqueness, for the recording of sensations, and the recording of experiences. The workings of the Whole also require the ego that is creating part of you, [who are] that part of the Whole whereby the Whole senses and records. Without that, we could be truly separate.

Think: it has often been said, that to the nucleus or core of the Whole there is no sensation of either good or bad, cold or warm, soft nor hard. This would be the case with our physical mind if it were not coupled with the whole body, to enable our mind to record these sensations. Those sensations are recordings for the core that supports us. The actions of the mind can be controlled by our judgements, and yet there can be control by the inspiration that comes from the heart, the Centre, the Space between. The mind, without reference to the heart, judges and causes us to act, and to destroy.

Judgement is not valid, because it destroys what the heart says: "Take, hold precious, enjoy and love, for this is the experience that must be recorded, by the Whole. For I say this: what catches you as beauty, causes a tear to fall with joy, that lifts your heart, that causes you to embrace, to reach out, to perform the necessary deeds with no thought of self, is what you have been led to do from the heart, from the Centre. All that causes you to destroy, to sneer, to injure, to speak unkind words, is the instrument of the mind being used by judgement.

[This concludes our account of what happened at Berlins, that evening of October 1, 1978. It can readily be grasped, how strong an experience it was, drawing us to a relationship to the One.]

122. The Five-Fives Puzzle.

To see what this Puzzle is about, we need to study five puzzle pieces discovered synchronisticly in five locations. I regard each puzzle piece as having its origin in the "Space Between" in the "Void" in the emptiness that is the true Substance. Let us see what picture can be made from the puzzle pieces.

This conversation with Stephen took place in Berlins on the West Coast of the South Island of New Zealand. A key item was Stephen's *five* words of Greek.

Let us call the Berlins conversation with Stephen, just related: "Location **One**".

Three parts are of particular interest:
  (1) Five Greek words were spoken.
  (2) the discussion about the Space Between
(3) the UFO theme, and *Close Encounters of the Third Kind,*
the film directed by Steven Spielberg,

It took two or three days before "chance" discoveries revealed what had been happening in four other locations in Christchurch, perhaps 150 miles away from Berlins, during that same evening that I had been talking with Stephen.

Location **Two**: at the house of Des and Jessie in Christchurch:.
On that same evening, Des had the urge to find *five* notes on the piano, without knowing why.
Location **Three** was at my future wife Gertrud's home in Spreydon, when on that same evening she had a dream.
In the dream, she came from a forest to a speckled stone near the sea, at the edge of the forest, on a beach, and in the stone were *five* plugs. These "plugs" were 1.Wisdom, 2. Ability to recognise Beauty, 3. Empathy with people, 4. Self-knowledge, and as for the 5th... what was this?... later she wondered whether it could have to do with relating to the Whole.
She could be plugged into this stone, and the connections would go in her side.
The "five" can again be noted. The dream is more obviously along the same theme as the Stephen conversation, with the unconscious, the Spiritual, or maybe the Space Between.

Considering the attachments to it, this sounds like the "Philosopher's Stone". J. E. Cirlot, in his *Dictionary of Symbols* p.314, writes: "....as for the philosopher's stone in alchemy, it represents the 'conjunction' of opposites, or the integration of the conscious self with the feminine or unconscious self.. it is then, a symbol of the All." (*Diccionario de símbolos* [*A Dictionary of Symbols*] (1958)

Location **Four** was at the classroom of a primary school teacher in Christchurch.

On this evening, the teacher was making a large UFO of speckled silver paper, on a netting base. It was speckled like Gertrud's spiritual stone. It had *five* strips of black polythene connecting it to the four walls of the classroom. I was able to see the teacher's handiwork when I conducted a Scripture class for his children a day or two later.

Des and Gertrud, although aware of Stephen, knew nothing of a conversation in Berlins. The teacher had neither knowledge of Stephen nor of our experiences; so for all three the events were private, so far as they were concerned. The teacher never found out how important he had been. Gertrud took time to accept that her personal dream could be part of a wider event. It was a new way of viewing things for her.

Jung came to consider UFOs to be symbols of polarity and integration within the Whole, and this is exactly the symbolism of the Philosopher's Stone. Thus the images in Gertrud's dream correspond closely to the symbolism of the Philosopher's Stone; the "speckling" of her stone, corresponds to that of the Teacher's "UFO", underlining that it too belongs to this synchronicity.

Location **Five** was at John and Mary's home, in another part of Christchurch.

On that same evening they had been consciously thinking of me at Berlins, and they were determined to share in that event.

They meditated, and felt led to the *Christian Science Monitor* that their friend Rene had lent to them. It was the issue of August 21, 1978, and at page 29 there was the following poem that they clipped out, feeling it to be important:

Message Received:
    Sudden sun bursts...in your thought
    The tree at your window... takes leaf in your book
    Unannounced five birds
    five shadows
    gather print in their wings
    move within the branches' tracery
    that grows through the words
    their meanings alight
    Notes on the stave of the tree, they remain
    after the birds are gone, after the words fly free.

The eye becomes the ear.
You're wondering why
in all this sun, in all this gentle urging
five sounds frame one
   dear
cosmic
    cry.

Ιαχω 'με θαινω σε φροντιζεσθε

'iácho/ me/ phaíno/ sé /phrontízesthe

Those five notes are the notes by which the *Close Encounters* UFO (mentioned in my conversation with Stephen) attuned itself to this world. They therefore specifically link this poem with the UFO film, and with the scene at Devil's Tower in the north of Wyoming. The five notes formed part of a piece of music that was being much played on the radio stations, for a long time afterwards.

123. Commentary.

[John and Mary were aware that there might be a conversation at Berlins, but had no knowledge of the questions. So it seems that "Chance" led myself to be apprised of the *fivefold* synchronicity, in which it took time for it to dawn on the other unconscious or conscious participants, what had happened.]

Sudden sun bursts in your thought: a new dimension of thought suddenly shows itself in one evening.

The tree at your window: This reminds me of the Tree of Life of the Cabala which has been the subject of prolonged and intense synchronicity in my life, and I understand it as a symbol for the All. Similarly Gertrud's stone, such a spiritual stone, unites all things together, like the symbolic Philosopher's Stone of the ancient Greeks.

Unannounced five birds like the aerial connections between the teacher's UFO and the walls,

five shadows: like the dream connections with the Philosopher's Stone, "gather print in their wings, move through the branches' tracery that grows through the (five) words".

their meanings alight: I translate the words and their full meaning gradually dawns upon me.

Notes on the stave of the tree: These notes Des had been trying to find, but they remain, repeatedly played over the radio as a popular single, [the UFO theme of *"Close Encounters"*] "after the birds are gone, after the words fly free..."

The eye becomes the ear. "You're wondering why, in all this sun, in all this gentle urging five sounds frame one dear cosmic cry."

Birds, shadows, notes, words and sounds spell the end of polarity, but rather frame the One.

I quote again the passage from T.S. Eliott:
"We must be still.. and still moving
Into a further intensity
For a further union, a deeper communion
Through the dark cold and the empty desolation,
The wave cry, the wind cry, the vast waters
Of the petrel and the porpoise. In the end was my beginning."

124. The UFO theme.

This was how it was to be. Soon the voice of Stephen was to be stilled. But over the next seven years the themes of his teaching were to be reinforced by a whole series of synchronisticly interlocking events of even greater complexity. The complex events followed each other, conveying an other-dimensional teaching in a logical way, bringing out a host of implications of Stephen's words both at "Location 1", and on nearly 200 other occasions.

More on the UFO theme.

A few months prior to the events surrounding the Five-Fives puzzle, I had a long series of dreams that seemed to foretell future events to do with UFOs. It was three weeks after the synchronicity of the Fives, that the Bass strait, Tasmania, UFO event occurred, and then three months later, those seen in Kaikoura, New Zealand. My dreams were to be seen to describe these events in a score of ways. These events led "into further intensity, for a further union, a deeper communion" over the next ten years. These events and the long series of complexly inter-locking synchronicities are described in an unpublished sequel to this book that I call *Into the Wider Dream.*

So, for the purposes of this book, I can say "In the end was my beginning."

Part Three
Actually partaking in the banquet

125. Actually partaking in the banquet..

Stephen: As we have talked with much seriousness tonight, let me
then, also be serious: I am reminded of a story that I heard from my
father about the many cooks who created a great and wonderful feast;
they admired what they had made - they spoke of its virtues and how
wonderful it must taste! But all of them forgot to eat it.

>   Or, are we not sometimes like the traveller who, when having
>   arrived at the destination, fails to leave the vehicle.

We have often been advised to look at everything that the Father
creates. We can see that of all the objects that we can perceive that
have remained as they were created, each functions perfectly, each is
in the [fits into the general] order of things, the purpose that they serve
is clear for all to see. Even with ourselves, we can see, like that meal,
the virtues that are us.

We understand (or we feel we understand) the journey that we must
take. What we must ask ourselves is "Have I tasted what I have prepared?" "Have I come to the end of my journey?"

Is it not time that I stepped from this vehicle which is my mind, and
which has carried me thus far?

I do not speak to puzzle, but each of us, having heard that perfection is
here and it is ours, feels a difficulty in tasting what has been prepared.

>   We can say often that indeed now,
>   as we always have been,
>   we are what the Father has created;
>   all that we must do is to be that.

We have heard that we must trust,
but we find that we are unable so to do.
While we are unable,
the Father brings as help the experiences we may need.
    We have been told that what we await is here,
that our journey is at an end,
yet again, we have difficulty in recognizing
that we have arrived.
Therefore, that was as it was before, so must it be again.
We must be shown and led into trusting,
shown that we are perfect in a way
that we more easily recognize.
All that we have said, that our Lord is with us, is true;
all that has been said concerning the perfection
of what the Father has created, must also be true.
    But without further guidance, it is difficult for us to taste [the meal], or to leave the vehicle that our minds have created,
for a journey that was non-existent.
    Be patient and happy, for in truth what we cannot recognise for ourselves, what we must know to be the truth, will be shown to us in its completeness. Then we will know what we are, and we will know that like the mountains, the sea, the sky, we are, as God has made us, perfect for his design, a reflection and image of his oneness. For we are equal as with all.
    God bless you.

126. Anxiety

Stephen: In what way may I assist?

Michael: By reassuring some of Michael's anxieties.

Stephen: Could Michael reassure Michael?

Michael: Michael would like to do so, but he wonders whether Stephen gets anxious about us.

Stephen: Perhaps Stephen might be anxious for himself.

Michael: I had not thought of you being anxious for yourself. Are you?

Stephen: I am not... more than Michael. [*M. laughs*]

Michael: I do not feel anxiety with you. I feel comfortable with you. You don't give me discomfort.

127. The sense of being an 'I'.

Olive: We were wondering whether you would talk on what we term "I", and whether you give us this sense of "I" and of personality?

Stephen: There is still confusion in your mind as to which is the created and which is the Creator. Of which "I" did you wish me to speak?

Olive: You call yourself "I, Stephen," and I call myself "I, Olive."

Stephen: When I refer to Stephen as "I", I speak generally of the personality and the ego, and the understanding that was the experience of Stephen.

But the "I" which we all have in common ... Let us use the term as you have been using, the "spiritual I". These two "I's" are not one and the same, for the "physical I" is the one that records experiences.

It has been said even in this night that the physical I is in each different, and that the spiritual I is all one. Let me try to make this more clear.

You have spoken recently of your incarnations: we have said often before that now Olive is Olive, no more and no less. This Olive that we speak of is the physical I of Olive, quite unique for she is but one.

But we talk now about what she has in common with the other lives and experiences, and this is where the confusion lies. Olive herself may have some characteristics in common with those of a previous life, but physically, as a physical I, they are as separate as two trees in different countries. And this is a good example, for they are both trees. They both grow from the same soil, they are both nourished by the same thing. Yet one must bear the fruit that is suitable for that land and for that time in which it grows; the other the fruit that is suitable for its environment and time.

Now, because of this conscious and physical separation of the truth, each I of the physical of these trees will be and is separate. The tree does stand alone, not self-sufficient but alone. This is one consciousness. In that consciousness the experiences that each of these separate trees undergoes, cause a reaction from these trees. Whereas the leaves, when the cold weather comes, will fall. [Perhaps referring to the fact that the physical mind survives the death of the body.]

If sufficient rain falls upon the ground, then the tree will blossom and give its fruit. All of these are reactions to experience.

If there is insufficient rain, and when nourishment is not taken by the roots, then the tree will change its form, become no longer a tree, but another element that will experience in its particular way.

So it is with the physical I. The physical I is emotionally involved with its experiences and reacts in a way that can be beneficial by being content, or non-beneficial, by losing that contentment.

Therefore we need the guidance and the help of the spiritual I, which does not itself have experiences, for it is.

It [the Spiritual I] cannot react one against another for it is *one*.

The experiences of the physical I are important to what is spiritual. If we wish, and we can become conscious, we can sometimes thank the emotional experience that would be the spiritual I.

When I speak as Stephen, I speak as a physical I, that understands and can often see from the point of view of the spiritual.

And often whilst using [in the mode of] the spiritual point of view, I have no understanding of happiness or unhappiness, contentment or discontent.

We hear and often have spoken of the time that just is, which is neither good nor bad, sad nor happy in relationship to all that is physical.

[We find sadness and happiness, good and bad, only] in relationship to our own point of view, the physical I that is.

Whereas the spiritual I does not have a point of view,

It simply *is*.

When we can reconcile the point of view of the physical to the spiritual,

then we will not have much difficulty either living as an incarnate being, or *not* living as an incarnate being, for both would be the same.

[The spiritual I is] not negative but neutral, because the spiritual I does not react, for it is the creator of experiences, rather than *being* the experiences.

Therefore Stephen is no more or no less than you are. [Thinking physically of] Stephen: I am but that tree in a far country that you have become conscious of.

In the spiritual I, I am you. So you see that the various experiences and understandings that you have had in recent hours and days can but confirm this. I will leave you to discuss and talk. God bless you.

128. Viewing things from the Spiritual.

Stephen: I am sorry that I didn't bring the fertility symbol with me! [The bull, the subject of some group receiving]

Olive: After you talked last time, it seemed that we would be much more content, if we could view things from the spiritual. How best could we do this?

Stephen How do we become the Father, how do we become the Source, how do we become the Whole?

Our Lord has taught us that we become this thing by being ourselves. This puzzles you. For what we are is what we should be.

The difficulty that we find is that often we are not true to ourselves.

We are true only to the concept, and to the self that we have built in our minds. Doing this leads us to see ourselves as alone; and we build a concept of ourselves as being insignificant. We are doing nothing more than attempting to create our lives as we believe we should.

We look and see clearly from the Eye of the Source;

it is only when we face ourselves as such,

[that] our conscious mind decides that we are insignificant.

Our Lord has told us that the meek and humble are those that are blessed.[44]

[But] what is "meek and humble" but to be content with what you are? For this is the way to heritage. We do not step back.

We do not perform rituals, for all that is necessary is that you are, and that you believe yourself to be that implement you were created to be. This will take away ambition, for any ambition comes from the ego.

[The ego] is not a driving force for what you are.

What you will become, is what you should be, and what you will be. Recognise the simplicity of what you are, for "simplicity" and "simple" are not derogatory terms, but the truth, stated as the truth.

You have had much discussion. Many of you over the past two days have had some insight into what we might be.

But in your minds you have confused meekness and simplicity with insignificance. In the pattern of all creation, not one thing, not one of the created things, can be described as insignificant.

Think on this and practise more often being what you are, and being content with that being, for you have no journey to make.

129. The Image of the Pen and Paper.

[The group had been sharing thoughts on how reality influences us, and how we may influence our reality. We speculated that we would hear from Christ, if it was to Christ that we turned our attention. But it is Stephen who speaks:]

Stephen: Then I shall enjoy being an anticlimax!
It is not that I purposely tease.
There is much that I wish to say that can add
to the many, many true things that have been said tonight
by each of you in the way that you feel
and in the way that you understand.
This is what I have: that we use the term
of each of us being a part or an instrument
or a thought of something that we can call the Whole.
We are not the tree, we are not the mount
or if we were [seen] from the point of view of the tree or the mountain,
then we could but just stand there and let what was be.
We are different, for we have thoughts, and we have emotions, and we have reactions.
So the instrument we are is a Pen
and the Paper that is written on.
For we are both as we would choose to be
as we think of ourselves at that particular time.
The God we have is the Ink that will record on the Paper.
Think now of the negative of these two:
For without the Pen and without the Paper,
as with[out] the Ink, there would be no record of what there is.
Together the Thought:
And that is of the Hand that writes,
that holds the Pen,
that causes the Ink to flow upon the Paper:
that is to think beyond what we grasp, often.

The Ink, when it has recorded, can,
if we have accepted our experiences,
with the trust that we have been asked,
be indelible.

If we fetch to ourselves a God we do not trust,
this Ink will in time fade.

Many of us look to the indelible recording of others;
if it is indelible, we say, "Then it must surely have been true."

But I say this to you that each of you will choose eventually,
if you have not already chosen,
the ink that is indelible,

For as often as the ink that you recorded, faded before,
so you have come again to record.

You will not always consciously choose at any particular
time,
whether you are the Pen or the Paper;
you will even feel that there is no way
that you may control or choose the Ink.
So often to help you, you have had others to come close to.
Each one is this duality.
You have gained from the writing and the recording,
of each one, and you will gain.

When you see an Ink that to you is indelible,
then surely you will follow this Ink.

For only your own experience is going to prove or disprove,
that indelibility.
And this is not a cruel... this is not a perverse God saying,
"Why do I not just make my indelibility available?"
For the supreme experience that one can have is to choose and
to know what is indelible. God bless you all.

130. Praying for the Water.

Stephen: I wonder if the prayer might be for the water that I have
displaced.[45]

In what way may I assist?

Michael: Would you explain what you have just said?

Stephen: We have spoken of prayer and we have broadened our
views much, but not to the point of unselfishness.

We have said, "Help in accepting the experience". We have even condescended to judge.

We have not prayed for the water,
or the life that is that water,
that it may be calm?
This is the expansion of our thinking,
For we have said All is One.
We speak of experience
and that experience must be of the Whole.
Simply that we might speak,
might communicate with each other in this manner,
and might feel, understand,
show, and have emotions,
does not make us greater
nor even lesser than all else that is.
And our Lord said,
"Not one bird would fall from the air
that is not known by the Whole
and is not the experience of the Whole."

Michael: Would you speak of the Ink?

Stephen: We have spoken much this night of the Ink.

We have understood that which to us in our minds, and even in our hearts, can be understandable.

The indelibility of the ink becomes more with our greater understanding. We must understand our oneness with the Whole.

Do not think that I preach that we must consciously and purposively step forward to lose self for this is not possible;

the mere act of stepping forward to lose yourself proves yourself, and clothes you more in that self. It is to be open to understanding to be receptive and learn through your experiences, to accept those same experiences and trust even that those experiences will come.

Michael: These experiences come, they come from all quarters, they come and they make a whole pattern in my mind. I do not know that I cause them to come but I play my part in their coming. I am a sense organ for the Whole, but I do not know the Whole, and could I ever as such?

Stephen: I will attack if I may
the first words of your sentence.
For we have forgotten our lesson with the boat.
We say we are not conscious of making them come,
these experiences,
but they come, and we say also,
that we may have caused unconsciously
those experiences to happen.
What is to cause?
Understand this more fully.
　　For until you begin to understand this, the second part of what
you say is unanswerable.

Michael: What is it to cause, did you say? Then I can't answer what is to
cause, because the Whole is the Whole, and to me it all dovetails and relates.
I was wondering, as we are speaking now, perhaps it feels to me that is all
just happening. It is the Whole acting, and we are an aspect of the Whole.
Do I cause you to come? Do you cause me to come? We are just here.

Stephen: We are come. Did you cause each other to be born?

Michael: I lapse into not knowing,
Just waiting for the next thing to come.

Stephen: Then the prayer is more like praying for the water.

Michael: Praying for the water to... ?

Stephen: Just praying for the water.
Not to cause that the water
should have [something] done to it
or fail to have done to it,
be saved from either contamination
or be protected from non-contamination
but simply [pray for it as] it is.

Michael: What is the water, Stephen?

Stephen: The water is the Whole
and the boat is that body which you wear

with you in that boat, that does pray is the mind and the personality of that body.

Michael: Can we therefore have hierarchies, adepts, stages, and "higher and lower" in this?

> Stephen: If you wish, and if you so choose,
> But if the water is no greater than the boat,
> And if the boat is the servant of your mind,
> and your personality,
> where should we start this hierarchy?
> At what stage would one be greater than the other?
> Must one drown? Or must one float?
> Float well, and God bless you!

131. The Second Coming.

Stephen: See how obediently I wait! In what way may I be of assistance?

Michael: People in a prayer group seem to feel that the test of my being a Christian was whether I would agree with St Paul, writing in the *First Epistle to the Thessalonians* (4:13ff):

"The Lord Himself will descend from heaven with a shout, with the voice of an archangel, and the trump of God... and the dead in Christ shall rise up, and we which are alive and remain, shall be caught up together with them in the clouds, to meet the Lord in the air: and so shall we be ever with the Lord."

Michael: Well I don't quite know how to cope with that.

Stephen: I ask you a question: are we to meet up in the clouds with the Lord?

Michael: It doesn't fit my concepts at all.

Stephen: And you are perhaps a little worried that you might be wrong?

Michael: I would be open to what is true, but I would also like to be at one with my friends.

Stephen: I say this then, for this is what I believe: that the experience of the coming again of the Lord will be to each and every one, an experience which leaves nothing but awe and wonder. For it will unmistakably happen, and each of us will know.

Paul would have known how cities in his day greeted kings and great personages. Most people had seen triumphant arrivals of great lords and kings. People did indeed, in those days, come forth. You will have had similar experiences yourselves. People do come out. They make every effort to come and see a marvellous spectacle. And of course, if it were God who was arriving, then he would not come to our lowly home, but we would go to meet him. It is not surprising that Paul gave such a comparison.

Let me also give a Pauline concept that you might understand: suddenly from out of the sky a great light comes, with an enormous ship. We know that this ship is to take us to the Father; we know that all we have need of will be supplied; that there are no fears and dangers any more. [We know] that we are come up, and the ship and the light from it would cause us to rise up into it, when we had all come, to take us away from our tribulation. We might readily understand this concept; but it is a concept only, that we might think and that we might understand the breathless emotion, the exaltation that we will feel. [We know] that the dead will rise, for we can say: I am one of the dead. I too will feel this, and will know. We will rise together. We will understand truly that we are all one and brothers, and this love, that we cannot now feel for each and every one that we meet, or have experience of. We will find that we are given this love for all things, and then we will be able to return this love. We could neither receive all of this love now, and we could no more give what we have not received, than we could [demand] this and take away from somebody what they do not have. I say that Paul is right, for he speaks only of the triumph that he can conceive. I find this conception most helpful to me.

Olive: The picture of Paul is one thing, and the picture as if of a UFO, to use some people's concepts, conveys to me the feeling in some little measure. But we would not expect to see precisely a UFO to take us to the Father, as we might conceive of it in the physical.

Stephen: Many of those whom Paul spoke to and explained this to, did not share Paul's feeling, also. But they believed and formed their own concept. I say this now, because in your talk before there was a certain dejection, and feeling of hopelessness, that there can be no improvement.

If on the day that the Lord arrived, you had this hopelessness, your joy would be much greater. It has been promised, it is part of what is planned and what must happen. It is the plan that gives us in the best way, that we might understand, the joy that we have been promised. It will be, as Paul said, a wondrous time and a wondrous joy. Do not let us use concepts that cause us to be despondent. Do not let us analyse our environment and ourselves until in our minds we conceive an inevitable life or death of mundane happenings. For this cannot be so.

132. Peaks and Valleys.
Stephen: Remember this as a concept:
life, physical and spiritual,
flows in peaks and depths or valleys; not always do they coincide.
Although you cannot see it
there is balance running through these peaks and valleys.
Do not feel ashamed of all the material comforts
the physical peaks bring,
or feel deprived when you are living in the valley,
Remember always that you are given all you need.
Liken it to a diet - life knows all that you need to eat to keep you healthy and fit,
but Thomas says, "I think that kind of food will satisfy me more."
We tend to think like this about our spiritual life,
but whatever we may think, we are always given the right amount of food.
You are in a peak physically, but in a valley spiritually,
and so are our friends.
Although they try, by much imagining,
their small but sufficient diet
will not turn into a banquet by doing this.
When you need to have faith, you have sufficient.
You and Thomas are good at this:
any fear and straight away Thomas turns to his Father with complete trust, like a little boy who waits for his father to lift him down from a high fence.
Have patience and do not look into the valley while you are on the peak. Enjoy the peak. Also, when you are in the valley, do not look back

at the peak... and surely... "the mountains will be laid low, and the valleys lifted up." [*Isa 40:3 quoted Lk 3:5*]

133. Not feeling in tune with other Christians..

[Thomas, Olive and Michael have been talking frustratedly about feeling failures, not bearing the fruits of the spirit, and feeling generally disappointed.]

Stephen: And it came to pass that Daniel did enter into the lions' den! In what way might I help?

Michael: If you mean that you are Daniel and I am the lion, I owe too much to you to want to eat you. Stephen. I find I disagree with almost none of it, and feel very much in tune with it, but you may be aware that we don't feel in step with other Christians throughout the world. For instance, the Charismatic movement is very strong throughout the world. And here are we, apparently isolated, part of nothing in a certain sense. I know that the Father is working in us all. I do not mean separate in that sense. But I find that we cannot identify ourselves with other Christians, as a movement, so I wonder why it is that we are out of step, and looking at ourselves rather wryly; we wonder about the lack of fruits in ourselves, the fruits of the Spirit. And we wonder how the Father can possibly use us, and we wonder if we haven't failed him in many ways. We would like you to talk to us straightly, so that we may know where we have failed, and fail him the less.

Stephen: Firstly, then let me correct one misconception. We talk of the movement of a great number of people whom we refer to as Christians, and that this movement is strong throughout the world, and that it is by far in the great majority... these people. That a great majority of Christians are these people.

Of course, this is not so. Greater numbers by far of those that, were they asked to declare their allegiance, would call themselves Christians, the vast number would not belong to a church or to an organisation, in the belonging sense that we talk of in these others. The majority of people, including the three of you, [Tom, Olive, and Michael] and those you come in contact with, are not of this category of belonging in the full sense of the word to this or that sect.

The greater majority of those who would call themselves Christians are, as you yourselves put it, out of step with these movements, and with the churches. They feel out of step with these organisations, and, in most cases, there is a little feeling of guilt, for under certain circumstances they feel that they are bound to use these organisations, for such ceremonies [such as] marriages and deaths, and on very special religious occasions and anniversaries. But these are the only times that they feel in step. So I will contradict you in your feeling of separateness...that is the wrong word....in your feeling not completely joined unto these, that does not make you in a minority, but in the majority.

So I shall talk more about this majority of which you are part. Each individual in that majority has some theory, feeling, and hope, that is deeply remembered inside them. And they know that they do belong to what we call the Whole. They feel dissatisfied because they do not feel that they belong to the self appointed guardians, or organisations, that lay down codes of spiritual behaviour upon their followers; and those that are sincere unto themselves, and cannot agree with these codes of behaviour. [They] feel that because of the teachings of these organisations, they are the ones who are not in step. It is a little like the soldier, out of step, who said that all of the other troops should come into line, and say, "step like me, and come into line!"

So therefore we can say that one of the fruits of your learning and your behaviour, is that in spite of the pressures that may have been placed upon you through your calling, and through an allegiance, is that you have remained in step. Not an unworthy fruit, I would choose to judge, if I were to judge.

We are inclined to forget what we know of husbandry, of which we have often spoken before, that the plant grows, and, in time, it bears the fruit. When the labourer starts with the plough and cuts that part of the furrows that he must do, he cannot look back and say, "I have ploughed this field," until indeed the field is ploughed. He might say, "I am ploughing this field, and I can see some furrows." It would be even more foolish to look at the furrows and expect to see the corn.

Now you wish to ask me further.

Michael: Well, what you have said so far, Stephen, I feel to be true, and that settles my mind, thank you very much. As you have pointed out in the past, I tend to inflict guilt upon myself, and so do Thomas and Olive. But do I fail? Or am I doing as I should be doing?

Stephen: One cannot judge the success or failure until that task is completed. It would be foolish of you in the middle of your preaching, if you stopped and said "Have I failed to convey the lesson which I wish to give?" before the lesson was given. I can no more judge my success or failure in what I do, for I have not yet completed what I must do.

134. The rings.

Stephen: I really must be a spirit, for my feet no longer touch the ground! [Stephen is joking: Thomas is in trance sitting on a high chair, feet dangling.]

Michael: In your opinion, what has been happening in our group in the last three years? What have we been on about?

Stephen: We must think of our three rings, not static or material rings that enclosed or in one [particular] place, but similar to the rings of a [radio] signal that go out from the source of that signal. They grow wider and as the circles of the signal will travel. Each time that these rings or part of a ring comes to an object of experience, [like radar] the echo or the memory of that experience goes back to the Source.

We are not the whole of these three rings, but a small part of each moving in one of all those directions.

The things that we come into contact with, will as with ourselves, be transmitted back to that Source. Much of our experience, now and in the future, will be similar to but not exactly the same as experiences return-signalled previously. If the experiences were exactly the same, it would be pointless for that signal to be sent out.

The knowledge thus gained, or the echo received back from these signals, is the experience of the Source. And is the experience of the Whole.

[That knowledge would influence] the next signal that is sent out, and the next, and the next.

What are we about? We are recording experiences, in many, many different ways. Even our reaction to an experience is itself an experience.

Think back long ago, of what we have spoken about the pebble in the water, and the rings that this sends out. [Pause]

You hesitate Michael.

Michael: Relating to the question of time and timelessness, in what you are saying.

Stephen: In the signal there is no such thing as time, for the instant that is [as it] was generated, is that instant now, and will always be. As with the echo that comes to be received, time is part of the experience inasmuch as our reaction causes time.

We say this experience was when I was younger. We say that I was taken back to the time when I was a child. When we look at our lives we could answer this question very easily by saying, "Who am I?"

What we mean to say
is that the receiving of these signals
remembers [records] a message received from a child
in a certain experience;
but we can more be that child
than we can be each other in a physical sense.
And yet we are [indeed] that child.

We spoke many times of that Michael that was at school and now we have a different Michael physically. And a different Michael in his reaction to experience. Next week we have even another Michael.

Michael: True. It seems to me that when we look at our experiences, there is a thing in common between one experience and another; the more that I go inwards, it seems, the more abstract it becomes.

It is like preachers who talk about "doubting Thomas" or "perfidious Judas" and are fond of comparing their congregations to these two people or to other people. There is a kind of abstraction as we go inwards. Jung I think referred to these as archetypes. [i.e. "a collectively inherited unconscious idea, pattern of thought, image, etc., universally present in individual psyches."]

Stephen: Let us look at it like this: Each of us sometimes has cut or wounded a finger. The way in which this happens shows many variations. The reaction to the cut was quite different: when the child Michael cut his finger and bled, it caused a greater reaction than if the Michael of now cut the same finger in the same manner and bled also.

And this is why all experiences may have been similar to other experiences, but it is the *reaction* to these experiences that is the record that is returned.

Michael: It is the *reaction* to the experience being returned, that is the key thing?

Stephen: The experiences are bound to happen if the signal is sent out, but if there is no return or if what is returned was known before the signal is sent out, it would be a pointless exercise.

Michael: In the book which I have on my lap, it says many things which I feel summarise what you have been saying, and yet there is one thing that said, is that we are absolutely determined beings. We are absolutely convinced that Thomas goes to Berlins because it was ordained, in human terms, a thousand years ago. And he could have no choice but to go to Berlins.

Stephen: ...so that the cell may be strengthened in what it knows. Not even that the cell may be strengthened, but that the cell may grow in experience, and react. For life truly in the whole of the universe, and all that there is, is life, and life is movement.

True life is all movement. The whole of life must be the whole of movement.

[David Bohm, op.cit, calls this the "Holomovement"]

135. Blasphemy against the Holy Spirit.

Olive: Can you help me to understand these words of Jesus, "Whoever blasphemes against the Holy Spirit, never has forgiveness but is guilty of eternal sin." What is that blasphemy?

Stephen: [Blasphemy against the Holy Spirit] occurs on the day when we are questioned and, in spite of our testimony, in spite of its being known, and in spite of our hearts, we stand before that which is not of the Lord, and beg forgiveness for our belief. To deny that which is in your heart, to save yourself from persecution, that is the blasphemy which is referred to.

You have separated yourself in these circumstances irrevocably, for, in full knowledge and with the strength of the Lord with you, you turn away from Him in fear and blaspheme His Love, to give obedience [to the other]. That is the time when your cell of influence can no longer record the experience of that body and that mind and would withdraw. But take not this as a judgement on those who are foolish and who with little thought and little intention speak of the Lord and use the Lord's name in derogatory terms, for at this time they are deaf in their ears, and the words come only from the surface of their tongues, not from their hearts. There is greater blasphemy and many will commit this blasphemy and their bodies will be left without the guiding spirit, and the cell of influence until they are (in the little time that remains to them) just the mind of Man with all its corruption, its fears, all its uncertainties, and its complete lack of knowledge. It is the dross that is shed in the foundry, to separate what is pure from what is not.

136. Eternal Life.

Olive: When Jesus offered us eternal life, was he speaking to me, Olive, or to the cell of influence which is eternal anyway?

Stephen: If you think in your time, or you speak of the physical, when did our Lord speak these words? Two thousand years ago. Therefore He must have spoken these words to that which is continuous. He did not promise that this eternal life was some attribute that was to come in the future, but made a simple statement that this was so, as you have stated yourself, that the cell of influence does have eternal life. These words were given to us so that in our physical minds we would understand that nothing of this Earth could keep us from that life eternal with the Father. For it is the Father's and it lives forever. But these words were given to us, so that we would not despair in our physical suffering; for all the discomforts that might come upon a physical body or a physical mind, are but a drought in the life of that which we call our soul. Remember this, for this is oft misunderstood, that [eternal life] was not a promise as a reward, but a statement of what has been the case, "in the beginning, and is now, and every shall be. Amen."

137. A healing. Wish to be at home with God. The Millennium. Not just a few saved. Eternal life.

Olive: The other night I was given a wonderful healing for my ear by our Lord. Afterwards I wept a lot and felt a desperate yearning to go home. This, I felt, was not Olive who yearned to go home. it was very strange. What did it mean, Stephen?

Stephen: To receive this experience and this healing it would be necessary for your spirit to be uplifted; you would be very close to home, but you needed to come back from the peace and contentment of all things perfect, back to where you do not know this peace. [That] would I think compel you to weep. So that which did speak and cry was truly Olive.

Olive (on behalf of Michael): "The last session upset me, for it appeared to imply and affirm the salvation of just the few, just as many sects state. Although I stand up for Christ, my behaviour, and putting into practice leaves a lot to be desired" Tom and I agree with this also. Can you help us?

Stephen: Firstly I must take away the misapprehension that just a few will be saved. The scriptures and the Revelations, teach us that [about] the few who are mistakenly interpreted as being all of them.[?] We are told that they come to the Lord and rise up with him before the time of the tribulation. It is also written that during and at the end of the time of tribulation many more will come to and be with the Lord; because of their experiences at this time, and even after that, after what is given to us in the dream as the Millennium, there will be another resurrection of those who even in the last moments of breath did accept the truth that is very obvious to all of us who know the Lord. For they would have met him face to face, and would have known.

Those are spoken of as being the people who will not come with the Lord are those who through their own choice even after all the experiences that are to come, would still from their own choice and preference accept that which is the opposite of the Kingdom. The choice will be plainly theirs; some will even live and receive all the benefits of the Millennium, of all that which is perfect: the perfect government of the Lord, the perfect health, the perfect Love, when all things are as they were in the beginning. But after this time, when they know in their hearts that which is the Kingdom, that which is undeniable, then they will deny this and utter and perform the blasphemy that cannot be forgiven. For to be forgiven is to accept and want this forgiveness. It is not a punishment, it is a desire of each one and their choice, their preference, not in ignorance, not in mistaken loyalty to others, not without the full knowledge of our Lord, but armed with all of these they will deny and choose unto themselves the alternative to Perfection.

Those of us who love the Lord may ask ourselves how it could be possible to see such Perfection, to feel such love and yet deny for the third time, but some people will do so. All others will be with the Father. So, I stress again, those who are faithful to our Lord, those of us that are not perfect in all that we do but who rely on our Lord Jesus Christ and his sacrifice for our salvation, these before the Millennium, will not need to have the question put to them again. The second time and the second question are called or are known on the day of tribulation. The first question was on the day that our Lord Jesus Christ was crucified for us. The third question of course will be at the end of the Millennium when even those who during the time of the Millennium have lived in and with a body, have experienced [much], and these bodies in perfection will last one thousand years. And those who at the end of the tribulation, at the end of the second question have died, they will become conscious again, at the end of the third question, and the choice will be theirs. Not one will be condemned to their own choice without first knowing, without first experiencing that Kingdom which is perfection. Since it is a Kingdom of perfection, all must be in harmony, all must love willingly, all must give to receive, all must be perfect peace and harmony. Therefore ask yourself, if someone cannot accept all of these things, and cannot come into this perfection, wanting and longing to go home to that perfection, then they must, of necessity, even for themselves accept the alternative: namely the judgement from Him who is to come as Judge. The words He will say will mean this: "I will offer to you, and give unto you all of this that you have experienced, or any such other that you may desire."

And so we have all the experiences through the many lives of souls, who both have engaged with a mind and desires that are *not* of the Kingdom, and have also had the full experience of that which is the Kingdom. Their judgement then is that they should choose which of these they desire.

No one can influence another in that true choice, for by this time the Lord has called to them, has loved them. If they refuse this love, then what is of the Lord, he willl take back into his fold, where they must remain with him for ever. What is not of Him is free to choose of itself the kingdom which it desires, and remains so for ever.

For the Lord truly will gather in all that, that is His. His flock will be safe, for those are his sheep. That which is not of His flock can never be of that flock, but must dwell amongst its own kind. Amen, so be it.

138. Christ is not in us, we are in Him.

Olive: A lot of problems seem to stem from whether it is a Christ from within or without.

Stephen: Those who look only for Christ within themselves, are worshipping that which is their desires, for as we are in sin, we know much that we desire is not of our Lord. We read his words, we learn of his teachings, and we know that our desires, what we feel within ourselves as our desires, are an abomination in his sight.

He comes <u>into</u> us but he is not <u>within</u> us; [rather] we are from <u>within him</u>. Be not deceived with this corruption of words: the Tempter will tempt you to think that within you, you will find all that is good. This contradicts the words of our Lord when he tells us [that] all that is good comes to us from <u>without</u>, from the Father <u>into</u> us, should we desire to receive and act and feel.

Olive Yes, I agree with that, for the only time I have ever felt any true good within me, is when I have been keenly aware of our Lord's presence.

Stephen: What is good within you and what is part of the Kingdom, awaken at the touch or at the word. That part that awakens is of the Kingdom. Therefore we look to put this part closer to the Lord; when we do we feel the response of the part of us that is of the Kingdom. Then we know that which is of the Truth, for were the Lord to be here now, and say the word "Anne,"* unto you, the part that is in you that we call Love would gos out to join that which is Love.

Many words of others who deceive themselves, also deceive us; much thinking restricts the All which is the Kingdom, which is the Lord and God our Father, to an insignificance that can be contained within ourselves.
[The tape ran out at this point. Briefly what was said was:]
"Salvation is not within ourselves but in the acceptance of that which is the Father's, and the outstretching of ourselves to the Father."

139. May 31, 1980: The conversations with Stephen end.
Stephen: Let us then thank Thomas for putting behind *his* ego, and allowing me to come. Dear Michael, ask your question.

Michael: Dear Stephen, thank you for being a friend over these years, You are much in my mind, and always continue to be much in my mind. Stephen, about the *ego*. I have become quite aware of this boat which protects me from the waters. I become more and more aware of the forces within me, the madness within me, which keep me from surrendering to who I really am. Would you like to talk to me about this, to help me become clearer in my thinking?

---

* A former self of Olive.]

Stephen: The boat, you will recall, I said would separate you from your element. It was an unnecessary protection that you have for yourself. There is one misconception that I feel that you have, and let me correct this if I may: it is that the ego is the product of your mind and its concepts.

That mind, that body, and those concepts, must also be of the Whole. Is this not so? For nothing can exist that is not part of the Whole.

You have spoken of the dissipation of this ego and yet have not considered that this is also an instrument of the Whole..

For we have spoken about the recording of experiences that are necessary for the Whole. For why would what is perfect need to have created all that we consider material, which includes the mind and the product of that mind which is the ego, if these experiences were not only desirable but necessary?

We might as well say of a body with a limb that is useless, that cannot function, that that limb should be cut out and destroyed.

Think when I speak about the misconception and the disservice that you give to your own mind, and what it creates. It is indeed the instrument of experience, and is your unique contribution to the Whole.

Similarly, as each part of your body, being part of a whole, is also unique.

The workings of the Whole create the workings of that part of each body for its uniqueness, the recording of sensations and the recording of experiences.

So now, we will see what the answer to Olive's question would be: Without the ego, the creating instrument of you that part of the Whole whereby the Whole senses, and regards,

without that then, we would be truly separate.

Think... it has often been said that in the nucleus or the core of the Whole, there is no sensation of either good or bad, cold nor warm, soft nor hard. It would be the same with our mind, if it were not coupled with the body to enable our mind to record these sensations.

What must be removed is the ego's judgement on those sensations. For those sensations are the recordings for the core that support us. For the sensation of taste, sight, sound, smell and touch enables us to take in sustenance, to support the tongue, the eyes, the ears, and the hand, that they might perform their various functions.

Michael: You are using this as an analogy for the body of the Whole?

Stephen: For in what other way can we say that we are in the image of our creator? Think not that this is an idle saying: "The Whole is as we are. We are as is the Whole."

The body is therefore no misconception of our minds; it is no mistake; and it is part of the wish of the Whole. We had been talking earlier almost as if it would be a good thing if we got rid of our bodies.

At times, as with myself, when Thomas is kind enough to loan me the body that I now use, now it is mine, it can hear, touch, smell, and even see. Then I have another body that enables me to record sensations that are beyond the abilities of this body of Thomas's. These sensations are recorded, as also are the sensations in other stages*.

Michael: Stages?

Stephen: How can I put this so that you will understand? For the talk of bodies could then lose the concept?

Ah, I will talk of the Blood, the other stages that the Blood travels, each particle of that blood being the body within a body, changing from material as you would understand it to non-material in the way that I understand it. The difference between us is that I understand because I live in the state of non-material and have lived in the state of material. I can understand the body that I have now, and the way that it needs to be fed, as you must also.

For we cannot be part of that perfect Whole if we become passively non-active, and waste away our own bodies [Words lost here] .

All that we are asked to do, and what we pray for, what we long for, if we analyse it deeply enough, we will know that it is the ability not to judge, but to *love*.

The judgmental conclusions of the mind conflict with what comes from the cell of influence. What comes from the cell of influence is [in conflict with] the physical mind that creates judgemental thoughts and causes us to act in the way which destroys or attempts unsuccessfully to destroy.

Take, hold precious, enjoy and love, for this is the experience that must come back to the Whole. So I say this, that what catches you as beauty, causes the tear to fall with joy, lifts your heart, causes you to embrace, to reach out to perform necessary deeds with no thought of self, is what you have been led to do by the cell of influence.

* See Section 58. Trinity: the Bodies, Skins, Stages, that underlie the physical mind.

Everything which causes you to destroy, to sneer, to injure, to speak unkind words, is the instrument of the mind being used by the judgement. All these words are complicated so therefore we who must teach, and this includes all of us here, must from necessity simplify that teaching, as only the simplest teaching can be; and that is the perfect teaching. Think of the words of our Lord, what he has taught. He has said much more in five words, than I have said over five years.

Michael: I cannot comment on that.. You have been of great help.

Could you comment on a discipline that I am following *A Course in Miracles* in three volumes. Can you discern whether this is a sound discipline?

Stephen: You will come to a point in these books where you will decide and see very clearly if at that point it advocates that judgement is right, and emotion is wrong; Do not refer back to me, but refer to the teacher of clarity, you will then know for yourself, the value of these books. But do not judge them.

Michael: You are saying, not to refer back to you in general, but only on this issue?

Stephen: *In general*, because my words have been many, not that I disclaim responsibility for my words, but my words are too numerous to be sufficient to answer at that time your question. For what truth I speak is but *my* truth; my truth comes only from my experience, and alas, my judgements. God bless you all.

140. A brief reunion. May 3, 1993.

[Many years have now elapsed since our last conversation with Stephen. I have not seen Thomas and Olive for perhaps ten years, since they are living in Nelson. But my intention to publish a record of our conversations with Stephen led me to think that it would not be right to do so without Thomas's and Olive's full consent. It seemed imperative that we should meet and talk about the whole experience.

They were in fact happy that we should publish. It had been hard to enter Stephen's reality, and for many reasons it had seemed hard to put into practice. Private emotional difficulties had got in the way; there was lack of clarity about how to convey Stephen's message to others.

We recognised the great value of what Stephen was saying. Yes, indeed let us try to publish. It would relieve us of some guilt, if at least some others had a chance to read Stephen's words for themselves.

Yes, also we agreed that we would try to make contact with Stephen once again after all these years. How was he feeling about the situation? Could he help us to progress?

We met together for brief prayer, and Thomas laid himself open for trance. He became a little pale, but it was not immediately apparent that Stephen had taken over. We did not see his usual smile, and he gave us no greeting. But Thomas's right hand pointed towards me, and Olive suggested that Stephen might be in the process of coming, and that I should ask my question.]

Michael: Stephen, welcome. I want to give you, if you can hear me, my deepest thanks for your spiritual help over the years.

Because I have been retyping the whole of our past conversations with you, with the possibility that they might be published, I have come to a clearer understanding of what you have been presenting, and am feeling it more deeply. But this has led me to a feeling of sadness and guilt that we have not been able better to build on what has been happening in the past thirteen years, so far as I am concerned. I think we are asking you if you can help us to progress beyond the feeling of separation, and of inadequacy we now feel.

I would like you to know that I was very fond of you, and still am, for the help and sharing that you have granted. That is what I want to start off to say to you. To say thank you, and ask, can you help us?

Stephen: To do what?

Michael: To overcome whatever may separate us from our growth. I have been talking with some of my friends, and we find that some of us feel that we cannot love as much as we would like to love, because of continuing and repeated hurts in our lives, and so that the commandment to love almost seems like a judgement.

Stephen: You wish then to win the war?

Michael: We wish very much to win the war. We do not want to be defeated, because we were given such good ammunition in this war, to start off with. We would like to continue to use that ammunition.

Stephen: In which direction do you wish to travel so as to win this war?

Michael: I have been thinking in terms of Spirit as being like the General of an army, and the individual soldier being like us. And I feel that we may have been confused. We have been waiting for instructions from the General about how, in our own ways, we should progress. But then I begin to think that the responsibility lies with the individual soldier, holding the hand, nevertheless, of the General.

Stephen: I was referring to your concept, with the war..[long pause] ...Forgive the time.... It is difficult.... We shall get there. I shall win this war...

You speak of love much as if this were but one thing. You worry that you are unable to love as our Lord had loved. Love for us must necessarily be confined and directed.

That direction [of love] is the objective that the soldier may wish to see or feel is his duty to proceed to, overcome, and conquer.

It is a little like when you do not have directions and you ask and receive directions but your instincts lead you in another direction.

It is a little like coming down from a circular tower and taking the wrong path,.. but you get there in the end.

You must be clear in your mind what you wish to achieve. It must have purpose. We say, friends, that we have listened well but we have not yet achieved. Achieved what? What do each of you wish to achieve? How courageous are you, to use what you feel to achieve an object? Why do we always compromise? Why are we afraid of disapproval, in what we have to say? .. or in the object that we wish to achieve? Look round at the achievers. These then that we may even despise, who appear to achieve, have a clear object. They pursue it, in spite of criticism, or opposition, until apparently they achieve their object.

If those with objectives so wrong as to exclude love, if they can follow an objective, may not we also, if that is the direction in which we must travel? And that is the direction we should go.

This is not meant as a criticism, but before you know where and why you want to go, you cannot travel in the right direction.

You wish to heal in special ways? How often have you thought and stopped yourself from doing it, because your opinions would not be received with any approval? How often have you compromised your teaching, because it would not meet with approval?

If your objective towards which you would wish to travel, were clearly in your hearts, and in your minds, and you followed in that direction - you all have experiences where this has led to achieving..... I hear from Thomas. [Pause]... Yes your Minister of Social Welfare does not appear to love but she does appear to believe in her objectives. Her motives are not known. Myself, I cannot and will not judge.

Michael: I think when I have been looking over what we have been hearing, you have been presenting us with a picture of reality in which we live and move and have our being. And we have had confirmation from our synchronistic experiences that this is in fact is the nature of this reality. There is left in my mind a feeling of more at-oneness with the universe and with Christ.

But then we think: Is it that we should teach this reality to others, because when we try, we find that others have preconceptions and beliefs of their own, which impede their hearing us? And then, on the other hand, if we were to take the simple teaching of Christ, of surrender, love, forgiveness, non-judgement, then this is a prescription for daily life, which we would like to live by. We can but feel that there is such a richness in what we have been experiencing amongst ourselves and from you, and such a vision of things, that we find it difficult to get an objective. Do you see my problem?

Stephen: If your objective is elusive, look more into your motives, and what your aims should be. When you have discovered these, your direction should be clear. Always remember that you lead from the front not from the rear.

We have often spoken of the positive and negative, the male and the female as being opposites. Then where you have one you must have the other on your outline. Where you have the concave you must also have your convex. The actions of others are like the convex, and our approval or disapproval are like the concave.

Michael: We get caught in the same thing that they are doing.

Stephen: We get caught in looking at the particular circumstance, narrowing our vision until we see a spot. Look closely next time with a glass at your hand, narrow down and look at one spot, and I assure you Michael, you will see nothing but a ghastly hole.

Michael: Are you happy Stephen that we should...
[Stephen beckons to Olive for support: "Help this body."]... [Pause]

We must consider Thomas and so I must leave you.

Depend not only on me. Many, many times have I spoken in these stagnant years. Listen to me always in everything. We have not been separated. You have not been abandoned. But sometimes the hearing may be affected by other noise..... God bless you.

Part Four
Discoveries about Stephen's early life

Chapter 1

Stephen, the Essenes, and the Dead Sea Scrolls

Note:

In this section of the book Stephen tells many things about his life on earth, what he has to say is moving and of great interest. He speaks about his childhood, how he apparently joined a Jewish sect called the Essenes, how he became a disciple of Jesus and how he was martyred for his faith.

At the same time as this story is told, historical and linguistic evidence is adduced to show that it is a true story, and that we are in fact hearing from that Stephen who had died for his faith.

In the process the book may provide far more evidence than most readers can cope with. Of course readers know what to do when this sort of thing happens – skip over the fine print to the next point of interest.

For those who have the interest and the patience to explore the fine print, some explanations may be necessary.

The Dead Sea Scrolls that were discovered in eleven caves along the northwest shore of the Dead Sea between the years 1947 and 1956 at Khirbet Qumran. The scrolls along with numerous portions of the Hebrew Bible as well as many documents connected with the Essene sect were found in high and inaccessible caves. An Essene monastery had been in the vicinity, and perhaps facing annihilation by the Romans, the Essenes hid their precious documents in the caves. This is the source of documents including *The Manual of Discipline*, to be quoted later.

141. After the wedding breakfast, Stephen sets his Greek puzzle.

Thomas (through whom Stephen spoke) and his wife Olive have already been introduced. Now it might be helpful to gain an impression of a typical gathering, where Thomas would be taken over by Stephen.

What are they like as people? Olive, the New Zealander, is dark, vivacious, much smaller than Thomas, warm and deeply religious. Thomas, the Londoner, looks and behaves like the businessman, or high-class hotelkeeper that he has been. Dresses smartly, a good speaker, and always seems in charge of the situation. He gives little hint of being introspective or a mystic, yet is in fact devoutly spiritual.

Members of our informal group have arrived, hoping that Stephen may be willing to communicate. Thomas and Olive are only marginally well off, but the home has a neat, cheerful feel about it, and we are welcome. The handful of guests is religious, but free thinking. They are perhaps all creative in their various ways, and come from a wide variety of religious backgrounds. Ordinary mainline churchgoers, a Liberal Catholic priest, a Buddhist, and so on.

At first we have refreshments and chat about this and that as people do in almost any group. But then we earnestly discuss the transcripts of recordings of the last conversation with Stephen. From our discussion questions arise. These are more usually put to Stephen by Olive or myself.

The time comes to invite Stephen. There is a period of prayer and meditation. Then Thomas prays for spiritual protection prior to allowing himself to fall into trance. He becomes pale, he is unconscious, then there is a slight jerk in his body and he appears to change before our eyes to become a smiling visitor who nevertheless keeps his eyes shut. Visitor Stephen usually jokes a little before coming down to the serious business.

Here, though, I want to talk about a very special day. May 13, 1974. It was on the day of the marriage of Thomas and Olive. The wedding breakfast was over. It was evening, and the usual people who had been questioning Stephen were assembled to hear from him once more. Perhaps it was that we wanted to include Stephen in the party. Thomas was tired, of course, and had just a little too much to drink. Even so Stephen was in no way hindered. He began by uttering a number of Greek words in what turned out to be a less-known dialect of 2000 years ago.

Three of us were later to make a painstaking transcript of them from a tape-recording. Thirty years of detective work with the words have revealed a great deal about Stephen's life, which could be backed up with hard facts from scholarly and ancient sources. Stephen was able to convey these words through Thomas (who knew no Greek,) and lead us to information which makes it virtually certain that it is the spirit of Stephen who was speaking, and no other.

Stephen: Kárno dióti diéta dióti, kárno dióti borô zélai Leneká mélla diésta(sthai?).[46]

Καρνω διοτι, διετα διοτι, Καρνω διοτι βορω ζελαι Λενεκα μελλα διεστα (εσθαι ?)

But it would be better, I think, were I to speak with words that would bring a greater emotive response.

[In telling the story, I find the enemy to be its bewildering complexity. To keep the story simple, I shall leave out the rest of the conversation. Six days were to elapse, during which time attempts were made to translate these words.

For easier reading I shall continue to present the main story in normal type, with supporting data in small print, just for the record.]

142. This is what Stephen's words mean, and imply:

My research helps to confirm that Stephen was accurate when he said that his Greek words had originally been spoken to Joseph the father of Jesus, and that Joseph had been an Essene at the time.

Stephen would have spoken those words to Joseph, just before he himself was accepted into the same group of Essenes as Joseph, after serving a two years' probation.

The Essenes had a Communion service, with bread and diluted grape-juice, and a convert was not entitled to take part in that service unless they had had two years' preparation and probation. When finally accepted as an Essene, grape-juice was diluted ready for the ceremony.

Stephen said that he had been born in the Ancyra (modern Ankara) area of Galatia, and that his given name, Stenen, was Thracian. As Stephen spoke the Greek dialect found in Thrace (some hundreds of kilometers from Ancyra), and as he refers to himself as a Celt, it can be assumed that his parents were Celtic and Jewish, and that one or both of them had come to Ancyra from Thrace. It is a fact that many Jews and Celts in Ancyra intermarried.

A number of modern scholars do think that Stephen had been an Essene, before he became a follower of Jesus.

It is necessary to know all the above and more, before we can understand the proper translation, which is:

"For the Carnyx*/Celt [like For the Kiwi/New Zealander], the two years [of the probation] having passed, for this Carnyx, the wine** of the juice of the newly-pressed grape of the Lenaia*** must now be mixed with water [as it always was in the Messianic Communion].

Stephen's own words about his childhood can be found later in this part.

143. Discussing the Greek Puzzle with Stephen.

[I check out a first effort at translation with Stephen]

[Prior to this session I had done much research into the meaning of Stephen's Greek words, and now felt ready to come up with a translation. I had noted that the word for *wine* (zélai) was a Thracian word, and mistakenly thought *for the Celtic born* was the right meaning for *kárno*. I had learnt that there had been Celts in Thrace (in the far north of Greece), and also in Galatia, in Asia Minor, and that Celtic tribes had conquered Thrace early in the 3rd cent. BCE. They had proceeded to overrun much of Asia Minor, only later to be confined to Phrygia, which was renamed Galatia, after the Latin for Celts, *Galli*. I had understood that *Lenaïká* referred to the Lenaea, a Dionysian festival, and that the Celts had a bad name for drunkenness. I had *reasoned* that Stephen was not from Thrace, but from Galatia.]

Stephen: I believe much study has been apparent these days, since last we have spoken!

---

* A Celtic war trumpet that Romans and others saw as a symbol of the Celts.

** A native Thracian (not Greek) word is used.

*** The Lenaia were ceremonies celebrating the juice of the newly-pressed grape. They were in honour of the god Dionysus. Stephen would have found it a suitable Greek translation of the Aramaic names of the grape-juice festival of the Essenes, reference to the Communion service in which the diluted grape-juice was the main thing.]

Michael: Indeed there has! Stephen, might we check with you the results of our studies? Are you aware of the interpretation of your Greek?

Stephen: I would prefer that you would give me one of these interpretations.

Michael: "And so, for the Gallic [*Celtic*]-born, and for the two-year-old, for the Gallic-born, for the glutton, the Bacchanalian [*Dionysian*] wines should be diluted".

Stephen: And the conclusions from this interpretation that you came to?

Michael: The historical conclusion leads me to guess that when you were last on earth - last 'shackled' - you were a Greek-speaking Jew, using the Thracian-type dialect, spoken by the native inhabitants of Galatia, and that it was in that province that you spent your childhood.

Stephen: The childhood I spent in Ancyra[47].

Michael: Did you?! And now the other conclusion is that the reason why you spoke of "Greater emotive response" [in **141**][48] was that the people of Galatia had bad feelings about the Gallic-born [Celts] whom they thought to be rough and uncouth masters - that is why their wine had to be diluted.

Stephen: I would not be so unkind! The emotive response that was required was from you. If I speak in a tongue with which all of you are unfamiliar, then we would not *feel* as we do now.
Your interpretation is close to that which I intended. The only deep significance was that of an exercise,[49] firstly that I might test myself. For to use these words *that have not been with Thomas for many, many generations,* was an achievement for both Thomas and myself, and excellent practice for you.

[Stephen is stating that Joseph, the father of Jesus, *had* known those words many generations before, and that the Thomas of today is very closely related to him in "the Communion of Saints". This is a key point in interpreting the Greek.]

Michael: I was surprised that you were able to use words that Thomas did not know..

Stephen: Might I, then, at this stage, use the opportunity to tell you more of Stephen? It has been of concern that it should be one that was known and has been written of, that should come to you in this way.

[There were indeed people in the group, especially in the early stages, who quite reasonably felt most bothered by the fact that we seemed to be receiving communications from such a famous personality.]

Stephen: It is for a simple reason - not that Stephen is great, only that he may be recognised as an *instrument*.

I will give you a comparison of the power - I should say better – the gifts of Stephen, for which he was chosen for the tasks that were to be performed. It was spoken of Stephen that he was often "with spirit". Look then, now, at the body of Thomas. Is it not also "with spirit"? There are many, and there have been many before, through whom the Father has chosen to communicate with many, for his purposes - many at the time when Stephen was chosen for the task. Therefore be sure in your minds that there are many now who could undertake this task, and the tasks that Stephen could undertake. But they gain not their position by their own choosing.

You have this day listened to the words of the teaching that explains to you that when the Father calls, He chooses the instrument, or the priest, or the bishop. It would be better always if we understood that Stephen, like Thomas, has been used for a particular purpose of the Father.

The knowledge that may be attributed to Stephen, and to many others, comes whence all knowledge comes. Your own knowledge - to be able to trace and find out from small clues - is an achievement. Looked at in the physical, and by the physical minds only, it could be said that Michael is extremely clever, for I assure you that, to my knowledge, no living soul could tell you this day where Stephen spent his childhood. But if then, we consider Michael the instrument, who is susceptible to guidance, and is open, then the mystery becomes then again, in proportion.

Should we say that because Thomas's voice speaks a strange language, that Thomas is clever? Instead, we often give the glory to Stephen. This is not so [appropriate], for when you find more of Stephen in the writings, you will find mistakes were made by Stephen in what he taught, for Stephen, like all of us and all of you, can form conclusions that are often incorrect".

144. Stephen's own moving words about his childhood and youth:

Stephen: Olive has a question. She wishes to know more of Stephen. My answer is that she wishes to understand how and why I feel things, why I might say things, and to whom I might speak; what emotions I might have, if I have any anger, and what my doubts might be. Then perhaps she will understand herself better, and she knows another a little more closely. She might understand then, when she feels despondent, and feels that much is not worth while, when she sees that another has felt this way, has risen above it, and has gained help, and can give help. Then perhaps it might be that the readers of the book that you might write, might also feel this.

Would you know of the times when Stephen was in doubt? When he walked and preached and still he doubted?

Of the great fear, and the knowledge of tragedy that was in Stephen's heart? Or the tears that Stephen shed for himself? Of the ambitions, as your own, that were unrealized?

Of the terror of death, of the fear of the opinions of others, the ambitions to wealth and fame, of the love of another that Stephen felt? Does this sound unfamiliar to you?

This is how it was for Stephen, a young man, spoken of by his elders. I recall that he was considered untidy, that he showed not the respect for his parents that he might, that he stole as a child foolish things, he gave away what did not belong to him, his taste for music was indifferent, he had many dislikes of the foods that he ate, he would wish for fine horses, but needed to pretend with a mule; he had ambitions of being a great soldier.

We could then count Stephen as failing in many of his ambitions, much to his gain. Stephen did not see success in much that he tried to accomplish. Often his testimony was mistaken. Very seldom was it well received. He had many moments of foolishness, and a great deal of laughter. He was inexpert when he travelled, and often he was unwise in his companionship. This then is Stephen. Is there more that you wish to know?

145. Stephen's Awareness 1.

Olive: Your awareness now.

Stephen: The awareness that I have is the gift of, and is part of the Father, as are we all. We think perhaps that Stephen is separated and that he is aware of everything in the way that Olive might be aware, or feels that she is aware. But this of course is not so. [It is true that] for a long period of what we might call time, after the death of his body, Stephen was separated, as many still are.

In his so-called separateness, Stephen attempted to be of service to the Father. But then in the course of what we call time, Stephen let go of the personality of Stephen, the tent which the Father had given him in which to be housed. And thus unclothed, he gave up his separateness to be one with the Whole. You will understand that when I speak to you, I re-enter this tent, I put on again the clothes of Stephen, I put on the robes of a saint, in order that you may feel comfortable, in order that you may walk with me in a way that to you is familiar.

Michael: It makes me feel really scared to hear you talk like this. That this Stephen to whom we talk is only a puppet of personality manipulated by the Whole. It reminds me that I, Michael, would be such a puppet too. I get really scared of losing what is me, what I think of as me, and jumping into the void.

Stephen: Then take the comfort that the Father has given you; accept the security of your tent. Return to the tent that is Michael when you wish. It is there for your use. But as for me, I have left my Stephen behind, and I have life that belongs to the Whole, to the Father. Now I can be present in the lives of a thousand others.

Stephen's Awareness 2.

Stephen: We are a little out of practice! In what way may I assist?

John: I take it that you are in a time, space, and awareness that is different from ours. How much are you yourself aware of our particular time, space, and consciousness? How much are you aware of what is actually going on in our planet?

Stephen: Firstly, I must disagree with you. You are in a particular time and place with a lack of awareness, and your conscious mind does not always recall.

But your awareness is such that many things, (even though not seen and observed) are apparent to you. You ask of my awareness, of this as a planet. The awareness is of much more, that of a Whole, rather than that of a separate planet.

You too, as you think, are aware of much wider fields than just this planet. You know for certain that this is a part of the universe, and you are aware of the universe. My awareness is not greatly different from yours, except that I do not have some of your restrictions. I do not need to touch, for to know; I do not need to sit, to be aware, I do not need to taste, to be fulfilled, and know what satisfies.

Each of you now - each of you now close your eyes. You are using only some of your senses now, and you are aware not only of what is in this room, but of your vehicles outside, in some cases the families that are at home. You know of a certainty that these things are there. Such is my awareness of what I know exists.

Miriam: Could Stephen tell me what God is then?

Stephen: God is everything that you see, and more. It is all that you cannot imagine, all that you cannot conceive.

Miriam: That is how I feel. I feel that I am part of that.

Stephen: You must be part of that, for there are many who cannot conceive Miriam, nor perceive Miriam. You are part of that, that cannot be seen, touched or conceived, and much of what we call creation, so that we cannot even separate ourselves in this way. We are also the unknown, as well as the known. Can we conceive of Stephen? Is he known to all? Can we feel and touch him? Nevertheless, we have Stephen here.

Miriam: Do we have Stephen here separate in the sense that Michael is separate?

Stephen: Separate only because we choose to say that Stephen is separate, for none of us is separate from each other. On the other hand, within metres of this place there are many people gathered [in a church] who would deny his very existence, and who would not be able even to conceive this Stephen that we have.

Michael: I continue to confuse myself, for I say to the group that I can infer that I am part of the Whole, that you are also a part of the Whole, but I cannot switch me off.

Stephen: It is [the truth of] your experience of the moment that you are Michael, and I am Stephen.
Why deny what is given to you for experience?
For it is [just as] true as the discussion that would go on with this other group of people, were they to deny the existence of Stephen, for to them Stephen cannot and does not exist.

Michael: Do you feel "Stephen" or do you feel "The Whole?" Or do you feel a figment of my imagination?

Stephen: For if I say that I am Stephen, I must first create Stephen, and be he. For I cannot be nothing. For once I decided I was nothingness, then I have learned nothing of nothing. I will say this however for your guidance, and accept this humble advice: do not feel that you must throw a concept to the winds or feel that things that you know have been taken from you. For as I am real to you now, all those concepts that are real to you, are part of your needs. They are your clothing, they are your life and they are what supply your needs.

Michael: Now I think I can take this in. Now I am asking a test question: are you real to yourself? In the sense that I say this of myself?

Stephen: In the sense that you say this of yourself.

Olive: Do I conjure up my picture of Jesus?

Stephen: Did you conjure Stephen up for us? [Olive: No]
Then no more did you conjure up for us our Lord, or have I conjured up falsehood. He is real to you and to me. Blessed, holy, real, even so, for he should not be denied. For if you deny it when you feel the real gifts, then you deny what is yourself.

Olive: This is where we seem to be tangling ourselves. For in one sense it is easy for me to feel Jesus as you, and John, and to feel Him in this way, and in another way we might feel Jesus within, as part of us. Now there is a certain truth there too, but we tangle ourselves.

Stephen: You cannot say that you are Jesus, any more than Thomas can say that he is Stephen, even though the body be of Thomas, and the voice that I call Stephen comes from... but they are not separate, neither are you.

Michael: A picture I use when talking to people is to use that of the fingers of the hand. I say you are the thumb, you are the forefinger and you are the ring finger, but there is one hand. Is that a useful image?

Stephen: Put the hand in a room, and say of all, "You are the room". In one way you restrict your outlook and, in another way you expand it beyond your own comprehension. You have what you need. What you have, what you feel, what you love, is there for your needs.

Michael: Now this I accept from one angle, but this leaves me still confused because you Stephen, while in Tom, are part of this room; and even when you are not in Tom, you are part of us. Yet you are Stephen, and I am Michael, yet you are part of us. Yet you are Stephen, I am Michael, and Jesus is Jesus. But the room and Jesus together...

Stephen: We need first to put Michael and Stephen together, for Michael has a need for the words that Stephen will say, and the concepts that he must give. Therefore, Michael has Stephen. You have Jesus in the same way. You have God in the same way, if you choose. You have yourself in that way.

146. On his language:

Stephen: We often say that the language that Stephen speaks is his language when I do not have a language. For language is but sound and sound needs a throat a tongue and an ear with which to listen. Of these things I have none. Would the gift be of use to us if the language could not be understood and when the words were spoken, there was no emotion felt?

We use our bodies as we might use an instrument to catch what we must feel. That the mind [of Thomas] that I use, has a store of sounds that can be used and understood by the ear, makes the instrument useful, for words by themselves when they are spoken or written separately mean little, but together, (when Stephen speaks), with what is in our hearts, what has been previously in our minds and in our thoughts since we last spoke; these sounds for the ear can reach the heart."

147. More on his martyrdom.

Stephen: After two thousand years you would think that one would give up hope!

Michael: But I would think... oh!...I am just thinking of you as being two thousand years old, although I know that this could be said of us all. But you have felt successful sometimes during those two thousand years?

Stephen: Occasionally I have felt that I have been worthy in a small way of doing the work of the Lord. Even then you may have read of my failure.

Michael: That was very much in my mind at that point. Does the Bible report what happened at the stoning accurately?

Stephen: Quite accurately.

Michael: You... What pain... then... did you feel?

Stephen: Only for a short time was there pain. The Lord is more merciful than you would imagine. That each one, under these circumstances, is taken apart from himself. Even now, should injury come to Thomas' body he would not feel that... I do not suggest that we injure him, for he must come back!

Michael: Stephen, no questions are coming to my mind.. but feelings are coming into my mind... to my inner self... that I think I am getting the Brother feeling.. I cannot put it better into words.

Stephen: This is how the feeling should be, for we are brothers. I shall depart. Continue with your feeling. Feel thus, when you pray. And bless each of you.

148. Christ speaks about Stephen:

"The task of your servant Stephen is that of messenger and he speaks with great authority. The task of yourselves is the decision as to which way you choose to use those messages. I say this unto you, that if your choice be wise, you will indeed see the fire in my eyes. You will indeed recognize the feet that are burnished bronze. Wonder not but proceed with courage, for thus far, we are well pleased".

149. Celts and Jews in Galatia:

That dialect of Greek must be Stephen's own because people don't usually mimic the dialect of someone else. The dialect was *Koine* or the international form of Greek spoken hundreds of years after Classical times, in the first century C.E. It was *Koine* but with the local variants characteristic of Thrace and perhaps Macedonia. That was why I at first connected Stephen with Thrace.

Those readers familiar with the Greek of that period, can read in the Appendix a full analysis showing Stephen's words to be genuinely of Stephen's time and place, corroborated by experts in ancient Greek. All the words can be looked up in Liddell and Scott's *Greek-English Lexicon*.

One of Stephen's Greek words was *karnon/karno* or *carnyx*. The word itself is a Celtic loan word, and it does refer to a strange-looking trumpet used in battle. It can be successfully argued that it also means *Celt*, because Roman coins and triumphal sculptures do show the trumpet or carnyx to *symbolise* the Celt, the Celt beaten by the Romans in battle. The carnyx was a potent image, because the Celts were known for being aggressive warriors, and it was their musical instrument used for psychological warfare.[50]

Photo: Urban

Mannequin depicting an aide-de-camp of the chief éduen Dumnorix.[51]

The carnyx[52] was played with the stem pointing vertically upwards, with the round trumpet mouth replaced by a bellowing animal's head, facing forwards. The trumpet looks like a bellowing or talking instrument, or a puppet being manipulated from below. A very good metaphor for the "instrument" that St Stephen would have himself recognised as, and the instrument that Thomas was.

In *Grove's Dictionary of Musical Instruments*, it is recorded that "the carnyx is frequently depicted on Roman coins and monumental sculptures showing victories over the Celts, particularly on Trajan's column, which celebrated the Dacian campaign."

Thus the carnyx was very much a symbol of the Celts. So what does this reveal about Stephen? Plainly it connected him to the Celts, and, because his word for wine was in the native Thracian language, then Stephen must in some way have been connected to Thrace.

At that time it occurred to me that Stephen may have actually been born in Galatia on the misapprehension that there were Christians in Galatia during Stephen's childhood. "Galatia" is based on the word for Gauls, or Celts. That is why I guessed that he had lived there.

Even though there were no Christians in Galatia, Stephen nevertheless confirmed my guess by saying that he was born in Ancyra (modern Ankara).

150. So then, how was it that the Celts came to Thrace and then to Galatia?

The Encyclopaedia Britannica 2000 records that in the third century BCE, certain warrior tribes had migrated to the East.

"Irruptions of Gallic or Celtic tribes into the eastern parts of Europe are first recorded in 281 BCE when a small army under Cambaules, attacked Thrace.[53] Three years later their soldiers swept through a large area of northern Asia Minor. After much conflict they were eventually settled in northern Phrygia, which was called *Galatia*, after the Roman word *Galli* meaning *Celts*."

"The population in this area consisted of the original Phrygians of the old Anatolia, the invading Celts and settler Greeks, to whom were afterwards added a considerable sprinkling of Romans and a smaller number of Jews. At the time of St Paul and St Stephen there was probably a marked difference between the rural Celtic population of Galatia, who were comparative barbarians, little affected by Greek manners, and the population of the cities, who were Greek, the majority of whom were not of Celtic origin. But while continuing Celts in feeling, the Celtic tribes in CE 30 who had intermarried with the people of the land, must have been assimilated to a large extent into Greek life and culture during the three centuries spent as a conquering caste amid more civilised peoples." [See article by William M. Ramsay on Galatia, in op.cit.]

The next word of interest is boro, which can *mean for the drunkard?* Would this be appropriate? Would Stephen be implying that he was a "drunken Celt"?

Not necessarily. It is true that Celts *did not* dilute their wine at the time that Stephen was alive, as was customary in the ancient world. Wine cups found are so large that they could not have been used for wine, drunk undiluted. Indeed drinking undiluted wine was frowned upon. When there was a party, the president of the party decided the proportion of water that should be mixed with the wine.

Map showing the Black Sea, Thrace, to the west of the Dardanelles, Galatia, to the east of Bithynia. (Ancyra cap. of Galatia).[54]

In fact the Celts' very bad name was widespread in the civilised world. They were regarded as barbarous, exceptionally hard drinkers, and most warlike.[55] As noted, their braying beast-mouthed battle trumpet was used as a fitting symbol for them on numbers of ancient Roman coins.

Another possible translation might be:

"For this reason, for the Celt, two years having passed, for this reason, for the greedy Celt, the Dionysian wine shall be diluted".

That translation makes some kind of sense in the above context. It has already been noted that the Celts were often a drunken lot. There was speculation at the time that Stephen was having a sly dig at Tom and Olive, who had a great deat of wine at their wedding breakfast, suggesting that they were behaving like drunken Celts. Stephen, however, was later to give another picture. "Yes," to "Celt", "No," to "drunken.". This will be discussed later when we have Celtic Stephen in Judaea, in reach of Jerusalem. But Stephen's words do imply that he had some sort of connection with the Celts. However he was also know to be a Jew. So how did the Jews find themselves in Thrace and in Galatia? This is answered in the following quotation:

"The enormous extent of the Jewish Diaspora in comparison with the petty mother country presents an enigma to historical inquiry which it is unable to solve with certainty... At the beginning of the Greek period the rulers sought, in the interests of consolidation of their dominions, to effect the greatest possible intermixture of populations, and with a view to this they incited and favoured general migrations, by guaranteeing certain privileges and by other means." [E.Schürer: "Diaspora" James Hastings Dict. of the Bible, Extra vol. p.91][56]

That was the general picture, but with regard specifically to Asia Minor, we read:

"Here we have numerous testimonies, and are able to demonstrate the presence of Jews in almost every quarter. They were most thickly settled in Phrygia [later *Galatia*] and Lydia, and we know further how they came there. Antiochus the Great transplanted two thousand Jewish families from Mesopotamia and Babylonia to Lydia and Phrygia, because he considered them more loyal subjects than the Lydians and Phrygians." [57] [Again from E.Schürer]

With regard to Thrace, it appears that hard evidence is lacking about Jews there. On complex evidence, Schürer infers that neighbouring Macedonia had a number of Jews. Later he infers that many were descended from prisoners of war of the Maccabaean period who had been sold into slavery in Greece.

151. Stephen in Ancyra

Stephen's Greek dialect belongs to Thrace, so his family must have come from there. It can be assumed that Stephen called himself a "Carnyx" or "Celt", and that he also saw himself as a Jew, (see Acts 6), and he did say he was born in Ancyra, in Galatia. (Modern Ankara).

What languages would have been employed in that city? Schürer writes:

"In Galatia, the most general language was Greek. But there were still Phrygian speakers (a language that scholars used to consider to be linked to Thracian or Illyrian but [they] now view Phrygian as a separate Indo-European language that shares a number of isoglosses with ancient Greek.) No doubt some people understood Latin and Hebrew."

Possible Celtic ancestors for Stephen would have begun coming to Galatia almost three hundred years previously. But from their Thracian dialect, Stephen's parents must have been first generation settlers. The reasoning is that Stephen was to say that his real name was Stenen, and that it was Thracian. Having a Thracian name, using a Thracian word, also implies that his parents had family connections with Thrace, and had come from there. They may have been Jews, or Celic converts to Judaism. On the possibility that one of his parents had been born in Ancyra, then there would also have been a good chance of a Babylonian origin.

Jews of all periods of time are seen as being steadfast in asserting their Jewishness. So how likely is it that Stephen as a Jew in Ancyra, would refer to himself as a Celt? In answer, William M. Ramsay[58] writes: [op. cit.]

"The Jewish colonists [in North Galatia] undoubtedly exercised great influence on the development of Asia Minor in the Roman period; but they have left few conspicuous traces of their presence. They adopted Greek and Roman names (at least in public life ["Stephen" is a Greek name meaning "Crown"]) and it is doubtful how far they retained any knowledge of Hebrew; hence they are hardly to be distinguished from the ordinary citizens".

Ramsay states two other important things: namely (1) that Celts were very thinly distributed through Galatia, except in Ancyra where there was a greater concentration of them. There, they constituted an upper class, over the mass of people who were Phrygians and Greeks. (2) Ramsay speculates that several upper class and noble families were Jewish. Thus Ramsay gives persuasive reasons for supposing that Stephen saw himself firstly as a Celt, and secondly as a Jew, much as Jews in the United States, see themselves primarily as US citizens, and secondarily as Jews. It is likely that Stephen belonged to this putative upper class, if *Acts* is right in recording that he was later chosen by the twelve apostles for his leadership abilities. The speeches credited to him in the book of *Acts*, in themselves, would presuppose that Stephen was literate and that he was obviously a leader.

Not so long after our session with Stephen in which we discussed my first attempt at a translation of his Greek, Thomas was to "receive" concerning the early life of Stephen. As I said earlier, he received with his conscious mind, and this was checked when he was in trance and we were speaking to Stephen.

152. One day Thomas consciously attuned his mind to Stephen, and attempted to intuit more of his history.

[In giving an account of the resulting intuitions of Thomas, I present just one, or a pair, at a time. I then relate how we attempted to evaluate the intuition(s) in question.]

Thomas: "Stephen... no, that did not seem right..Stenen.. another of us is *Stenen*... how strange."

[Later we had a conversation with Stephen to check all this, and I asked him whether "Stenen" was right.]

Stephen: It would be correct..

Michael: And the origin of the name?

Stephen: It was a Thracian name and quite common.[59]

Michael: And when did you change it? Was it when you became a Christian?

Stephen: I never did change this name. Others may have changed it for me. For often the name by which we are called did not find favour with those that we must speak to. I believe this would still be common practice.

Michael: Stalin being an example...

Stephen: I am not familiar with the name.

Michael: Stalin was the Russian leader of some years ago, who was called Dzhugashvili, but changed his name to Stalin, the man of Steel.

...

"A Greek-speaking Jew": wrote Thomas.

[Yes, we know this also from the *Book of Acts*, chapter 6. Stephen was appointed to help the apostles minister to the Greek-speaking widows joining the followers of Jesus who were missing out on help, because the apostles were Aramaic speakers.]

Thomas: "born in the small village of Seletar, on the outskirts of Ancyra in the province of Galatia, i.e. near Ankara in what is now modern Turkey".

[Stephen had said Ancyra. But this is not really a contradiction. I phoned Thomas later and asked him whether he could say more about Seletar, and after meditating a short time he answered that it was to the NE of Ancyra,[60] on the outskirts, a small village, extending along the bank of the river, making the shape of a capital D with the straight side along the bank of the river. On the Seletar side of the river it was reasonably flat, whereas the land on the opposite side of the river is hilly, rocky and barren. The buildings were mainly white, and low, with the streets geometrically laid out, with wider streets running parallel to the river. There were four of these wider streets; but at the wider part of the D, these wider streets parallel to the river were augmented by three of four narrower streets.

The letter D seemed to bother Tom. It was a peculiar shaped D. It was important... perhaps it wasn't a D after all, but a numeral.

I pointed out to Tom that the cursive Greek D (δ) was used to represent the number 4, and so I wondered whether the name Seletar had some connection with the number 4.]

"Were you born in Seletar?" I asked Stephen later.

Stephen: The name, in spite of the contradiction that might be in your mind is indeed Seletar.

Michael: And did the name have a meaning?

Stephen: An obscure one I believe: it was "The Fourth Landing-place".

Michael: Seletar, does it mean "fourth" in the Thracian dialect?

Stephen: It does, the fourth place.

Tom said that the place was north east of Ancyra, along the river, and that the village, which was in the shape of the letter D faced north across the river to the hilly country. Could you confirm that?

Stephen: The village was to the north, and to the east of Ancyra, but was not on the same bank as Ancyra.

[As stated, Seletar would have been on more level ground, whereas on the other side of the river, it was hilly, with Ancyra or Ulus being built on steep hills.

I became a little confused about the picture, and I wondered whether Thomas had made a mistake. To which Stephen replied:]

Stephen: Then we shall forgive him! For even though I was born there, such accuracy has needed much accuracy in recall. Can you describe for me the village in which you were born, the meaning and the name of the village, and its geographical location? Thomas has done so.

[I thought I should check the meaning that Stephen gave for the name "Seletar" through Thomas, in trance. He pronounced it *sell*-e-tar..

In Liddell and Scott's *Lexicon* 1867, there is listed the word σηλια "selia" untranslated, with reference to an Attic form of the word τηλια meaning "any flat board, tray or table with a raised rim or edge". As the Greek for "four" is "tessares" = τεσσαρες or "tettares"= τετταρες I thought that we might not get confirmation for "tar" meaning "fourth", but the writer Amphis in 335 AD uses the root "ταρ" = tar- = "four". Anything of course can happen with dialectical forms. "Tar-" could have been used in the local version of Koine Greek; "board with raised edges" could have acquired an extended meaning of "landing-stage".]

153. A cross-correspondence with "Stephen"*

A member of our group at that time was Michael McGaw. Michael had not been present at the Stephen-session where we spoke of Tom's spiritual receiving with regard to Stephen's biography, and when Michael spoke to me, he had just received the transcript of the session. It appeared that a week before, just about the time that this information concerning Stephen's life was coming into Tom's mind, Michael had felt inspired to write a science-fiction story. It was about an extra-terrestrial race of "Thracians", inhabiting a planet on another solar system, whose technical advances were similar to our own, with one striking difference: and that was that the Messiah, Jesus Christ, had not made himself known there. The main character of that other world was a man called "Stenen", medium-tall, blue-black hair, steel-blue eyes, and the colour of which was considered a mutation that was unfavourable, with the consequence that he was an outcast.

The exact parallels are clear: Thracian, Stenen, main character, outcast = stoned. "Colour of eyes unfavourable mutation" could be seen as parallel to Stephen's seeing of the spirit, causing him to be stoned. And we can note the coinciding with Tom's receiving.

At a meeting of our group Michael McGaw's writing aroused great interest.

154. The possibility that Stephen and his parents came to Judaea because they were sympathisers with the Essenes.

Stephen agreed that he was a Galatian. But it is known that he was martyred outside Jerusalem. How was it that he travelled to Judaea? No one knows, of course. It is possible that Stephen was with his parents on their way to becoming pious settlers in Jerusalem, so that they could be close to the Temple. Foreign Jews often did this so that they could participate in the Temple worship. It is possible that Stephen journeyed to Palestine alone or with other companions. No one knows. But we have a question to consider. Stephen said that those Greek words had been spoken to Joseph the father of Jesus, and, in another context, that Joseph was an *Essene*.(Sections 30, 142 and 157) Which kind of Essenes, though? It should be remembered that Joseph was *married* to Mary: therefore they did not belong to the main body of celibate Essenes at Qumran by the Dead Sea. On the contrary, it is clear from their *Zadokite document* that the married were in Essene "camps" both in towns and villages.[61]

155. Joseph and Mary as Essenes.

I have quoted Stephen as saying that in addition to Joseph and Mary, some of the disciples of Jesus had belonged to the Essenes, and this is also the opinion of a number of New Testament scholars. Kittler pointed out something very interesting, that Joseph and Mary then would have belonged to a sect that expected a *Messiah to come from their own midst*. It would not therefore have seemed incredible to Mary, that an angel should announce to her that she would become mother to the Messiah, who in turn was connected with Mary and Joseph, and the Essene community.

At Heading 30 reference is made to the time when Stephen had said that he, Joseph and Mary, and also Judas, belonged to the same spiritual group. At the time I took this to mean, "belong spiritually together". But perhaps he also meant that they had been all together amongst people who had been connected with the Essenes.

156. The Essenes in general.

In his *A history of Christianity*,[62] Paul Johnson notes that "Palestine Judaism was not a unitary religion but a collection of sects... as many as twenty-four."

"The Essenes did not recognize the Temple... and they were agreed to be the purest and strictest sects."

"The Essenes existed for 150 years by the time of Jesus' birth – they wanted a theocratic state and to purify the Temple – but by going to Qumran (near the Dead Sea) they opened Judaism to universalism by making the physical location less important"

"There arose a new idea that the Temple is not the building, but the worshippers"

"The Essenes...developed the regular practice of a sacral meal of bread and wine..." [It has been termed a "Messianic Feast service"]

"The Essenes were incredibly intolerant. They had a war plan and were an extremist apocalyptic-eschatalogical[63] sect, who expected their triumph to come soon."

"The individual is nothing; the pure community (and a community of birth and race) is all."

There is some information to begin with. They were the "purest and strictest of sects", "incredibly intolerant", and exclusive. But there is much more of interest that we shall explore in due course.

157. Putting detail into our picture.

Quite early in our conversations with Stephen, I asked him whether I had been present at the time of our Lord, and he said Yes. He said that he and others had been members of a (presumably reincarnational) group at that time. Once I asked;:

Michael: I would like to ask you, Who are in my group? Can you tell me that?

Stephen: I for one, Mary for another, Joseph. for another, a relatively small number, but then we are discussing a group in physical terms [for which I am the memory]"

On another occasion I asked Stephen more specifically::

Michael: Could you confirm my supposed receiving that Thomas had belonged to the Essenes when he wore the personality of Joseph?

Stephen: The body of Joseph was indeed connected with those that believed as the Essenes did.

Michael: And Mary, Jesus' mother, also belonged to the Essenes?

Stephen: It is the case that this was so.

[Thus, if we accept the accuracy of Stephen's words, then (1) Joseph and Mary were Essenes (2) Stephen implies that he and the version of myself alive at that time were also Essenes. (3) As the words are in Stephen's own dialect and, as he was an Essene, then it is reasonably certain that it was he who spoke those Greek words to Joseph, prior to being received into their particular Essene group.

If that is true, then we can arrive at the right translation.. The key is the word *boro*. Professor Robin Bond, whose help I have acknowledged earlier, has pointed out that it has a second meaning, namely, *"with the juice of the freshly pressed grape".*

To try another translation: *"For the Celt, wherefore, two years having passed, mark you, for the Celt, with the juice of the freshly pressed grape of the Lenaïa [a Dionysian festival of the newly pressed grape, in fact] wine shall be diluted."*

But why should grape-juice be diluted "for the Celt"? They were such odd words. And especially odd, it would appear, if spoken to Jewish Essene Joseph. Plainly one cannot get drunk on grape-juice, so there is no need for dilution. Moreover what had the grape-juice of the Lenaïa to do with Joseph and the Essenes?

In 1995 I was thinking about this grape-juice, also called "must", and had the conundrum on my mind, when a friend lent me Glenn D. Kittler's: *Edgar Cayce on the Dead Sea Scrolls* in a Swedish translation printed in 1978. Kittler's preface helped me connect "Lenaïka [pertaining to the Lenaïa] and the must" with "Essenes".]

158. The Essenes' expectation of a Messiah with their Messianic Feast (like a Communion service):

Firstly, as stated, Kittler pointed out that the Essenes expected to produce a Messiah from their own number, and that one of their women members would be mother to the Messiah or *Christ*. ("Messiah" is Aramaic, "Christ" is Greek, and means "The Anointed One." Later, Christians were to confine the word "Messiah" to Jesus Christ, the Saviour. But before His birth, the Essenes could envisage a number of Messiahs or "Christs".)

Then Kittler describes the Essene Messianic Feast: [and I translate back into English]:

[Page 110] So it is quite clear that the Essenes expected to find a Messiah from amongst their own number. Moreover they were expecting a Messiah to come very soon. It was clear that they expected that he would be a layman, a royal Messiah, a worldly leader, and of the house of David. This is quite evident in their *Manual of Discipline* - namely in the part that deals with rituals at mealtimes. It is always the priest who blesses the bread and *the must* [or grape juice, new wine, (which we have been associating with the Lenaïa) which the priest *dilutes*], and who first partakes. Even with a Messianic feast, even in the presence of the Messiah, it was still the priest who pronounced the blessing, and who first partook of the bread and must. Only then was the Messiah served and the others.[64]

Stephen is quoting Greek words spoken to Aramaic speaking Joseph (who may well have been familiar with Greek. He has to find a Greek word for the ceremony involving grape juice. The Lenaïa with its grape juice is a close parallel. The best analogy, surely. And it would apply also to the annual Festival of the Grape Juice of the Essenes. (They had three main feasts, each separated by a "Pentecost" of fifty days, and one of these feasts was the feast of the *New Wine or Must*. Truly, New Wine was an idea central to the Essenes. Joseph in his language would have used the words "yayin hadash" or "mô'ed hattîrôs")

[See Joseph A. Fitzmyer: in his *Responses to 101 Questions on the Dead Sea Scrolls:* London: Geoffrey Chapman, 1992 (p.74) '"mention is made of tîrôsh, "must, fresh wine"' He implies that the "new wine" may be taken as meaning "must".'

(p.75) 'In 11Q *Temple* the Feast of New Wine (19:14) mentions *yayin hadash*, lit. "new wine," but later on it is called *mô'ed hattîrôs*, "Feast of Must". (43:8-9)

'The use of this calendar is also confirmed by the regulations for the sacrifices given in the Feast-Day Calendar of 11QTemple 13:8-30:2, according to which we learn that the community also celebrated feasts not recognized by other Jews. '[p.86]

'What is striking here is the celebration of three Pentecosts: the Pentecost of Wheat, the Pentecost of Wine, and the Pentecost of Oil, each clearly marked as "fifty days" from the preceding feast, beginning with the Sheaf Waving or First Fruits of Barley. Pentekoste is the Greek name for the "fiftieth" day, which the LXX [Septuagint translation] of *Tobit* 2:1 describes as "the sacred (festival) of the Seven Weeks." Its post biblical Aramaic name was 'asarta ', or in Greek Asartha, as used by Josephus (*Antiquities*. 3.10.6 § 252), which means "(the feast of) the Gathering" or "Assembly." It was to be fifty days from Passover, but reckoned according to Lev 23:15-16, "from the morrow after the sabbath (mim-mohorat hassabbat), from the day that you brought the sheaf of the wave offering: seven full weeks shall they be, counting fifty days to the morrow of the seventh sabbath." (pages 86-87)]

This brings us back to a study of our translation of Stephen's Greek words, i.e. *For this reason, for the Carnyx/Celtic trumpet/Celt, two years having passed, for the Carnyx,(mark you) with the juice of the freshly pressed grape, (as in the Dionysian Lenaia festival) the wine of the Messianic Feast shall be diluted.*

As already noted, Professor Bond had pointed out that *borós* could both mean "drunkard" or "*juice of pressed grapes, or must*". He suggested "Again, in the spirit of oracular/mystic utterances, a pun ambiguity may be intended". It is truly ambiguous: on the one hand, it is a fact that the Celts were seen as drunkards; and *borô /glutton* would be rubbing this in. On the other hand (still with likely uncomplimentary overtones with regard to the Celts) it does most likely refer to the juice of pressed grapes present at the scene when the words were spoken. In the latter case *borô/grape juice* would fit in nicely with the two words that follow: *"Zélai Lenaïká/new wine of the Essene Messianic Feast.".*

This allows a translation that makes much better sense:

For this reason, for the Celt, two years [of the Novitiate] having passed, for this reason, for the Celt, with the juice of the pressed grape, the new wine of the Messianic Feast [seen as parallel to the Lenaia] shall be diluted.

It seems strange that Stephen used a Thracian word for "wine" in this Judean context. Perhaps it was so natural for him that he was unaware that "*zélai*"/"wine" would not be understood. Perhaps he knew Joseph well, and had used the word before in his presence.

159. Stephen as a novice, and his acceptance as an Essene

When Stephen was speaking of his youth, he mentioned that he was fourteen years old, when J esus was crucified. That would be one year after Stephen would by custom have become a religious adult. But children and teenagers could never be classed as Essenes. If Stephen had wished to join the Essenes, he could have begun a novitiate at the age of eighteen and been accepted at the age of twenty.

"At the age of twenty years (he shall be) enrolled" (*Rule of the Congregation* l, 8-9, 1QSa) and only "at the age of twenty-five years he may take his place among the foundations (i.e. the officials) of the holy congregation to work in the service of the congregation" (ibid., l, 12-13). In addition, "No boy or woman shall enter their camps, from the time they march out of Jerusalem to war until they return" (*War Rule* VII, 3-4).[65]

I have taken Stephen's Greek words as implying that he would have just completed a "novitiate" of two years [*two years having passed*] and that he had been accepted as a full member of the Essenes. Nothing else makes sense of the "two years".

The Qumran *Manual of Discipline* vi,13-23, as summarised in *A guide to the scrolls* by A.R.C.Leaney and others[66] gives details of what was required of such a novice.

A novice had to spend a year of probation, before he was publicly examined. If he passed the test he was allowed to live within the community and to share food with those members who belonged to the lower orders of the group. After another probationary period and passing a second test, he could then join the community as a full member, and at last was allowed to share food* with even those members called *rabbim* who constituted a 'council of elders'**. Their standing was the highest in the group, and from them were chosen three priests and twelve lay members in whose hands was the supreme administration of the group.

Cf. *Of postulants and novices* vi,13-23 : "If any man in Israel wish to be affiliated to the formal congregation of the community, the superintendent of the general membership is to examine him as to his intelligence and his actions and, if he then embark on a course of training, he is to have him enter into a covenant to return to the truth and turn away from all perversity. Then he is to apprise him of all the rules of the community. §Subsequently, when that man comes to present himself to the general membership, everyone is to be asked his opinion about him, and his admission to or rejection from the formal congregation of the community is to be determined by general

---

* Heb. Original is "drink". This agrees with Stephen's Greek words implying *"now that the novitiate is over, let the unfermented wine be mixed."*
** This sharing of food or drink implies taking part in the Essene Messianic Feast with the *rabbim* and the priests.

vote. §No candidate, however, is to be admitted to the formal state of purity enjoyed by the general membership of the community until, at the completion of a full year, his spiritual attitude and his performance have been duly reviewed. Meanwhile he is to have no stake in the common funds. §After he has spent a full year in the midst of the community, the members are jointly to review his case, as to his understanding and performance in matters of doctrine. If it then be voted by the opinion of the priest and the majority of their co-covenanters to admit him to the sodality, they are to have him bring with him all his property and the tools of his profession. . . §Not until the completion of a second year among the members of the community is the candidate to be admitted to the common board [Hebr. "drink"] When, however, the second year has been completed, he is to be subjected to a further review by the general membership, and, if it then be voted to admit him to the community, he is to be registered in the due order of rank which he is to occupy among his brethren in all matters pertaining to doctrine, judicial procedure, degree of purity and share in the common funds. Thenceforth his counsel and judgment are to be at the disposal of the community." *The Scriptures of the Dead Sea Sect in English Translation.* Translation, Introduction and Notes by Theodore H. Gaster. 1957. pp. 60-61]

160. We can now try yet another translation:

"Therefore, for the Celt, now that the two years [of the novitiate] have passed, for the Celt (mark you) with the juice of pressed grapes, let's dilute the new wine of the Messianic Feast [with water.]"

161. The village community that Stephen would have joined.

If Stephen were in fact joining with Joseph and Mary, he would have been joining a village community. It may be of interest to learn about such communities.

This is what Magen Broshi writes in his paper, *Village Essenes*:

"For a village Essene matters were less rigid but many requirements were the same as those for the monastic order. Both branches considered themselves the true Israel; followed the Zadokite priesthood—every group of ten or more had to include a priest; partook of a common meal; arranged themselves in a strict hierarchy; insisted on a correct interpretation and strict adherence to the Laws of Moses; swore to uphold the New Covenant; followed a solar calendar precisely so as not to deviate from his [Moses'?] appointed times, including holding an annual congregation.

The children of any Jew (those who had entered the covenant granted to all Israel forever) could become an Essene by swearing an oath on their reaching twenty—the age of enrolment. Before then nothing of the statutes was to be revealed to them. Particular rules for village Essenes were given in the Damascus Rule and the Rule of the Congregation, or the Messianic Rule as Vermes has renamed it.

Members had to cleave to the laws of Moses; the Mebaqqer of the camp or village community was its head, its teacher and its director; he allowed commerce with the impure and the imperfect but had absolute power over it, permitting no casual contacts; temple sacrifice was permitted and demanded absolute ritual purity; full maturity was reached according to the Rule of the Congregation only at the age of 30; observance of the Sabbath was strict, the rule expressly forbidding the picking and eating of fruits from the fields; members were not allowed to bear witness in the courts of the gentiles —the Romans. The punishment was death but since the Community had no powers of capital punishment it is plain that expulsion was meant. Expulsion was eternal death, but for a strict Essene was often physical death too.

Note that village Essenes brought up in an Essene community were not considered mature until the age of thirty, the age at which Jesus was baptized. No Jewish priest was allowed to enter office until he was thirty years old and the Essenes were a priestly sect.

Village Essenes, unlike the monastic variety, owned their own property. Instead of holding goods in common they donated two days' wages a month into a common fund to provide for orphans, the old and needy and widows. The Community whether in the monastery or the camps was bonded by a common meal. Only the perfect were allowed to partake of it and in particular to partake of the 'new wine' which is to say the unfermented grape juice of the congregation." [67]

This completes our investigation of the puzzling Greek words that Stephen originally spoke through the mouth of Thomas Ashman. A careful reader might rightly complain that there is speculation here. We cannot check with Stephen and ask "Did you mean this or that?" "Were they actually your words to Joseph?" "Were the words actually spoken in the context we suspect?" Unless we could ask these quesstions, we cannot have certainty. On the other hand, the words are correct grammar, can bear the meaning we ascribe to them, and they *do* fit if we believe Stephen when he says they were known to Essene Joseph.

162. Why were these words so memorable?

If in fact Stephen is quoting words that he himself said to Joseph they will have been words of huge emotional impact, and, as such, truly unforgettable. Here is Greek-speaking Stephen with mixed Celtic-Jewish ancestry actually gaining acceptance and membership of a group of Essenes in Judaea, in spite of their racism, and their despising of foreign born Jews. He is gaining acceptance after a two year initiation. He is speaking those words to the father of Jesus, the Jesus in whose cause, Stephen is to be martyred.

Truly unforgettable indeed.

Chapter 2

Stephen's Ministry and Martyrdom

163. Stephen's Greek fits one situation only: that he was about to be received as a full member of the Essenes..

We know the rules that governed the lives of Essene communities. If the Essene community to which Stephen belonged kept to these rules, then we have quite a clear impression of the religious structure in which he would have lived.

If we can agree that Stephen's Greek words were repeating what he had said to Joseph almost 2000 years ago, then it seems that he was joining the Village Essenes, perhaps at the earliest age possible, the age of twenty. Stephen said he was fourteen years old when Jesus was crucified. Five years later, at the age of nineteen, he said he began to "receive" and become aware of Divine guidance. We might guess that his family had migrated to Palestine, and that perhaps they had become village Essenes themselves.

Scholars do paint differing pictures of the Essenes. The possibility has been raised that they were like our contemporary Catholic Church, with its monasteries and convents, its priesthood, its communion service, but also with its ordinary members. If Stephen had Essene parents, he could have recognized the crucified Jesus as the Messiah, without ceasing to be a practising Essene. After all the apostles in Jerusalem continued in their own form of Judaism, including worship at the Temple. Stephen could have been martyred for his faith in the Risen Christ, while still being an Essene. It is indeed true that members of Essene group had rules of strict obedience to the leader, but perhaps Stephen had sufficient learning, and spiritual authority to be given his head. Essenes were human and probably different from community to community in their practices. We may recall that Stephen said that he was nearly twenty-two years old when he was martyred.

164. What St. Luke has to say about Stephen.

Luke writes in *Acts 6.1* that "some time later" after the coming of the Holy Spirit (was this months or even years?) there was a quarrel between Greek-speaking and native Jews about the care of Greek widows. Luke says that the apostles after due process selected Stephen and six others for this work. Stephen was no newcomer, but, as he himself implies, he was personally known to the father of the Messiah. (The confusing thing however, is that there is no mention of Stephen working for the widows. It is clear that he was an evangelist, doing what the apostles do.)

From St Luke's *Acts of the Apostles*, Chapter 6, it is clear that Stephen has accepted Jesus as the Messiah and Saviour. Whether or not he had broken with the Essenes, we do not know, but he is described as an evangelist for the risen Christ, preaching with great power. There are hints in the Acts story though, that he was a leader of a group of followers of Christ who were not in agreement with the rest of the Jerusalem Christians, who continued worshipping in the temple like all other Jews.

These are words said to have been spoken by Stephen shortly before he was stoned: *Acts 7.48-50* "However, the Most High does not live in houses made by men: as the prophet says, "Heaven is my throne and earth my footstool. What kind of house will you build for me, says the Lord; where is my resting–place? Are not all these things of my own making?" . . .

These sentiments would be in line with Essene belief.

Acts 11.19-21 seems to imply that he was a leader of a group of evangelists[68]. He seems to have been opposed to the church of the Judaean Christians in Jerusalem, headed by James, the brother of Jesus, Peter and John. Paul makes no reference to Stephen, in his own writings. We may guess that Stephen had his own version of the Gospel, tinged with an Essenism modified by a thorough universalism. As a Hellenistic Jew, brought up in a land far distant from Israel, it would be hard for him to have had too parochial a God.

165. Thomas Ashman's Intuitions about Stephen's Life and Ministry, discussed with Stephen.

The group of us who met regularly to hear and question Stephen, had been focusing on his earthly life. Tom Ashman, in private meditation, intuited the statements printed *in italics*. For convenience I present each of *Thomas' intuitions* interspersed with the comments that Stephen made at a later date.

Tom: Stephen knew from his receivings that Jesus was the Messiah.

Stephen: I am aware of the questions that you would ask. In general, the details of "Stenen" (Stephen) would be correct, although the importance of these details is slight. The intention of Thomas, I feel sure, was that, as with himself and others, others of us could associate a little and know a little. The book you write is not a biography of those associated together. The book is to convey to others what we have come to know so that they may examine this knowledge also. But pray, do clarify in your mind the other details, for by now I feel that these details will have aroused much curiosity.

Michael: Indeed they have!

Stephen: I perceive Thomas to say that he would wish it.

Thomas: He travelled to and joined the Christians at Sardis.

If his starting point were Ancyra, then it is a fact that there was a good main road between Ancyra and Sardis on the West Coast of Asia Minor.

Thomas: His receivings became known at the nearby church of Thyatira [a day's journey from Sardis by the direct route north] where the disciple Joseph known as Barnabas or "son of a prophet" taught on several occasions.

These last two statements cannot be confirmed from Scripture, but are possibly accurate for three reasons:

Although New Testament chronologies are constructed from particular dates that are reasonably well accepted, nevertheless there is controversy. C.H. Turner, who wrote in the five volume Hastings *Dictionary of the Bible*, put the crucifixion at 29 AD, and Stephen's martyrdom and Paul's conversion at 36 AD These dates agree with Stephen's words, that he was 14 when Jesus was crucified, say, in AD 29).

I have presented reasons for thinking that Stephen turned from the Essenes to be the follower of Jesus, after the resurrection. But he may have stayed an Essene, while still believing Jesus to be the Messiah. Stephen agrees that he became "an active receiver at the age of nineteen", presumably meaning that he became an active receiver of personal revelation. Presumably this marked the beginning of his capacity for inspired preaching. In short, Stephen had perhaps three years in which to preach, either in or near Jerusalem, or in Asia Minor. He would have used the Greek language, abroad, perhaps without reference to the Jerusalem church.

Joseph Barnabas, is mentioned in Acts 4:36-7. A Greek-speaker, like Stephen, he was nicknamed "Son of Exhortation" or more accurately "Son of the Prophet" or "the Prophetic One" by the apostles. Shortly after the Pentecost, the occasion of the coming of the Holy Spirit upon the apostles, he sold an estate and gave the money to the apostles. We know that after Paul's conversion, he preached the gospel both together with him, and separately. He seemed from the first to have formed a high opinion of Paul's ability and energy, and it was he who sought him out in Antioch (*Acts* 11.25), and seems to have formed a special friendship with him. The two lived in close fellowship with the congregation in Antioch for two years. Such being the "prophetic one", it is not at all impossible that he could have been in Thyatira prior to Paul's conversion.

The receiving seems to say that Stephen had preached or prophesied in Sardis, and his prophecies became known in Thyatira, where Barnabas also preached. I have already noted S.G.F. Brandon's view, supported by words in *Acts* 11 that Stephen was actually leading a movement of his own, and had fellow evangelists who continued their work after Stephen's death.

Earlier I recalled how Stephen has said that he had been in his fifteenth year when Jesus was crucified. From the book of Acts we do get the impression that Stephen could have been stoned to death perhaps even in the same year that Jesus was crucified, perhaps 29 or 30 AD, which is how the scholar Harnack, for example, took it. But if Stephen had in fact been accepted as an Essene at the age of 20, that date would be impossible.

[A weakness in this possible chronology is that in Essene *monasteries* one could not become a full member so early. We have no information about the rules in *camps* where families lived together. The rules for families may well have been less demanding.]

Other inconsistencies are found in Acts (7:54-60). There we are told that Saul, later called Paul, watched the stoning of Stephen, and even held the cloaks of those doing the stoning. Further, the *Acts* story suggests that the example that Stephen gave in dying, would have been in Saul's mind at least after his vision of Christ on the road to Damascus. If one accepted the Bible picture we might imagine that the crucifixion, stoning, and Paul's conversion all happened in the same year.

In contrast, biblical scholars, Biblical scholars, like Ramsay and Lightfoot, put Stephen's death at 33 or 34 AD. Even this theory does not square with Stephen's words, for he would still have only been 18 or 19 at the time of his death.

The choice of dates of C.H. Turner, namely, that Jesus was crucified in CE 29 or 30 and Paul.s conversion took place in CE 35 or 36 support Stephen's claim that he was 14 when Jesus was crucified in say CE 29. [69] and Stephen's martyrdom and Paul's conversion at 36 CE. This would make Stephen aged 21, at his death.

166. Stephen on his Martyrdom.

Stephen's own words, in reply to my questioning, were consistent with this dating. At the same time he said a most surprising thing.

Michael: "When was Paul converted?[70] When you were 21?" - a backhanded way of asking Stephen when he had died. I think I could not quite bring myself to refer to his martyrdom directly.

Stephen: I was not present at Paul's conversion.

Michael: Your dreadful day had occurred... when? Were you 21 on the day that you died?

Stephen: I was late in my 21st year, and soon it would have been my 22nd. I believe four days separated that occurrence from the date that I would celebrate my birth. The timing was considerably bad!

The conversion of Paul, and I understand your meaning of conversion, on the road to Damascus, would precede my 22nd birthday by several months, fifteen in all.

Michael: It is said that Paul was much influenced by what led up to your own witness for the Lord [your martyrdom]; but I would understand you to say that he had been spoken to by our Lord before your own witness.

Stephen: I would indeed, be sure of this. It is not to my knowledge, and I have doubt in my mind, that Paul had any association with the events prior to the celebration of my birthday. You see, Michael, I refuse to die!

[The Bible story in Acts is so definite that Paul was consenting in Stephen's murder, and had not yet seen the vision of Christ on the road to Damascus. Either the Acts story or Stephen's words are mistaken.
S.G.F. Brandon was inclined not to accept the Acts version. He wrote:

"The nature of Paul's participation is singularly passive and artificial, and, as we have seen, there is good reason to doubt its historicity. However it has an important function in the narrative of the Acts, being clearly employed to introduce a portrait of Paul as the most notorious persecutor of the church." ... "a later attempt to connect Paul to the protomartyr Stephen, and was probably made in ignorance of the direct contradiction it thus constituted to Paul's own explicit statement in the Galatian Epistle that he was unknown personally to the Palestinian Christians until some three years after his conversion." *The Fall of Jerusalem and the Christian Church*, SPCK 1951.] pp.89-92

Chapter 3

Additional Articles

167. How much can we rely on the historical accuracy of *The Acts of the Apostles*?

It is plain from a study of Acts that we have on the one hand the original Christian church in Jerusalem, headed by James and Peter. On the other we have the churches founded by Paul. We note that there are several references to antagonism between the Jerusalem church and the movement begun by Paul. Luke, the author of Acts is writing after 70 AD when the original Jerusalem church was massacred along with the rest of the population, by the Romans. Thus Luke, a companion of Paul, in the latter part of his journeys, is writing history from the point of view of the surviving Christians, the Gentile followers of Paul. It is a history written for the edification of the Pauline churches, and after the actual events. Luke's memory may serve him well when he recounts the times that he accompanied Paul on his missionary journeys, but accounts of earlier events are likely to contain historical fiction, a probable example being the putting of Paul at the place of Stephen's martyrdom. F.J. Foakes-Jackson remarks that determining sources of historical information in the New Testament is largely guesswork.

"It was the practice of ancient historians. . . to tell part of their narrative by means of speeches put into the mouth of the chief actors, and it seems that they did not intend their readers to believe that these were other than their own compositions."

Thus Stephen's speech at the trial would be such a composition. If the composition conveys any true impression of his words, and it well may, then we would gather that (1) he expressed hostility to the Jewish church in Jerusalem (2) that he nevertheless regarded the law as perfect: "you who got the law the angels transmitted, and have not obeyed it!" (This would also differentiate him from Paul, who regarded the law as good, but having no saving power. It could characterise Stephen as an Essene.)

Similarly, Luke has the contradictory story, on the one hand that Stephen was appointed by the Apostles for social work amongst Greek speaking widows, but on the other that Stephen "full of grace and power, began to work great miracles". Luke says that Stephen argued for the faith against other Hellenistic Jews who "could not hold their own against the inspired wisdom with which he spoke." (6:8-10)

Following clues given by Luke, S.G.F. Brandon (op.cit.p.161) writes:

"It would consequently appear that the movement of which Stephen was the most notable champion was one which was distinctly separate from that of the original community and its followers, and was even distinguished by a certain amount of hostility to Jewish Christianity, with its continuing attachment to the national cultus. What was the exact significance of the new movement it is impossible to determine on the evidence available, but it should be noted that Paul in all his disputes with the Jewish Christians, so far as they have been recorded in his extant writings, never once invokes the example of Stephen in support of his own cause." [71]

168. Scholars' thoughts on Stephen as an Essene.

An interesting paper by the Rev. Peter J. Blackburn discusses the likelihood of Stephen being an Essene. He draws on the work of a number of notable scholars[72]. Amongst the points raised, is the fact that Stephen's speech about the spiritual history of Israel as recorded in *Acts 7* is very similar to a history in *Hebrews 11*.

"The feature of Stephen's speech and of Heb. 11. . . is their eschatological progression. The examples of hard-heartedness move forward to a signal example of faith in the faith of Christ who is in fact the author and finisher of faith. This eschatological [*having to do with the Second Coming*] note is in keeping with the Qumran [*Essene*] literature, though in Qumran exegesis historical significance seems to be lost in eschatological fulfillment. In Heb. 11 they are kept together." [73]

Johnson once more: "The Essenes did not recognize the Temple.. and they were agreed to be the purest and strictest sects."

Blackburn writes: "The relation between the Fourth Gospel and the Hellenists is seen in the *spiritual approach to worship* in the discourse with the Samaritan woman (Jn 4.20-24). This is parallel to the attitude of Stephen, . . .

Cullmann considers that Stephen asserts that the *construction of the Temple was the height of Israel's resistance to the divine law* (Acts 7.47ff)." ....Another similarity of Stephen to the Essenes.

And a further one would be *universalism.* Johnson again: "by going to Qumran (near the Dead Sea) they opened Judaism to universalism by making the physical location less important". See Acts 7.49: "Heaven is my throne, and earth is my footstool: what house will you build me? saith the Lord: or what is the place of my rest?"

Many other points are made, but suffice it to say that numbers of scholars see a possible connection between Stephen and the Essenes. Scholarship supports rather than otherwise, what our own evidence shows, that Stephen had been an Essene. [See endnote 68 at the beginning of this section.]

These scholars assume that Acts 7 gives an accurate picture of what Stephen thought, and what he is reported as saying before his martyrdom. It may do so, but in the absence of stenographers, Luke, the author of *Acts*, must have been reconstructing a speech which he believed to be in line with his understanding of Stephen's thinking. As previously suggested, there seems to be some scholarly agreement, that sometimes Luke is accurate, and that sometimes his writing is fictional - the story of St Paul being present at Stephen's martyrdom being an instance.

The primary interest here of course is the revelation of Spirit that has been coming through the Stephen experience. Our research into Stephen's Greek words has uncovered many mutually confirming facts, giving us glimpses into Stephen's earthly life. We have also shown that detective work of scholars into matters relating to Stephen's life, has produced a picture consistent with our own.

169. How it may have been with the Holy Family.
(Joseph and Mary, and the brothers of Jesus)

Joseph. Stephen's words that he had said were "known" to Joseph were in Greek. This would indicate that Joseph, an Aramaic speaker, was no simple carpenter, but an educated person. The tone of these words might imply that Joseph was well aware of the Celtic reputation in Asia Minor.. His world was by no means confined to his village, but through his Greek, would have a much wider world. The words imply at least that Joseph and Mary were members of a small Essene village. No doubt he, amongst others, had the power to say yes or no, to Stephen becoming an Essene.

To say that Joseph was a carpenter ("τεκτον"/ "a craftsman in wood"), has no bearing on whether or not he had standing, and was well educated. It can be noted that the second son of Joseph and Mary, James, had sufficient Greek to write the *Epistle of James*, retained in the New Testament. James was at least bilingual, an accomplished writer, and had the ability to lead the Christian church, after the crucifixion of Jesus. If James had this education, surely the first born, Jesus, plainly also with leadership ability, would have been similarly educated, and bilingual.[74]

After all, St Paul, obviously highly educated, was a tent-maker, and of course was highly educated. Everyone in those days had to earn a living somehow.

What about Jesus then? Did he simply explode on the world like a supernova, or did he have an Essenic grounding at the hands of his parents, as well as others? With what education behind him, did Jesus converse with the learned people in the temple, at the age of twelve?

(*Luke 2:46-7* AV: And it came to pass, that after three days they found him in the temple, sitting in the midst of the doctors, both hearing them and asking them questions. And all that heard him were astonished at his understanding and answers.)

Think of other great religious leaders, such as Martin Luther. As a Catholic monk, he was very well educated. From that basis, he emerged as a reformer who changed the face of much of Europe. So our thesis here, is that Joseph and Mary were parents of standing and education amongst the Essenes, and it was from the starting point of their upbringing that Jesus developed into a reformer, a Messiah, bearing witness to the universal love of the Father.

Education in the Holy Family, yes. And there would have been strife also, as we shall see.

Edward H. Sugden[75] gives a succinct summary of what is known of the Holy Family:

"Joseph was a "just man" (Mt.1:19), i.e. a strict observer of the Law; the names of his children are those of the forefather of his race, and of three of the patriarchs; and they were doubtless brought up in the atmosphere of rigorous Judaism. Along with Mary they regarded the early ministry of Jesus with suspicion and sought to restrain him (Mt. 12:47 Mk.3:20-33). They did not believe in him (Jn.7:5), and therefore cannot have been amongst his apostles. Hence on the cross Jesus committed the care of his mother, not to them, but to the apostle John (Jn.19:26). After his resurrection Jesus appeared to James (1 Cor.15:7), and resulting in the latter's conversion, so that he and his brothers immediately associated themselves with the apostles (Acts1:14). [James'] character and his relationship to our Lord secured for him the leadership of the church in Jerusalem... There can be little hesitation in claiming him as the ...author [of the Epistle of James]"

The scriptural passages that Sugden cites state that Jesus' brothers, and presumably Joseph, remained committed to the old beliefs, until after the crucifixion and resurrection of Jesus.

It has been noted that Mary initially withheld recognition of Jesus as Messiah. *John's Gospel* depicts her (later,) apparently accepting him, at the Wedding at Cana[76]. As an Essene, she could indeed accept the possibility of giving birth to a Messiah. And the story of the Annunciation, her vision of the angel, may be true. Perhaps it was that the ministry of Jesus did not conform to the messianic beliefs of the Essenes that made it initially impossible for her to accept his Messiahship. If *John's* testimony is accepted that Mary* and John the beloved disciple were at the foot of the cross, we still notice the absence of her other children, and her husband Joseph. We notice that Jesus is concerned for her welfare, and asks John to treat Mary as his mother, and John to be seen as her son. It would appear that Joseph and his other sons had cast Mary out of the family. The Essene communities were so strict and exclusive, that this is how they would behave. And it must have been a great grief to Jesus, to be rejected too.

---

* Mary is not present in *Mt. 27:55-6, Mk.15:40, Lk. 23:49* amongst numbers of women followers present at the crucifixion. In *Jn* 19:25 Jesus' mother, his mother's sister and John are present. There is always scholarly controversy as to which parts of the synoptic gospels (*Matthew, Mark and Luke*) and *John* are historical. *Matthew* and *Luke* are dependent on *Mark. John* is independent, but written still later, possibly containing memories of the apostle John. There seems to be some consensus that where *John* differs from the synoptics, he may sometimes present a historical fact. In short all gospels agree about the absence of Joseph and the brothers of Jesus at the crucifixion. *John* alone places her there. Whichever the case, the truth still seems to be that Jesus was rejected by his own family.

If, as Stephen says, he was fourteen when Jesus was crucified, he may have turned to the risen Christ as the Messiah about the same time as the brothers of Jesus, after the appearance of Jesus to James. It may have been later. The first language of Jesus and James was Aramaic, whereas it was Greek with Stephen. Jesus and James were born in Palestine, Stephen in Galatia. Stephen was very much his own person, and had an understanding of Christ, which differed from the early Christians native to Jerusalem.

(As I pointed out earlier, Scripture is silent as to Joseph. My scenarios demand that he was alive one year before the crucifixion and perhaps several years afterwards. When he died, we do not know.)

Part Six

Some essays about the Stephen experience

170. The Testimony of the Perennial Philosophy: Michael Cocks.

Stephen talks about Reality from his point of view. Who else shares that point of view? The basic teachings of all the great religions have much in common. The philosopher Leibniz in the 1600's coined the phrase "the Perennial Philosophy" to describe such teachings. The term was popularised by Aldous Huxley in his book by that name (1945)

Here is a brief summary of the Perennial Philosophy. We can treat it as a kind of picture of what Stephen has been saying.

The Perennial Philosophy holds that our normal human identification with body and with mind contents is an error that induces us to fear death, suffer, and cause others to suffer. The remedy, variously called *enlightenment, liberation, or self-realisation* involves a deep shift of identification to the Ground itself. Huxley put it this way:

"The ground in which the multifarious and time-bound psyche is rooted is a simple, timeless awareness. By making us pure in heart and poor in spirit we can discover and be identified with this awareness. In the spirit we not only have, but are, the unitive knowledge of the divine Ground." [Huxley 1945, p. 29]

Ken Wilber (*op.cit.* p.161) characterises the philosophy thus: "'In the beginning' there is only Consciousness as Such, timeless, space-less, infinite and eternal. For no reason that can be stated in words, a subtle ripple is generated in this infinite ocean. This ripple could not in itself detract from infinity, for the infinite can embrace any and all entities. But this subtle ripple, awakening to itself, *forgets* the infinite sea of which it is just a gesture. The ripple therefore feels set apart from infinity, isolated, separate... This is not only the beginning of narcissism and the battle against death, it is a *reduced* or *restricted* view of consciousness, because no longer is the ripple one with the ocean, it is trying itself to be the ocean."

Compare *Genesis* 1:1-2: [King JamesVersion] "In the beginning God created the heaven and the earth, and the earth was without form and void, and darkness was upon the face of the deep".

Genesis 3 describes how human beings separated themselves from their oneness with the Creator, deciding what was right and wrong for themselves." See Jesus' prayer in *John* 17.21: "that they may all be one; as Thou Father, art in me, and I in Thee, that they may also be one in us", and *Ephesians* 4:6: "One God and Father of all, who is above all, and through all, and in you all."

Compare also Shankara (Founder of Vedanta): "Though One, Brahman is the cause of the many. There is no other cause. The Atman is that by which the universe is pervaded, but which nothing pervades; which causes all things to shine, but which other things cannot make to shine. It is ignorance which causes us to identify ourselves with the body, the ego, the senses, or anything that is not Atman."

Compare also Chuang Tzu (Taoism): "Do not ask whether the Principle is in this or in that; it is in all things. It is on this account that we apply to it the epithets of supreme, universal, total. All proceeds from it and is under its influence. It is in all things but is not identical with beings because it is neither differentiated nor limited."

The last two quotations are cited from Huxley's book. He quotes also a number of Christian mystics saying much the same thing.

The above quotations do represent part of Stephen's thought, but with one major exception:

> *Stephen:* "The ego is the product of your mind and its concepts.
> That mind, and that body, and those concepts,
> must also be of the Whole. Is this not so?
> For nothing can exist that is not part of the Whole.
> You have spoken of the dissipation of this ego
> and yet have not considered that this is also an instrument of the Whole. For we have spoken about the recording of experiences that are necessary for the Whole.

171. Definition of "Synchronicity".

We have already mentioned synchronicity. C.G. Jung coined the word, referring to "meaningful coincidence". Writers on synchronicity often refer to the sense of the numinous, the presence of the Divine, in such an event. The "Five-fives" events described in Part Two could be termed "Synchronicity". One way of describing this, is as a meaningful orchestration of several events from another dimension.

172. What some Quantum Mechanics theorists suggest.

The picture of reality of QM theorists has a much in common with that of the Perennial Philosophy, and that implied by the teachings of Stephen. Albert Einstein must be named, and his opponent Niels Bohr, together with Werner Heisenberg, Wolfgang Pauli, John Bell, Jack Sarfatti, David Bohm and others. The reality they depict is so much at odds with the old fashioned mechanistic world-view, that academic and practical physicists are often reluctant to accept it. There is wide acceptance nevertheless.

I have neither the space nor the competence, to give an accurate account of their theories and the experimental work on which they are based. The following does however give a clear impression of what their teaching implies.

173. Quotations from a summary of *Bohm's Gnosis*, by Beatrix Murrell:[77]

1. Any individual element [of totality] could reveal "detailed information about every other element in the universe"
2. "The unbroken wholeness of the totality of existence as an undivided flowing movement without borders"
3. Two subatomic particles that have once interacted can instantaneously "respond to each other's motions thousands of years later when they are light years apart." [Stephen: "The furthest sun is closer to you than your tongue" Section 79]
4. Space and time might actually be derived from an even deeper level of objective reality. This reality he calls the Implicate Order.
5. Within the Implicate Order everything is connected, and, in theory, any individual element could reveal information about every other element in the universe.
6. The Hologram is Bohm's favourite metaphor for conveying the structure of the Implicate Order. "Everything is enfolded into everything". The totality of the movement of enfoldment and unfoldment

may go immensely beyond what has revealed itself to our observations. We call this totality by the name "holomovement". This is the "fundamental ground of all matter" The holomovement is ground for both life and matter.

[Stephen said, two years before Bohm's work was published, "True life is all movement. The whole of life must be the whole of movement" Section 139]

7. "What is is always a totality of ensembles, all present together, in an orderly series of stages of enfoldment and unfoldment, which intermingle and interpenetrate each other in principle throughout the whole of space."

8. The individual is in total contact with the Implicate Order, the individual is part of the whole of humanity, and he is the "focus for something beyond humanity"

9. It is this collective consciousness of humanity that is truly significant for Bohm. It is this collective consciousness that is truly one and indivisible, and it is the responsibility of each human person to contribute towards this consciousness of humanity, this noösphere.

10. Bohm also believes that the individual will eventually be fulfilled upon the completion of cosmic noögenesis.

11. Intelligence has always been at the very core of the Implicate Order.

12. It will be ultimately misleading and indeed wrong to suppose... that each human being is an independent actuality who interacts with other human beings and with nature. Rather, all these are *projections of a single totality.*

Notwithstanding all this, it should be said that with Stephen it is primarily *experience* with which we have to do. Experience through his personality, his love, his poetry, his stories and parables, through experiences of meaningful coincidence that show us to be bound up with him in something greater.

The feelings that his teaching evokes, the challenges to us to turn our understandings on their head, the strange puzzles that he set that required the activity of a wider consciousness to solve. It is all this that is involved in our experience with Stephen. These other happenings seem designed to give us actual experience of what Stephen's words imply.

174. St. Stephen and Philosophy - Prof. Richard M. Cocks Ph.D.

Probably the most compelling aspect of Stephen is the warmth of his personality, his consistently loving attitude and the gentle humor that pervades what he says. Autobiographically, Stephen was important in helping me overcome what philosophers call the scientific world-view, accepting the reality of an afterlife, and interpreting Christianity in a way that I found congenial. Philosophically I found his teachings very impressive, combining as it does some of my most cherished ideas about life. In what follows I try to place Stephen in the context of Western thought.

To begin with the pre-Socratics, Stephen is similar to Heraclitus with his emphasis on growth, movement, and change. Heraclitus also says "Listening not to me but to the Logos it is wise to agree that all things are one." Stephen too recognizes the level of the relative, where we are each individuals confronting other individuals and the absolute in which we get the ultimate indivisibility of the divine.

More specifically, Stephen's account of reincarnation and knowledge as memory is Platonic in nature. In Book X of Plato's *Republic* is the Myth of Er in which a man of that name, being placed on the funeral pyre is found to be alive. He gives an account of the afterlife in which the dead are judged and are offered the opportunity to become incarnate once again. But before they do so, they must be immersed in the River of Lethe. *Lethe* means forgetfulness and *aletheia* is its opposite, to remember. Interestingly, it also means truth and reality which follows the Platonic doctrine that to know the truth, what is real, is to remember. Stephen's teachings concur with this and suggest that what we need to remember will be revealed to us. "Feel within, *recall* the knowledge which you have."

So, what are we remembering? What is this truth that we can re-discover? In the end perhaps, it is the holist's intuition that all is one. That separateness is an illusion. An illusion that is necessary perhaps for the possibility of experience, but one that can be dangerous if we forget that it is an illusion and act as though we are separate from other people and from nature. If all is one, how can competition be based on reality? How can there be not enough? And how can any part of God's creation be rejected? To reject one part is to reject all.

Corollaries to Stephen's teachings can also be found among the Stoics. Epictetus in particular suggests that events themselves are neutral. It is only our judgement of those events that leads us to consider them positively or negatively. In this case, no experience comes with a judgment already stamped upon it. So, consistent with the Christian dictum to judge not, Epictetus suggests that at the beginning of our education we still blame others for 'bad' things that happen to us. It represents progress if instead we blame ourselves for negative experiences and the end of our education is when we blame no one. Stephen also thinks that no one *has* to view any experience as bad and argues that Jesus' response to crucifixion was continued love and continued acceptance. He rejected nothing, neither the events, nor those whom we would call his persecutors, nor God, nor his destiny.

Stephen's notion of experience also has close similarities to the philosophy of John Dewey, a twentieth century holistic philosopher whom Sidney Hook called the American Buddha. Dewey views experience as an interaction between the 'organism' and the 'environment.' Experience represents a contribution from both. What this means for a Stoic is that control of the 'organism' is in principle sufficient to keep experience from becoming 'suffering,' or 'undesirable.' We cannot control external events, such as disease, death, poverty, or false accusations, however we can, in principle, choose our attitude to these events. For Stephen, if we refuse to deviate from a loving attitude, from acceptance (non-rejection), thus from reality, if in fact all is one, then no experience can be 'bad.'

This however, does not mean that Stephen is a quietist. He says: "The starving masses do starve because we in the West choose to let them starve. In that sense the sin of not recognizing their at-oneness with ourselves, as a product of the human mind, does cause or allow their suffering. It is not God as love that is responsible for their suffering. If they continue to love God, being able to bear the pain, they surely contribute in a striking manner to experience of God's love. God does not *need* this suffering - his love would be manifest anyway.

"It seems plausible to say that that which we may need may not be what our physical selves may want. That we may cry out that we are no longer loved when we in fact are."

Stephen's notion that the only sin is stagnation is also consistent with Dewey. Stephen says "Sin consists of attempts at 'stagnation,' or non-growth along the path set each one of us individually and corporately 'by the Father'." Dewey also rejects stagnation in the following passages.

"In . . . *The Dawn of Conscience* James Henry Breasted refers to Haeckel as saying that the question he would most wish to have answered is this: Is the universe friendly to man? The question is an ambiguous one. Friendly to man in what respect? With respect to ease and comfort, to material success, to egoistic ambitions? . . .Mr. Breasted's answer . . . is that nature has been friendly to the emergence and development of conscience and character. Those who will have all or nothing cannot be satisfied with this answer. Emergence and growth are not enough for them. They want something more than growth accompanied by toil and pain. They want final achievement [but] . . . morally speaking, growth is a higher value and ideal than is sheer attainment (55 - 56)."

"The live being recurrently loses and re-establishes equilibrium with its surroundings. The moment of passage from disturbance into harmony is that of intensest life" (*Art as Experience*, 17).

"Instead of signifying being shut up within one's own private feelings and sensations, [experience] signifies active and alert commerce with the world; at its height, it signifies complete interpenetration of self and the world of objects and events. Instead of signifying surrender to caprice and disorder, it affords our sole demonstration of a stability that is not stagnation but is rhythmic and developing (*ibid*, 19)."

Stephen also stresses the importance of feeling. "If you *feel*, it is much better, than being able to hold with the physical mind. For as some insight comes in, other insight may begin to escape you."

Dewey's philosophy gives enormous importance to feelings and rescues them from the dustbin of subjectivity to which the scientific revolution had relegated them.

For Dewey, emotions are not to be thought of as discrete states of mind with a "cognitive content." Instead, the idea is that a coherent experience involves a selection and arrangement of qualities of the world in an interactive stance. Emotions play a role in this selection and arrangement. The qualities selected and arranged are real, existential qualities of the world. For this reason, emotions reveal real aspects of the world that would otherwise not be noticed. For instance, if one is "in love," in a strong occurrent sense, one notices all the charms of one's loved one. The loved one's charming and lovable characteristics are noticed and selected. When one falls out of love, the same person's displeasing qualities may be noticed for the first time. Both emotions, love, and hatred due to betrayal, open up different contexts in which the person is revealed. The noticed qualities are never perceived as discrete and separate items, (although one might choose to *consider* them reflectively like that), but as features of people within a contextualized point of view.

Combining Dewey and Stephen one might say, as you feel so will you see. If you can feel love, then you will perceive God as manifest. A feeling reveals the world in a certain way. By feeling, we will perceive the loving interconnectedness of things, rather than merely accepting this as an intellectual doctrine. According to Stephen, we will then perceive truly.

Plato and Aristotle also emphasized the role of emotion in our lives. Both believed that children must be trained to take pleasure in virtue and to feel pained by vice. Parents can help to reinforce the connection. Without the help of our emotions, we don't act. Having a purely intellectual awareness of what you ought to do does not mean you will do it. Empathy too has an emotional content; one *feels* it. If you are aware of your connection with others both intellectually and emotionally, then you will act well.

For me at least, perhaps the most attractive philosophical idea that is represented in Stephen's teachings is something akin to Hegel's notion of God, what Hegel called the absolute spirit. Hegel puts forward the idea that human experience is part of God coming to know his own nature. Experience is only possible if there is something doing the experiencing and something experienced. This requires the illusion of dualism. God therefore has to make nominal distinctions within himself. Of course, all of creation is still God and still within God. The purpose of creation, for Stephen, is to make God's love manifest and in fact is the result of a kind over-flowing of love. Physical reality is not some ghastly mistake, as the Gnostics believed. It is part of God experiencing himself. Our lives therefore have a larger all-encompassing purpose and that is as God's sense organs. Every experience we have contributes to God's ever-expanding awareness and experience of his own nature. Hegel believed God's ultimate nature is freedom and saw human history as a progressive realization of ever greater degrees of freedom, from primitive communal societies which were free but unconscious of their freedom, to slavery, feudalism, and so on. I suspect that Hegel may be right about God's nature as freedom, although I'm not so sure about his views of human history. I also suspect that the views that God is freedom, God is love, and God is life, are all the same thing. What this *really* means I am still attempting to discover. With regard to Stephen, he thinks that human experience contributes in this Hegelian fashion and also that we are intended to experience everything. What this ultimately means is that an enlightened life continues to have pain as well as leisure, wild unfounded recriminations as well as gentle appreciation lovingly expressed. One who is saved does not cease to be involved in turmoil. All that might change is one's attitude to these events. We can learn from trying circumstances. We learn what we currently think are our limits and hence where we still need to grow. Where we find ourselves judging people or events negatively, we are made aware of potential new avenues of growth. Christ's attitude to his own crucifixion being a wonderful example. If one imagines that trying circumstances cease after one is saved and one loves God with all one's heart, soul, mind and strength, just look what happened to God's most beloved son. Still less can we expect prosperity, ease, and material comfort. But we can expect to love our lives more regardless of circumstance.

I have found Stephen's teachings to be philosophically profound. My consistent attitude has been that this cannot be a hoax, in the same way that Shakespeare's plays are not a hoax, Machado's poetry is not a hoax, and Einstein's theorems are not a hoax. If Tom Ashman is a fake medium, the teachings expressed are fake in the same way Plato's philosophy is fake, Bach's *St Matthew Passion* is a fake and Thomas Mann's *The Magic Mountain* is a fake, i.e., not at all. Of all the things expressed in Stephen's teachings, as I said at the beginning, the consistently loving attitude he expresses in his replies to questions is the most convincing and inspiring of all his lessons.

175. Further study of Stephen's Greek in Part 4; and how much does it prove?

I want to warmly thank two specialists in ancient Greek, whom I asked to check my Greek translations, and to comment on some of the connections I have made to the historical and cultural background:

Associate Professor of Classics at the University of Canterbury N.Z., Dr. Robin P. Bond basically accepted the translations, agreed about the origin of anomalous dialectical word-endings, and for the sections of Part Two that I had asked if he would study, accepted at least some of my reasoning.

I needed checking, since my knowledge is only of New Testament Greek, and that of certain early Christian Fathers. I am neither qualified in classical Greek, nor in dialectical. Neither am I a specialist in the history of Asia Minor.

With regard to the eight different words in the Greek, anyone who knows basic *Koine* Greek (which theological students often learn) can look them up in Liddell and Scott's Greek-English lexicon, note the varying possible translations, and verify the simple grammar. Even with such limited understanding of the language, they can check my translations, and form an opinion on whether the evidence justifies or not the understanding of the context of the words: as being spoken as Stephen with Celtic/Jewish origins in Galatia, and as an Essene novice about to be accepted into communion with fully fledged Essenes.

Dr Paul McKechnie, Lecturer in Greek at the University of Auckland kindly read most of Part Six. He understandably thought the Greek strange, but did not challenge the translations or the word endings. He specifically said that he saw no reason to doubt the integrity either of myself or of Thomas Ashman, the channel. As he had not read the entire book, he could not come to conclusions about the reality of the identity of Stephen, or the reliability of statements attributed to him. Thus he could not have an opinion about my reasoning and speculation on the basis of the ancient texts. All the same, I have to thank him for helping me develop certain lines of thought.

The Greek words that we are studying

This is what Stephen said in what we believe to be the Koiné Greek as spoken in Thrace, as well as other northern states:

Stephen: Κάρνῳ διότι διέτᾳ διότι Κάρνῳ διότι βορῷ ζέλαι Ληνέ·κά μέλλᾳ διέστα [διέσθαι]

If the words had been spoken by an inhabitant of Athens, in the south, some of the endings would have been different. They are underlined in the Attic version. Furthermore the word ζέλαι would not have been used.

Attic Greek would read like this:
Stephen: Κάρνῳ διότι διέτει διότι Κάρνῳ διότι βορῷ [ζέλαι] Ληναϊκά μέλλῃ διέστα [διέσθαι]
Expressing this is our letters:
(a) Stephen: Kárno dióti, diéta dióti, Kárno dióti, borô zélai Leneká mélla diésta

284

(b) *Attic:* Kárno dióti, dié*tei* dióti, Kárno dióti, borô zélai Lenaïká mélle diésthai

What kind of Greek is this?

1: One of those words is not in fact Greek. The word for **wine/zelai** is a Thracian word. The existence of this word is attested to by Greek grammarian Choerobos, of the 6th cent. B.C.E. (This language has close genetic links with Latvian and Lithuanian).Thrace lay to the north of Greece, its territory next to Macedonia, and overlapping with modern Bulgaria. Thracian was never a written language, and so anyone using that word must almost certainly have lived in Thrace, or been connected to people who had lived there.

2: I had transliterated the words with great care from the tape recording. Two other persons checked with me, who heard the sounds as I did. In this case the long "ô" sound at the end of one word, was pronounced with a quick up and down inflection, indicated by the cir-**cumflex** (^) over the letter. A few days after Stephen uttered the words, a Greek scholar told me that the inflection was important: for that is what they did with that " ô " in Stephen's day. A century later, she said, people simply put a stress on the " ô ". So that places the words as not later than the first century C.E..

[Dr McKechnie remarks "I do not think your Greek scholar was right. See W.Sidney Allen *Vox Graeca* where it is stated that a stress accent instead of tonal accentuation came in the 4th/3rd centuries BCE." [But on a website advertising Allen's book, his views are termed "controversial".] Even if Allen is right, this may not apply to dialects other than the Attic. It is the nature of dialects to be different, and for older forms to persist away from the culture's centre. On the other hand, supposing that the view is correct, that the change occurred in the 1st cent. CE, such is the nature of dialects, we cannot be absolutely sure of the habit in Thrace. So, unfortunately, here we are dealing with a likely possibility, but not proof.]

3: Some word **endings** were unusual, and I could not explain the discrepancies. I was angry with myself for not consulting an advanced classical Greek grammar until 1997. If I had done so immediately I would not have had to live through more than twenty years of uncertainty. But eventually I consulted William W. Goodwin's *A Greek Grammar*, ed. 1894. From this Grammar I learned several important things: that

Attic Greek (known as the Common Dialect) was the educated version spoken in all Greek-speaking lands. But in each area local words crept in, and there were local vowel changes. Compare the transliterated Greek above in the Thracian version (a) with the Attic or Athenian version. Professor Bond points out that variations are common even in classical Greek. Doric vowels are found in the lyrics of Attic tragedies, for example.]

α=a substituted for η=e and α=a for ει=ei, is a mark of the versions of Koine Greek in the provinces surrounding Thrace, namely that of Thessaly in the north of Greece; the Aeolic dialect spoken in the island of Lesbos, and in which in turn had similarities with that of Macedonia. So it should not be surprising to find these same vowel changes in a supposed northern version of the "Common Dialect" in Thrace.

Ληνεκα instead of Ληναϊκα, on the other hand, can reasonably be attributed to lazy speech. It takes some effort to pronounce the αι. (This may or may not have been characteristic of the dialect).

Thus we have indications that we have are dealing with the Greek spoken in northern states, one pointing in particular to Thrace, and another possibly pointing to a period no later than the first century C.E.

THE ATTIC or ATHENS VERSION PARSED

Καρνω dative neut. 2nd decl., of τό Καρνον, v. Hesychius. (The word itself is Celtic, declined as in Greek.) At first wrongly translated "Celtic born" or "Celt". Many years later it was discovered that the proper translation should have been "Celtic horn, or trumpet". (As it is a symbol for the Celts, "Celtic horn" can also mean "Celt". It appears on Roman coins celebrating victories over the Celts) The word is related to καρνυξ masc. (see Diodorus Siculus, *Historicus*) whence the English "Carnyx" referring to this same Celtic horn. Within the context of the whole Greek sentence, Carnyx must be read as a symbol for the Celt.

διότι, because, for the reason that, wherefore, since.

διέτει dative m. f. or n. of διέτης meaning "of, or lasting two years, a period of two years." Grammatically, it is the "Dative of Contact, defining a point in time or space." Therefore I suggest the translation "at two years", "two years having passed", "a period of two years completed".

Βορῶ, dat. m. f. or n. sing. Parallel with Καρνω, or in apposition to ζέλαι Ληναϊκα. From βορός gluttonous, devouring, see

Aristophanes *Pax* 38, <u>or</u> juice of pressed grapes, see Hesychii Alexandrii *Lexicon*

Ζέλαι (The lexicon gives this word as neuter. Our parsing seems to show that Stephen is treating the word as feminine. As it is a foreign word, perhaps the gender was not fixed.) Thracian for οἶνος (wine). Choerobos in his Grammaticus ed. Gainsford (from about 590 BCE) p.124 assumes a nom. Ζέλας gen. Ζέλαι but the fragment he quotes shows that it was indeclinable, cf Hesychius et Photius. see ζίλαι, ζείλα. [Expansion of Liddell and Scott's Greek Lexicon 1869.] Ze/lai was what we heard, so we stick with it, treating it as if it were the nominative feminine singular. thus allowing Ληναϊκά [pronounced by Stephen "Lehneka"] to be parsed as the nom. sing. fem. adjective Ληναϊκός ά- όν, "of, or belonging to the Lenaia, an Athenian festival held in the month Ληναιον" (otherwise known as Gamelion) in honour of Ληναιός, the god of the wine-press, ie Dionysus or Bacchus. Gamelion was January, "the wine was just made and the presses ἱ ληνοί just cleaned up." "At these some of the new Tragedies and Comedies were performed, and a prize of the rich must was given." (Liddell and Scott, 1869, under Διονυσια.)

Μέλλη is the 3ʳᵈ person singular subjunctive of μέλλω "shall" thus agreeing with the above parsing of ζέλαι Ληναϊκά

The context seems to require that "διέστα" should read "διέσθαι", the present infinitive of διίημι, a verb that has several meanings: "1.Drive, thrust or pass through, give people a passage through 2. dismiss, disband. 3 soak, 4 dilute, mix" There could be several reasons for the need for the emendation of the suffix: that was dialectical form I could not understand, that the sounds on the tape were a little indistinct, or that, as is usual in most speech, it was not quite clearly articulated. But there is little doubt that it is a version of διίημι.

A **further note on** Ζέλαι: *In The Language of the Thracians*, Ivan Duridanov states that the natives of Thrace were not literate in their own language. **Only 23 of their words** are attested in ancient writers, of which "zelai" is one. There are a further 180 words reconstructed from modern Bulgarian place names and words. "It turned out that the Thracian language is in close genetic links with the Baltic languages ["For more details see my work: Thrakisch dakische Studien, I. Teil, Balkansko ezikoznanie,XIII, 2, Sofia, 1969"].

HOW MUCH DOES THE GREEK PROVE?

Firstly, it is most unfortunate that I did not keep the original tape. I was not aware how highly significant it would become.

But there are **reasons for us to suppose that we did record the words accurately:** (a) Now that we have fully understood them after all these years, we find they make perfect sense in the context indicated by Stephen. (b) Greek is a highly complex language, with just over 330 forms to a verb conjugation, 36 cases for the adjective, 14 for the noun. In light of this it is remarkable that the words are grammatically correct. One ending wrong, and the sentence would be suspect. (c) Not only meaningful, and correct, the sentence has a common theme, namely "wine". Historically "wine" is associated with the Celt, βορός can either mean "drunken" or "unfermented wine", Ληναϊκός is associated with Dionysis or Bacchus, the god of wine, and refers to a festival of unfermented wine; ζέλαι means "wine", διῖημι is the word you use for mixing the wine. (d) The "wrong" endings in διέτα and μέλλα were further evidence that my transcription was accurate. It is plain that had I misheard, or had I deceived myself into thinking that I had heard the "right" endings and then changed them, I would have destroyed important evidence. It was only 23 years later in 1997 that I discovered that the "wrong" endings were actually correct for Stephen's dialect. (e) From the study of the historical and cultural background presented in Chapter Two, we find all the data fits together in a perfect jigsaw puzzle.

True sceptics will be driven to accuse someone here of constructing a hoax. Against that hypothesis, (a) I can repeat that Thomas Ashman left school at sixteen, and had no education in Greek. It would have taken Thomas years of intense study of ancient Greek to have constructed such a hoax. (b) The jigsaw only fits together, if the original framer of those words had access to all the information I uncovered painfully slowly over a period of twenty-five years. Neither Thomas nor I had access to that information in 1974. (c) Moreover whoever the original framer of the sentence was, he knew the word Ze/lai. This word is only known because it appears in a manuscript glossary of Hesychius, in the 4th century CE.. Otherwise Thracian was not a written language. A person using it would have had to come from ancient Thrace, as the sentence implies. (d) If, on the other hand, I am accused of knowing everything from the beginning, then reference to my articles published in *The Journal of* the *Academy of Religion and Psychic Research*, April 1982, and *The Christian Parapsychologist*, June 1981, will give an inkling of the slow development of my solving the mystery, and the great number of discoveries then yet to be made. (e) If it was alleged that Thomas "found" this quotation somewhere; the argument against that is, firstly, that Ζέλαι does not occur in ancient Greek literature, thus it could not become part of such a quotation. Secondly, as I have shown, the quotation appeared to be part of the specific historical situation outlined in this book. Thirdly, are we to suppose that Thomas went to a huge amount of effort to find such an obscure quotation, say it almost by the way, without any assurance that I could translate it, and make sure that everything fitted together in the intricate way I have described, over the several years of communicating? Much of the Stephen story would have had to be constructed over those years, with a view to harmonising with those words, and also with what is now known to modern scholars.

In the first edition of this book my sceptical publisher was concerned that there be no possibility of hoax. Prior to reading Part Four, Dr McKechnie, did raise the possibility of a hoax. But not afterwards. He wrote that he saw no reason not to believe in the integrity of the people involved.

Positively: This study shows the Greek words to be genuinely of the first century CE, and not to have come from the mind of Thomas Ashman. He received it "paranormally".

176. Grateful thanks to:

Stephen, the first Christian martyr, for his patient teaching over so many years.

Thomas Ashman and his wife Olive, without whom, much of this experience would not have come to pass. Thanks to the group, who for several years in the '70's were regularly involved physically and in Spirit in the events as they unfolded. They were heady days!

Thanks to Marcia Admore who transcribed the majority of sessions from tape recording to Gestetner stencil, for circulation among those present.

To Jonathan Beecher of White Crow Books, both for publishing this edition and for helping to transform it into a much more readable and useful work.

To Graeme French, for spending an intensive week of proof reading prior to the publication of this book, finding many infelicities of expression, and numerous errors and repetitions to correct.

To my son Dr Richard Cocks, for his articles in the book, and for much helpful advice.

There were many others who also played a significant role, plainly also participating in these events of the Spirit. They include my wife Gertrud, Norman Kjome, Dr. John Moss who corresponded about it over 15 years and more, and wrote about it in his own work *What do you think of Christ?*, Dr. Mary Carman Rose who published two of my articles about our experience in *The Journal of Religion and Psychical Research* and corresponded over a long period, Hyacinth Österlin and members of her group who studied the material, the late Bill Henson who scrupulously proof-read the text, and made valuable suggestions. Thanks to Drs. Tore and Nancy Fjällbrant, Alan Taylor and David Wright; to Rene Hodgson and my brother Jonathan, for their work on the text; to journalist Kerstin Wallin who wrote a long article about it in *Göteborgs-Posten.*, and to Dr. Bill Peddie of "Kelso" for being prepared to publish first version of the book, and for supporting and advising me in the course of the preparation for publication. Thanks to members of the *Scientific and Medical Network*, the Rev Dr David Bell, and Dr Leo Hobbis for organising a seminar in Auckland NZ to study Parts Four and Six, on the evidence of the reality of Stephen, to the former Chairman of Trustees of the Scientific and Medical Network, Max Payne, and to the Rt.Rev Edward Holland, (former Asst. Bishop of the Anglican Diocese of Europe) for careful study of the material, encouragement and helpful advice.

177. Bibliography

Abingdon Bible Commentary, edited by Frederick Carl Eiselen [and others] New York, Abingdon Press, 1929.

Allen, W. Sidney. *Vox Graeca:* a guide to the pronunciation of classical Greek. 2nd ed. London; New York, Cambridge University Press, 1974.

Ashman, Olive. *Communion with a saint.* Ely, Cambridgeshire, Melrose Books, 2006.

Richard J. Bauckham *Jude and the relatives of Jesus in the early church."* London, T&T Clark 1990

Barrett, C. K. The historicity of Acts. Journal of theological studies, 50 (1999): 515-34

Blackburn, Peter.J. *Shadow and Reality* http://peterjblackburn.net/essays/hebrews.pdf

Bohm, David. *Wholeness and the implicate order.* London; Boston, Routledge & Kegan Paul, 1980.

Brandon, S. G. F.: *The Fall of Jerusalem and the Christian Church.* London, SPCK, 1951

Broshi, Magen: *Village Essenes*

Catholic encyclopedia: an international work of reference on the constitution, doctrine, discipline, and history of the Catholic church; edited by Charles G Herbermann [and others] New York, Appleton, 1907-1912. 15 vols.

Cirlot, J. E. *Dictionary of symbols.* New York, Philosophical Library, 1971.

Cocks, Michael Articles about Stephen's Greek words in *The Journal of the Academy of Religion and Psychic Research*, April 1982, and *The Christian Parapsychologist*, June 1981

II.Code for Urban Communities Chapters ix-xii III Code for Camp-Communities chapters xii-xiii

Duridanov, Ivan. *The language of the Thracians* (see) *Thrakisch dakische Studien*, I. Teil, Balkansko ezikoznanie,XIII, 2, So-fia, 1

Fitzmyer, Joseph A. *Responses to 101 questions on the Dead Sea Scrolls.* London, Geoffrey Chapman, 1992.

Foakes-Jackson, F. J. *The Acts of the Apostles.* London, Hodder and Stoughton, 1931.

Gaster, Theodore H. *The scriptures of the Dead Sea* Sect in English translation with introduction and notes by Theodore H. Gaster. London, Secker & Warburg, 1957.
"The Zadokite document": p.71-94.

Goodwin, William W. *A Greek grammar.* London, Macmillan, 1894.

Hastings, James. *A dictionary of the Bible dealing with its language, literature and contents including the biblical theology.* Edinburgh, Clark, 1898-1904. 5 vols.

Hey, Anthony (Tony) and Patrick Walters. *The quantum universe.* Cambridge, Cambridge University Press, 1987.

Huxley, Aldous. *The perennial philosophy.* New York, Harper, 1945.

Johnson, Paul. *A history of Christianity.* London, Weidenfeld & Nicolson, 1976.

Kittler, Glenn D. *Edgar Cayce on the Dead Sea Scrolls.*

Leaney, A. R. C. Hanson, J.Posen: *A Guide to the Scrolls.* London, SCM, 1958

Liddell, Henry George. *A Greek English lexicon* compiled by Henry George Liddell and Robert Scott. 7th ed. Oxford, Clarendon Press, 1883.

Man, myth & magic; an illustrated encyclopedia of the supernatural; editor Richard Cavendish. New York, Marshall Cavendish, 1970-

Manson, William. The epistle to the Hebrews. London, Hodder & Stoughton, 1951.

Murrell, Beatrix: . http://www.onedegreebeyond.com/library/murel6.htm

Moss, John. *What do you think of Christ?* Edinburgh Pentland Press, 1996

Needleman, Jacob: *Lost Christianity.* New York Doubleday 1980

"New Grove Dictionary of Musical Instruments".[1985]

Oxford classical dictionary; edited by M. Cary [and others] Oxford, Clarendon Press, 1949.

Pibram, Karl. Article in Wilber's book, below

Plato. *The Republic.*

Qumran *Manual of Discipline* vi,13-23 "Of postulants and novices"

Ramsay, William M. Galatia in Hastings (1898): vol. ii p.88

Sheldrake, Rupert. A new science of life; the hypothesis of formative causation. London, Blond & Briggs, 1981.

Schuerer, E. "Diaspora" in Hastings (1898) vol.5: p.91ff.

Sugden, Edward H. *"James"* in Abingdon Bible commentary (1929): p.1327, col.ii.

Turner, C. H. article in Hastings (1898) above

Underhill, Evelyn. *Mysticism; a study in the nature and development of man's spiritual consciousness.* 4th ed. London, Methuen, 1912.

Weatherhead, Leslie D. *The Christian agnostic.* London, Hodder & Stoughton, 1965.

Weber, Renee. *"Field consciousness and field ethics"* in Wilber (1982) .

Wilber, Ken (ed.) *The holographic paradigm and other paradoxes: exploring the leading edge of science,* edited by Ken Wilber. Boulder, Shambhala, 1982.

Yadin, Y. *The Scroll of War of the Sons of Light against the Sons of Darkness* (Oxford: Oxford University Press, 1962)

Zohar, Danar. *The quantum self.* New York: Quill/William Morrow 1990

Zukav, Gary. *The dancing WuLi masters.* London, Rider:Hutchinson, 1979.

Endnotes

1 http://commons.wikimedia.org/wiki/File:Hallein_Keltenmuseum_-_Lure.
   jpg

Wolfgang Sauber [Celtic museum in Hallein (Salzburg). Reconstruction]

Image credit: Wikimedia Commons, Creative Commons Attribution-Shar-
   ealike 3.0,

2 Acts 6:8, 7:54-8:1.(NEB) "Saul" was to become "St. Paul" the foremost teacher of Christianity.

3 Possibly "the individual mind will exist no longer."

4 "Source", "God", "All that is," "The Space Between", "Void" seem to mean
   the same for Stephen. In a moment he adds that to apply the term "father"
   is to use *a tangible image of what is intangible*. The intangible Source has so
   many qualities of a good father. These days when women and men are perceived as co-equal, we might have liked Stephen to have used both "mother" and "father" as images for the Source. But his meaning is plain.

2 We *"Sons" or "Daughters"* are created in the image of the "father" of "base
   material." Our baser emotions need refining by the emotions of the "soul",
   or "cell of influence" (also seen as the Holy Spirit). We have to "grow, learn
   and experience" (over many incarnations) until we become "fathers" and
   "mothers" whose feelings and reactions are perfectly in tune with the "Father", Source of which it is our destiny to be the image.

6 The "continuous self" is the created personality, spiritual body of an individual, which may persist through numbers of incarnations.

7 "Thus in the congregation, is the Holy Spirit"

[8] Perhaps the train of thought is that the power of Divine Love was manifested indeed because they could not contemplate such a death, for they are not separate, but one.

[9] The spiritual self would never kill, but the physical mind could certainly dream up reasons

[10] Elsewhere Stephen affirms that it was not the physical body that rose from the dead, but the spiritual; that the resurrection shows Jesus still to live, with a spiritual body; that the loss of the physical body is of no consequence.

[11] No doubt that Stephen is referring to the whole of Scripture. But we might compare it with Romans 8:6-7: "The mind of sinful man is death, but the mind controlled by the Spirit is life and peace; the sinful mind is hostile to God. It does not submit to God's law, nor can it do so." *Et passim*. But Stephen also emphasises that "karmic" debt can only be repaid in the coin of love to others, in the present.

[12] Paraphrase of Psalm 23

[13] *The Holographic Paradigm*, 1981, p. 161.

[14] Other terms Stephen uses are: "Source" "All that is". Any idea of God standing "over against" or "separate" from Creation, is quite alien to Stephen.

[15] Here Stephen refers to the story of the Garden of Eden. Genesis 2-3. They eat of the tree of knowledge of good and evil. Hence, the comparison.

[16] In the story they are thrown out of the Garden, with the way back barred by an angel with a flaming sword. In actual fact, we travel far through many lives.

[17] Where instead we accept in trust the projection, the image, the Christ.

[18] In his paraphrase of Psalm 23, Stephen pictures the Good Shepherd walking ahead of us on the path he wishes us to follow. We are not to look to the right or to the left (do not make comparisons, do not judge) but accept that our path is indeed our path. The Mirror story goes further, and affirms that we must accept our "fairness", our loveableness and perfection for the path that we are to follow.

[19] So the desert is "a wilderness of ignorance". Are we, or are we not, to call on Christ to be saved from this wilderness?

[20] Ch.10: *The Yoga of Heavenly Perfection (VibhutiYoga)*, Bhagavad Gita

[21] Through humour Stephen consistently presents himself as a spiritual brother rather than master. He suggests that we see ourselves as a group of friends, not to be quiet as if in a prayer meeting.

[22] Compare *1 Corinthians*. 8.8:"Food however, will not improve our relation with God, we shall not lose anything if we do not eat, nor shall we gain anything if we do eat. Cf verse 13 "So then, if food makes my brother sin, I will never eat meat again, so as not to make my brother fall into sin". Stephen spoke at length on this point in the course of a session on Sin and Suffering,

[23] Some very important issues are being raised here. See the short essay at the end of this chapter.

[24] Incarnational thread of being, with many time names: Judas, Charles, Michael.

[25] Cf. Karl Pibram who sees the brain as a microhologram being of the same pattern as the universe, also seen as a hologram.

[26] If we look at Stephen's account of the "Seven skins", later in this chapter, we could interpret "sense-consciousness" as the "non-physical senses" associated with the cell. However, the earlier context suggests that it refers to the senses associated with the physical mind.

[27] See what Stephen has been saying a little previously about "misarrangements". Can Stephen be paraphrased a little to say that he is *denying* that God brings on physical experiences that cause pain to the soul, so that the soul can learn.

[28] Cf *Romans* 7.15b "For what I would, that do I not; but what I hate, that do I" (King James Version)

[29] This seems to contradict what Stephen has just been saying."It must be so", as Stephen says, "that the Whole is not like an animal, which moves. Yet cannot the emotion of love, not belong to the Whole?"

[30] Stephen is re-telling the story about the correction of mis-arrangements in the soul, or cell of influence, where the influence of the Source can be diminished by the emotions and prejudices of the physical. The etymology of "Godhead" equates it with "Godhood" or divinity, but Stephen uses the "-head" to mean a "head" which has the Whole to act as its instruments. He retells the story in such a way that we have a different feeling about "at-onement". God is seen as an Artist.

[31] p.35 *The Holographic Paradigm*, ed. Ken Wilber 1982,

[32] See section 88.

[33] See www.thegroundoffaith.net/stephen

[34] This "simultaneous receiving" was in fact to be a major feature of the Stephen Experience in the coming years, and in the years after Stephen's voice was heard no more.

35 "pure nugget of gold"

36 And you notice that in this case I have not followed his advice, but retained the whole session. I have done so, because the words spoken appear to be true: the contradiction lies in the question, "Who was communicating?"

37 Recognise Spirit as opposed to "Flesh".

38 The voice of Christ marks this session as being of great importance: the setting of the puzzle about the Twelves, that takes very many years to finally solve. Christ's words are much closer to the true solution, than when Stephen leads us into temptation, in inviting us to choose twelve. *Why should Stephen mislead?*

39 It was at this point that Stephen set the first of the puzzles to which I have been referring, puzzles, which over the next fourteen years, would give us first-hand experience of the Marriage of the One and the Many. I call his first puzzle "The Puzzle of the Twelve". He presents the puzzle almost by the way; but it was not "by the way" - it was to be central. It takes a book to describe how this puzzle was to be solved. I mention it only to record that something very important was being left out of this book. After setting the puzzle Stephen remarked,

"Think not that we purposely confuse you, if we appear to withhold information. What I do say, and what does happen, is that you will always find you have felt what is taught, before. The teaching method that I employ is to bring to your mind some of the knowledge, which you left behind when you acquired a body in your material world. So, some of the things which may seem confusing to you now will become fully clear in due course. And the reason for my teaching in this way will become clear.

My teaching will confirm what you partly know already. My speaking will help to make real for you, the information you have regarding your previous selves; information that you cannot by yourselves believe."

40 The voice of Christ had bidden Michael take the hand of the entranced Thomas.

41 Stephen's answer could be seen to parallel Bohm Quotation 5: "Within the implicate order everything is connected, and in theory, any individual element could reveal information about every other element in the universe"

42 Bohm: "Any individual element could reveal information about every other element". Stephen, on the other hand, says that the individual receives what is given, as by an act of grace and favour. I myself feel that when I have received or intuited an answer, that the question was also received. I suspect that I have no powers to make answers come. It is indeed as if it all happens as an act of grace.

⁴³ A worldwide network of computer networks that use the TCP/IP network protocols to facilitate data transmission and exchange

⁴⁴ Matthew 5:3 ff

⁴⁵ Explanation comes later in this session.

⁴⁶ Κάρνῳ διότι διέτα διότι Κάρνῳ διότι βορῷ ζέλαι Ληναϊκά μέ λλα διέστα [διέσθαι]

⁴⁷ Modern Ankara.

⁴⁸ Looking back, I can see that Stephen is saying that meaningless words convey no insights, no feelings at depth.

⁴⁹ I accept that, for Stephen, it seemed thus to him. But in view of the continual expansion in the significance of his words, and continuing synchronicity or meaningful coincidence with them, then Spirit had a wider purpose with these words than had Stephen.

⁵⁰ Regarding the carnyx, another authority expands on our dictionary quotations:

"Although surviving examples are few, there are many depictions of Carnyces, especially on Roman triumphal sculpture and coinage; the legions encountered it in battle, and thought it so strange, *that it was used as an emblem of the tribes they fought.* This gives us a wide range of comparative material, of varying quality. Some factors in the reconstruction are inevitably speculative: the original length and diameter of the tube, for instance, is unknown, although the dimensions fall within the known range. More awkward is the nature of the mouthpiece, for which evidence is poor." *Fraser Hunter, Dept of Archaeology, National Museums of Scotland.*

⁵¹ http://www.carnyx.mcmail.com/carnyx.htm [My emphasis] Musée de la civlisation celtique, Bibracte, France. Photo by Urban, {{Pd-self}} http://commons.wikimedia.org/wiki/File:Bibracte_Dumnorix.jpg

⁵² It was not until 1992 that I discovered I had misread the dictionary. It was *Celtic horn (Carnyx)*, not *born*. A few days later it occurred to me to try and discover what a carnyx would look like. Without much hope, I visited the city library and was referred to the *"New Grove Dictionary of Musical Instruments".*[1985] On page 312 I found a picture of three carnyx players (in a detail from a Celtic silver cauldron of the 1ˢᵗ or 2ⁿᵈ century BCE, found at Gundestrup in Jutland).

⁵³ In 278 three Celtic tribes that had migrated across Europe to the Dardanelles were taken as allies by Nicomedes I of Bithynia. The Celts invaded and ravaged Anatolia until they were defeated by Antiochus in 275. Thereafter they were settled in northern Phrygia by Nicomedes and Mithradates,

where they served as a buffer against the Seleucids. The district they occupied was thereafter called Galatia (from Galli, the Latin word for Celts). [Encyclopaedia. Britannica,. 2000]

54 From Murray's *Small Classical Atlas* ed G.B. Grundy, 1917

55 Diodoros is shocked at the exorbitant price "Celts" of his day would pay for a jar or even a cup of wine, attributing it to monumental lust for wine on the part of the barbarians (V.26.3). Diodoros makes no bones about the consequences in Massalia:

> "The Gauls are exceedingly addicted to the use of wine and fill themselves with the wine which is brought into their country by merchants, drinking it unmixed, and since they partake of this drink without moderation by reason of their craving for it, when they are drunken they fall into a stupor or a state of madness. Consequently many of the Italian traders, induced by the love of money which characterizes them, believe that the love of wine of these Gauls is their own godsend. For these transport the wine on the navigable rivers by means of boats and through the level plain on wagons, and receive for it an incredible price; for in exchange for a jar of wine they receive a slave, getting a servant in return for the drink" (V.26.3)

56 E. Schürer "Diaspora" in James Hastings' *Dictionary. of the Bible*, extra vol p.91 ii

57 Ibid p. 93 i

58 Also in his article on Galatia, ibid, vol.2, p. 88 ii.

59 Ivan Duridanov, *The Language of the Thracians*, has a list of the few Thracian personal names now known. "Stenen" is not in this list. The sound combination "st" is found.

60 Modern Ankara is situated near the confluence of the Hatip, Ince Su and Cubuk streams. The latter flows into Ankara from the Northeast, and has been dammed six miles up stream from Ankara. This may be the river referred to in Thomas' receiving. Ancient Ancyra, is to be identified with Ulus, which is located on two steep hills, and where ancient sites can still be identified, in particular the temple dedicated to Caesar Augustus, the Roman emperor, who died in AD 15, not so long before Stephen would have been born.

61 II.Code for Urban Communities Chapters ix-xii III Code for Camp-Communities chapters xii-xiii

62 (1976) [pages 14-19]

63 "Revelation of hidden things" "dealing with the events of the last times of the world when the saving Messiah will be revealed"

[64] Joseph A. Fitzmyer: in his *Responses to 101 Questions on the Dead Sea Scrolls:* London: Geoffrey Chapman, 1992. at p.73 quotes from Appendix A of the Qumran Manual of Discipline 1QSa 2:11-22:

[Then shall be the as]sembly of the men of renown [summoned] to the meeting of the council of the community, when/if [God] begets the Messiah among them. There shall enter [the priest], the head of the whole congregation of Israel, and all [his]bro[thers, the sons of Aaron, the priests [summoned] to the meeting of men of renown. They shall sit be[fore him, each [according to his dignity. Afterwards there sh[all take his seat the Mes]siah of Israel. And the head[s of] the Th[ousands of Israel] shall sit before him, [ea]ch according to his dignity. And [when they] meet together [at tab]le [or to drink the ne]w wine and (when) the table is *prepared and [the new wine] is [mixed] for drinking,* [no]one shall [stretch forth] his hand to the first-fruits of the bread and [the new wine] before the priest; for [he it is who shall bl[ess the first-fruits of the bread and the new win[e and he shall stretch forth] his hand to the bread first. Afterwa[rd] the Messiah of Israel [will stre]tch for his hand to the bread. [And then] all the congregation of the community [shall ut]ter a blessing, ea[ch according to] his dignity. According to this regulation [they] shall act at every meal-prepar[ation when] at least ten me[n are ga]thered.

[65] Cf. Y. Yadin, *The Scroll of War of the Sons of Light against the Sons of Darkness* (Oxford: Oxford University Press, 1962), p. 71. It stands to reason that this prohibition stems from the fear of sexual attraction toward women and even children. Cf. Ibid., pp. 290-91.

[66] Leaney, A.R.C. (and others) *A Guide to the Scrolls.* London, SCM, 1958 p.44

[67] Magen Broshi, The Israel Museum, Jerusalem

[68] "Meanwhile those who had been scattered after the persecution that arose over Stephen made their way to Phoenicia, Cyprus, and Antioch, bringing the message to the Jews and to no others. But there were some natives of Cyprus and Cyrene among them, and these, when they arrived at Antioch, began to speak to Gentiles as well, telling them the good news of the Lord Jesus."

[69] "Hasting's five volume, *Dictionary of the Bible*

[70] Not a good question: the Acts story has Paul's conversion some time after Stephen's martyrdom.

[71] Op.cit. p.89 See also most recently C.K. Barrett: *The historicity of Acts. Journal of Theological Studies* 50 (1999) 515-34

[72] O. Cullmann, *"The Significance of the Qumran Texts for Research into the Beginnings of Christianity"* in K. Stendahl (ed.), *op. cit.; Expository Times* (T & T Clark, Edinburgh). LXXI, 1, pp. 8-11 2, pp. 39-42

O Cullmann, *"A New Approach to the Interpretation of the Fourth Gospel"* *Expository Times* 71 (1959-60), 8-12, 39-43

C. Spicq, "L'Épître aux Hébreux, Apollos, Jean-Baptiste, les Hellénistes et Qumrân," RQ, 1, 3 (Feb. 1959), pp. 365-390. A similar line is followed by S.E. Johnson in K. Stendahl, op. cit.; Wm. Manson, *The Epistle to the Hebrews* (London, Hodder & Stoughton, 1951), pp. 30-36 *et al.*, sees direct dependence between Stephen's message and the doctrine developed in Hebrews. M. Simon, *St. Stephen and the Hellenists in the Primitive Church* (London: Longmans 1958)

73 See http://peterjblackburn.net/essays/hebrews.pdf   A B.D. thesis for Univ. of Queensland

74 A scholarly correspondent had these comments to make: "The flight into Egypt is important. Many Jews lived in Egypt, most of them in Alexandria. For refugees, Alexandria is a more likely destination than somewhere up country. Therefore Joseph, Mary and Jesus probably lived in Alexandria, though no one knows for how long – and if they knew no Greek before, I bet they learned some there. That is why I distrust New Testament scholars who insist that Jesus can't have known Greek. In Alexandria, even Synagogue services were in Greek. Jesus and his parents, for my money, must have been at least functional Greek speakers. Mary was of a priestly family (Zechariah, Elizabeth) and Joseph was of the Davidic royal family. Jesus sent out his disciples "to teach" –therefore he was himself a teacher, and a teacher of teachers ie of high intellectual attainments in a society with a long and complex literate tradition. I would say he came from a literate, as well as observant, household. The recent book on this is: Richard J. Bauckham *Jude and the relatives of Jesus in the early church*." London, T&T Clark 1990

75 "James", p.1327, col.ii *The Abingdon Bible Commentary*, New York, Abingdon-Cokesbury Press 1929

76 John 2.1

77 [Quoted with permission from http://www.onedegreebeyond.com/library/murel6.htm]

78 See *Oxford Classical Dictionary*, ed. M.Cary et al. Clarendon 1949, p.735

79 3rd edition, 1987

Paperbacks also available from
White Crow Books

Marcus Aurelius—*Meditations*
ISBN 978-1-907355-20-2

Elsa Barker—*Letters from
a Living Dead Man*
ISBN 978-1-907355-83-7

Elsa Barker—*War Letters
from the Living Dead Man*
ISBN 978-1-907355-85-1

Elsa Barker—*Last Letters
from the Living Dead Man*
ISBN 978-1-907355-87-5

Richard Maurice Bucke—
Cosmic Consciousness
ISBN 978-1-907355-10-3

G. K. Chesterton—*Heretics*
ISBN 978-1-907355-02-8

G. K. Chesterton—*Orthodoxy*
ISBN 978-1-907355-01-1

Arthur Conan Doyle—*The
Edge of the Unknown*
ISBN 978-1-907355-14-1

Arthur Conan Doyle—
The New Revelation
ISBN 978-1-907355-12-7

Arthur Conan Doyle—
The Vital Message
ISBN 978-1-907355-13-4

Arthur Conan Doyle with
Simon Parke—*Conversations
with Arthur Conan Doyle*
ISBN 978-1-907355-80-6

Meister Eckhart with Simon Parke—
Conversations with Meister Eckhart
ISBN 978-1-907355-18-9

Kahlil Gibran—*The Forerunner*
ISBN 978-1-907355-06-6

Kahlil Gibran—*The Madman*
ISBN 978-1-907355-05-9

Kahlil Gibran—*The Prophet*
ISBN 978-1-907355-04-2

Kahlil Gibran—*Jesus the Son of Man*
ISBN 978-1-907355-08-0

Kahlil Gibran—*Spiritual World*
ISBN 978-1-907355-09-7

D. D. Home—*Incidents
in my Life Part 1*
ISBN 978-1-907355-15-8

Mme. Dunglas Home; edited,
with an Introduction, by Sir
Arthur Conan Doyle—*D. D.
Home: His Life and Mission*
ISBN 978-1-907355-16-5

Edward C. Randall—
Frontiers of the Afterlife
ISBN 978-1-907355-30-1

Lucius Annaeus Seneca—
On Benefits
ISBN 978-1-907355-19-6

Rebecca Ruter Springer—*Intra
Muros: My Dream of Heaven*
ISBN 978-1-907355-11-0

Leo Tolstoy, edited by Simon
Parke—*Forbidden Words*
ISBN 978-1-907355-00-4

Leo Tolstoy—*A Confession*
ISBN 978-1-907355-24-0

Leo Tolstoy—*The Gospel in Brief*
ISBN 978-1-907355-22-6

Leo Tolstoy—*The Kingdom
of God is Within You*
ISBN 978-1-907355-27-1

Leo Tolstoy—*My Religion:*
What I Believe
ISBN 978-1-907355-23-3

Leo Tolstoy—*On Life*
ISBN 978-1-907355-91-2

Leo Tolstoy—*Twenty-three Tales*
ISBN 978-1-907355-29-5

Leo Tolstoy—*What is Religion*
and other writings
ISBN 978-1-907355-28-8

Leo Tolstoy—*Work While*
Ye Have the Light
ISBN 978-1-907355-26-4

Leo Tolstoy with Simon Parke—
Conversations with Tolstoy
ISBN 978-1-907355-25-7

Vincent Van Gogh with
Simon Parke—*Conversations*
with Van Gogh
ISBN 978-1-907355-95-0

Howard Williams with an
Introduction by Leo Tolstoy—*The*
Ethics of Diet: An Anthology of
Vegetarian Thought
ISBN 978-1-907355-21-9

Allan Kardec—*The Spirits Book*
ISBN 978-1-907355-98-1

Wolfgang Amadeus Mozart
with Simon Parke—
Conversations with Mozart
ISBN 978-1-907661-38-9

Jesus of Nazareth with
Simon Parke—*Conversations*
with Jesus of Nazareth
ISBN 978-1-907661-41-9

Thomas à Kempis with Simon
Parke—*The Imitation of Christ*
ISBN 978-1-907661-58-7

Emanuel Swedenborg—
Heaven and Hell
ISBN 978-1-907661-55-6

P.D. Ouspensky—*Tertium Organum:*
The Third Canon of Thought
ISBN 978-1-907661-47-1

Dwight Goddard—*A Buddhist Bible*
ISBN 978-1-907661-44-0

Leo Tolstoy—*The Death*
of Ivan Ilyich
ISBN 978-1-907661-10-5

Leo Tolstoy—*Resurrection*
ISBN 978-1-907661-09-9

Michael Tymn—*The Afterlife*
Revealed
ISBN 978-1-970661-90-7

Guy L. Playfair—*If This Be Magic*
ISBN 978-1-907661-84-6

Julian of Norwich with
Simon Parke—*Revelations of*
Divine Love
ISBN 978-1-907661-88-4

Maurice Nicoll—*The New Man*
ISBN 978-1-907661-86-0

Carl Wickland, M.D.—*Thirty Years*
Among the Dead
ISBN 978-1-907661-72-3

Allan Kardec—*The Book on*
Mediums
ISBN 978-1-907661-75-4

John E. Mack—*Passport to the*
Cosmos
ISBN 978-1-907661-81-5

**All titles available as eBooks, and selected titles available in Hardback and
Audiobook formats from www.whitecrowbooks.com**

CPSIA information can be obtained
at www.ICGtesting.com
Printed in the USA
BVHW031519150620
581354BV00006B/41